The Life and Work of Joan Riviere

The Life and Work of Joan Riviere traces her journey from dressmaker's apprentice, and member of the Society for Psychical Research, to Sigmund Freud's patient and his favourite translator. Marion Bower examines Riviere's important legacy and contribution to the early development of psychoanalysis.

Riviere was also a close friend and colleague of Melanie Klein and wrote her own highly original and influential papers on female sexuality and other topics, in particular *Womanliness as a Masquerade* (1929). Her position in the British Psychoanalytic Society was unusual as a direct link between Freud and Klein. Her own papers were extraordinarily prescient of developments in psychoanalysis, as well as the social climate of the time. Riviere's experience as a dressmaker gave her an interest in female sexuality, and she proceeded to significantly challenge Freud's views. She also defended Klein from ferocious attacks by Melitta Schmideberg (Klein's daughter) and Anna Freud.

The Life and Work of Joan Riviere will appeal to anyone interested in the history of psychoanalysis as well as Riviere's highly original perspectives involving feminist thought and female sexuality.

Marion Bower has trained as a teacher, a social worker and an adult psychotherapist. She worked at the Tavistock Clinic for fourteen years and currently teaches at The Kleinian Association of Ireland, the British Psychotherapy Foundation and Making Research Count. She has edited or co-edited four books, including the Routledge titles *Addictive States of Mind* (2013) and *What Social Workers Need to Know* (2018).

The Life and Work of Joan Riviere

Freud, Klein and Female Sexuality

Marion Bower

Routledge
Taylor & Francis Group
LONDON AND NEW YORK

First published 2019
by Routledge
2 Park Square, Milton Park, Abingdon, Oxon OX14 4RN

and by Routledge
52 Vanderbilt Avenue, New York, NY 10017

Routledge is an imprint of the Taylor & Francis Group, an informa business

British Library Cataloguing in Publication Data
A catalogue record for this book is available from the British Library

Library of Congress Cataloging in Publication Data
A catalog record has been requested for this book

ISBN: 978-0-415-50768-4 (hbk)
ISBN: 978-0-415-50769-1 (pbk)
ISBN: 978-0-429-43030-5 (ebk)

Typeset in Times New Roman
by Out of House Publishing

For Steve

Contents

Acknowledgements

This book would not exist without the work of the psychoanalyst Athol Hughes. In 1991 she edited a collection of Joan Riviere's papers, complete with a biographical introduction. The papers and the account of Riviere's life were so fascinating that I wanted to know more. With great kindness Athol lent me her research materials and listened to me read chapters of the book.

My son Bruno turned my handwritten manuscripts into an exquisite typed document, as well as giving me much-needed advice. Steve, my husband, showed heroic patience during the seven years it took for this book to come into fruition. He chauffeured me round places where Joan lived as a child and read through the book. Jacob, my older son, always remembered to ask how the book was doing when skyping from San Francisco.

I have spent many hours in the following archives: Bedford Council, Brighton History Museum, Wycombe Abbey School, Newnham College and Trinity College Cambridge, the Institute of Psychoanalysis, Lewes County Record Office, the Wellcome Library, the British Library, the Society for Psychical Research, the Victoria and Albert Museum Theatre Archive and the Tate Britain Archive.

My friend and co-editor in other ventures Robin Solomon has encouraged me and made helpful comments. Roger and Liz researched census records for me.

My editors at Routledge, Kate Hawes and Charles Bath, have been *exceedingly* patient.

Special thanks to the trustees of the Melanie Klein Trust for permission to reproduce the photographs.

Prologue

On 22nd January, 1922, Ernest Jones, President of the British Psychoanalytic Society, wrote to Sigmund Freud:

> Dear Professor,
>
> I thought it would interest you if I told you a few words about your new patient Mrs Riviere, who is going to Vienna next week, as she plays a considerable part in the [psychoanalytic] society here. … Most of her neurosis goes into marked character reactions … I am specially interested in the case for it is the worst failure I have ever had. … I think she understands psa [psychoanalysis] better than any other member except perhaps Flugel. Incidentally she has a strong complex about being a well-born lady [county family] and despises all the rest of us, especially the women.
>
> (Paskauskas, 1993)

When Joan Riviere died in 1962 the *International Journal of Psychoanalysis* published three obituaries of her, two by people who did not know her very well, and one by someone who did, but claimed not to. James was the younger brother of Lytton Strachey, a product of the Victorian intelligentsia and Bloomsbury. Both Joan and James had made substantial contributions to the translation of Freud and other psychoanalysts. James produced the 'Standard Edition' of Freud, and Joan was the translations editor of the *International Journal* from 1922 to 1937. However, Joan was Freud's favourite translator. Her beautiful muscular prose was well suited to Freud's style. Not surprisingly, James's obituary seesaws between admiration and dismissal.

James skates briefly over Joan's ancestors. She was born Joan Verrall. The Verralls were an old Sussex family. Joan's branches were mainly centred round Lewes and Brighton. Joan's grandfather crept into the middle classes by becoming a solicitor. Another ancestor wrote a successful cookbook. A copy of this belonged to Thomas Grey, now in the British Museum. With a sigh of relief, James alights on the 'really celebrated' Verrall, A. W. Verrall, a classics scholar at Trinity College Cambridge, where James had been a student. James likens Arthur Verrall to Freud: 'He had a mind which cut through conventional attitudes and superficial shams'. James's conventional attitude leaves out Arthur's wife Margaret, also a classics scholar at the university. Joan visited her uncle and aunt often, and as we shall see, their influence was very important to her.

James subtly underplays Joan's education: 'she had not herself been to the university, and indeed her education had been a little irregular'. Wycombe Abbey School 'did not suit her'. This was the cutting edge of girls' education at the time, and Joan spent three years there, followed by a year in Gotha to learn German. On her return home, Joan struggled to find a purpose in her life. She drew, she designed dresses, she worked for various women's causes. Finally, Joan made the obvious move of a beautiful girl who is not sure what to do: she married a handsome man. Evelyn Riviere was a chancery barrister, the son of Briton Riviere, a well-known Victorian painter. She now moved on the fringes of the Bloomsbury group. Her path crossed with that of James Strachey again: 'I still have a vivid picture of her standing by the fireplace at an evening party, tall, strikingly handsome, distinguished looking and somehow "impressive"'.

The connection with Arthur and Margaret Verrall led both Joan and James in a rather unexpected direction. The Society for Psychical Research was the respectable wing of spiritualism. It was started by a group of Cambridge dons of an earlier generation. Now its activities centred on the Verrall family. Members of the society grasped the importance of the work of Freud and Breuer. Freud even contributed a paper to its *Proceedings* in 1912. Joan would have read it. It was the start of her life's work.

James's obituary was read at a memorial meeting at the Institute of Psychoanalysis. As he neared the end, he began to struggle for what to say. Finally he hit on an aspect of Joan's character he particularly admired:

> I think she also regretted my non-committal attitude to questions of psychoanalytic theory. Non-committal was the thing she could never be. And that I think was … what was so splendid about her … and what she believed she would say out and uncompromisingly.

A ripple must have passed among the audience. The elephant in the room was Melanie Klein, who had died two years previously.

In 1926, Klein came to England trailing clouds of controversy for her work with young children and a radical technique. It was a meeting of minds between the two women. Joan was intrigued by Klein's intense little patients. She was to become Klein's most able defender. In addition, she was to use Klein's theories to produce a series of brilliant and original papers of her own. Why did no Kleinians write an obituary for her?

Chapter 1

'A well born lady'

> She has a strong complex about being a well born lady.
>
> Ernest Jones

As an adult, Riviere was seen as snobbish and upper-class, an impression emphasised by her height, magnificent carriage and stylish clothes. The reality was less elevated. Essentially her family were tradesmen who rose into the professional middle classes. Her father's family had a long history in Sussex, originating in Lindfield in the thirteenth century. From the 1700s onwards there was a cluster of Verralls based in and around Lewes. There are a number of theories about the origins of the name, one suggested it was a corruption of Firle, a village not far from Lewes. Another theory was that the name was French in origin. Whichever is correct, the family was well-established in Lewes and had a strong tradition of public service in the town.

Lewes is built on a chalk promontory overlooking the River Ouse. There has been a town there since 900. By 1080 the Domesday Book records Lewes as a borough and liable to taxation. The taxes included a tax on porpoises, and, unlikely though this sounds, remains of porpoises have been found in the grounds of Lewes Priory. The streets of the town cluster tightly around the hill and give the impression of a town in the clouds. Approaching modern Lewes it is striking how close everything is. The High Street, the Bowling Green, the White Hart and Bull House are all a few minutes walk from each other. They are also important in the history of the Verralls. In the town's seventeenth- and eighteenth-century heyday the High Street was lined by vintners, grocers, butchers, saddlers, gunsmiths, drapers, milliners and shoemakers (it remains the same today but without the saddlers and gunsmiths). Balls were held in the Assembly Rooms when the moon was full. There were a number of hostelries such as the White Hart, whose master was Richard Verrall (Davey, 1977). Richard and Sarah Verrall are the first ancestors of Hugh Verrall, Joan's father, who can reliably be identified. Richard was a constable of Lewes in 1717, 1730 and 1735. The role of constable was a voluntary one, appointed yearly to keep law and order. Between 1686 and 1799, ten Verralls served as constable. This tradition of public service was continued by Hugh Verrall, and his father. One of his sisters was on the education board.

From 1733 the developing Lewes social scene was damaged by battles between Whigs and Tories. John Cripps, the landlord of The Star, was a Tory, and likewise John Lidgitter, who owned a coffee shop. To balance things out the Duke of Newcastle, the Whig godfather of Lewes, installed Richard Verall Junior in a coffee house for the Whigs. A later attempt by the Duke to establish a Whig Assembly Rooms was less successful, perhaps because of a lack of partners. The division was called off, and from 1740 onwards Whigs and Tories danced together. Richard Junior died young in 1742 and was succeeded by his brother Harry Verrall as proprietor of the Whig Coffee House. As we shall see, Harry had even more radical leanings and played a significant role in the genesis of Tom Paine's *Rights of Man*. Harry was not an ancestor that Joan would claim with pride. She once famously remarked that socialism was the 'religion of younger siblings'.

Lewes has a long tradition of independent thinking. In the sixteenth century, seventeen Protestant martyrs were burned at the stake during the reign of Queen Mary. They are still commemorated in modern Lewes when seventeen blazing crosses are carried round the town on bonfire night. In 1768 the Lewes townspeople elected two enlightened MPs: Thomas Hay and Thomas Hampden. Both voted against attempts to expel or imprison their fellow MP, John Wilkes, the champion of civil liberties. Wilkes visited Lewes in August 1770 and was given an enthusiastic welcome with thousands flocking to see him and church bells ringing. The author of *The Rights of Man* slipped into Lewes more quietly in 1768. Tom Paine had an unsettled life and he tried a number of different jobs, including that of corsets maker – not a very suitable job for someone who advocated freedom. Despite his beliefs he accepted a job with the excise at £50 a year. Paine soon found kindred spirits including Samuel Ollive, his landlord at Bull House. Ollive was a pillar of the dissenting chapel and a Senior High Constable. There was also a lively group of professional men who met at the White Hart and formed a debating club called 'The Headstrong Club'. The most argumentative debater was awarded an old copy of Homer they called the 'headstrong book'. Not surprisingly, the book was frequently awarded to Tom Paine. Paine married Ollive's daughter, and Harry Verrall was a witness at their wedding.

Harry Verrall and Tom Paine were also both members of the bowls club. One day they were both relaxing over a bowl of punch and Harry remarked that 'the King of Prussia was the best fellow in the world for a King, he had so much of the devil in him!' This observation led Paine to reflect that 'if it were necessary for a King to have so much of the devil in him, kings might very well be dispensed with!' By 1774, Paine had moved on to France and America where his revolutionary thinking was more influential. The large undulating bowling green still exists. When I visited Lewes, bowls were still being played with special balls designed to cope with the ups and downs of the green. Modern Lewes leans to the right politically, but they are still proud of Paine. On a handsome board outside Bull House it proclaims Tom Paine 'Writer and Revolutionary lived here'.

Edward Verrall, the second son of Richard and Sarah of the White Hart, struck out on his own and became a publisher and stationer. He was paid by the borough to print notices during outbreaks of smallpox in 1731. He was proprietor, publisher and editor of *The Lewes Journal*. This newspaper was distributed by newsmen who tramped the country laden with journals, spectacles, fiddle strings, elixirs and pamphlets. Like Amazon, Edward diversified. Edward and his wife had eight children. When he died he left instructions for his daughter Martha to be apprenticed to a milliner in Bond Street, London. This had echoes one hundred and fifty years later when Anna and Hugh Verrall arranged for Joan to be apprenticed to the fashionable dressmaker Mrs. Ida Nettleship on Wigmore Street in London. Richard and Sarah's fifth child was William, who was probably the relative Joan was happiest to claim. He inherited the mastership of the White Hart from his father. However, he wrote a successful cookery book, *A Complete System of Cookery*. His book claims that he learned his recipes while working for the Duke of Newcastle under the great chef Clouet. His book was sold by his brother Edward and John Rivington in St Paul's churchyard. There is a copy of this book, which belonged to the poet Thomas Grey, in the British Museum.

With Harry Verrall's children the ascent of the Verralls into the professional middle classes begins. In 1781 William Verrall married Mary – and they had one child, Henry Verrall, born in 1783. Henry moved from Lewes to Steyning. Henry was the first professional member of the family. He was a solicitor who continued the family tradition of public service. He was secretary to the Bramber Agricultural Association, who presented him with a silver bowl in recognition of his services. Henry married Sarah Newmuns in 1812. Their eldest son, William, became a doctor and moved to Brighton, and their daughter, Mary, was unmarried and remained at home. The youngest child was Henry Verrall, Joan's grandfather, who was a Brighton solicitor. In 1848 he married Anne Webb, daughter of John Webb Woolgar. Their children incorporated their mother's surname, Woolgar, into their own, a tradition that Joan's father and mother would also follow. Henry and Anne's eldest child Henry died during infancy, a tragedy which was to repeat itself in the next generation. The oldest surviving child, Arthur Woolgar Verrall, was the star of the family. He was the first family member to go to Cambridge, where he was Fellow and Tutor of Trinity College and the first King Edward VII Professor of English Literature. He also found time to follow his father's profession and was briefly a successful barrister at law. In 1882 he married Margaret de Gaudrion, daughter of Frederick Merrifield, a Brighton barrister. Margaret was a lecturer at Newnham College Cambridge. These two unusual people were to become an enormously important influence on Joan's life.

The second son of Henry and Anne Verrall was Thomas Woolgar Verrall, who became a doctor. Finally, we get to Hugh John Verrall, Joan's father, born in 1854. Like Arthur, he was sent to boarding school, in this case to Marlborough, which had a good reputation for turning out potential professional men. Hugh joined his father's firm and became a solicitor. As well as being a solicitor, Hugh was also a clerk of the peace and Lieutenant Colonel of the First Volunteer Rifle Brigade, Sussex Regiment. In view of Hugh's later ill-health this is a position it is hard to imagine him holding, but very much in the family tradition of public service. Hugh also had two sisters, Marian and Annette. Annette was a member of the Brighton School Board and Education Committee and later the East Sussex Education Committee. Before women got the vote this was one the few ways a woman could exercise civic power.

On 16th June 1881, Hugh Verrall married Anna Hodgson in the parish church of Chalgrave in Bedfordshire. The bride was a former governess and daughter of the vicar. The wedding was a source of excitement in the village and the church was packed with people. A detailed account appeared in the local paper. At eleven thirty the bride appeared leaning on the arm of her brother. She was attended by the two Misses Verrall and her sisters Marian, Edith, Daisy and Dora. Anna wore a handsome cream satin dress, trimmed with Duchesse lace, tulle and ribbon. The bridesmaids were dressed in pink zephyr and mob caps and carried baskets of 'choice' flowers. The service was read affectingly by the bride's father. The wedding party was confined to near relations. Some economy was necessary as the Reverend and Mrs Hodgson had thirteen children, ten of them girls. After a wedding breakfast at the Vicarage the new Mr and Mrs Verrall set off on a tour of the Lakes.

At first it was a mystery to me how Anna and Hugh could have met. Chalgrave is a long way from Brighton. However, examination of the census records throws some light on this. In contrast to the Verralls, who were firmly rooted in Sussex, John Willoughby Hodgson, the Vicar of Chalgrave, had led a mobile existence. The 1841 Census shows him living at the Grammar School for Reigate, Surrey, his occupation given as a Schoolmaster. In 1851 he is visiting Kirkford Vicarage, Petworth in Sussex, aged 31, and he is now the Curate of Kirkford. In 1851 he married Julia Tosswill of Broadclyst, Devon, who was ten years his junior. In 1861 Julia and John Hodgson were living in Brighton and John Hodgson was a clergyman without care of souls. At this point Anna was four and the fourth of six children. The family had six servants including a cook, housemaids and nursemaids. It is likely that these servants were not only necessary for the family but also for a large household of boarders. By 1871 the Hodgsons had fourteen boarders. After the Hodgsons left the house it was occupied by Mr Seaver's Boys School which gives some indication of its size. Perhaps it was snobbery about the boarders which created some of the tensions between the Hodgsons and the Verralls. This cannot have been insurmountable as, following the family tradition, Joan and her brother and sister were given their mother's surname as a middle name.

Finally, on the 24th February 1875, John Hodgson became Vicar of Chalgrave and made up for his wandering years by staying put as Vicar for twenty-three years and sixty-six days. The family further consolidated their social position by sending two of their sons to Cambridge. The Reverend Hodgson's salary was £250 per year, so it was likely he continued to take in boarders to keep his large family. For Anna, now in her early twenties, the move must have felt like an exile from the sparkling life of Brighton. Chalgrave remains a remote and scattered parish and the church is at the end of a long and isolated lane. Something of the flavour of life comes from the parish vestry book. The same four or five men met with the Vicar to decide on the parish rate and allocate parish roles. In one particularly poignant entry, John Hodgson wrote that 'no-one came, so no parish business could be transacted'. The only exciting event seems to have been the Sunday School picnic.

It was probably to get away from this stultifying life that Anna decided to become a governess. In some ways her situation was more fortunate than that of many governesses. Her father was still alive and able to support her (Hughes, K., 1993). By the standards of the time she had received a good education from her father, and had probably helped out in the Sunday School at Chalgrave. She was familiar, perhaps too familiar, with the needs and demands of small children. Best of all, she had contacts. The years in Brighton and the Reverend Hodgson's work had given them a wide acquaintance. During the 1850s the supply of women wishing to be governesses exceeded the places available. It was a buyer's market, and women could be put through humiliating steps to get a place. The Governesses Benevolent Institution ran an employment agency, but that was based in London. Many women were forced to advertise their services in newspapers. The ideal way of getting a place was through friends and people you knew. (This is the scene in Jane Austen's *Emma* when the odious Mrs Elton suggests a place for Jane Fairfax.)

It is quite likely that Anna already knew Hugh Verrall because of the Brighton connection. If Anna did work for a family in Malta, as the family story goes, it was a sensible move. Governesses occupied an uncomfortable middle ground between the family and the servants and were often paid less than senior servants. Families from abroad appreciated their English governess, and the loss of social status was less painful. Did Hugh and Anna write while Anna was away? It would have been natural for Anna to return to Brighton where she had friends and contacts if she wanted a post in England again. Alternatively, Hugh could have proposed by letter, in which case Anna would have returned to her family in Chalgrave. Anna's experiences as a governess seem to have given her confidence and a willingness to try new things. When she wanted to see Queen Victoria's funeral she travelled up to London on her own. She took up archery and learned to ride a bicycle. It is a very different picture to the fussy housewife that her granddaughter Diana paints. Anna's experiences cast another light on the Verralls' decision to send Joan to Gotha for a year when she was seventeen. They must have hoped that year abroad would give her confidence, and unlike Anna, she would not have had to look after children!

Although Joan would probably have preferred to be compared to her father, as she got older she showed her mother's willingness to launch herself into new experiences, her analysis with Ernest Jones (although as we shall see, psychoanalysis as a theory was not unknown to her), her journey to Vienna to be analysed by Freud, and her intellectual daring in taking up the new ideas of Melanie Klein.

Chapter 2

Joan

After the honeymoon, Anna and Hugh returned to Brighton and moved in with Hugh's parents, Henry and Anne at 26 Gloucester Place. There was plenty of room in the tall, thin house, although Hugh's two sisters continued to live there. Living with Hugh's parents cannot have been easy for Anna. She was a wife, but with no home of her own to run. Anne Verrall rustled up and downstairs giving orders to the cook and the housemaids. Annette and Marion, Hugh's sisters, both had their own public concerns to attend to. Neither became particularly friendly with Anna. Anna probably joined Mrs Verrall on her round of social calls. Hugh and Mr Verrall shared a solicitors' practice at 4 New Road. The office has now been knocked through to make a cafe; but even then it must have been a lively location, near the Pavilion and a short walk from Gloucester Place. Hugh had a successful career until he was hampered later by the debility caused by rheumatic fever. He does not seem to have had the drive of his 2 older brothers. Arthur was a barrister and lecturer at Trinity College. Thomas held senior posts in the medical profession. Like Thomas, he went to Marlborough School, which had the reputation of turning out boys who became successful members of the professions. Anna seems to have been a more vigorous personality, and maybe this was part of her attraction for Hugh.

Before long, Anna was pregnant. In the days before pregnancy tests many women were not aware of being pregnant until the baby started to move. As the middle child of a large family Anna was familiar with the early signs. She immediately became the focus of discreet attention, this would be the first grandchild for the Verralls. The Verralls enjoyed providing for their grandchildren, so it is possible that they bought the cradle for the new baby. A monthly nurse was engaged. The nurse arrived a month before the baby was due and stayed until the baby was three months old. She looked after mother and baby, cleaning the mother's room, washing the baby's clothes and caring for the baby. If the baby was bottle-fed the nurse would feed it; if it was breast-fed the nurse would bring it in. The whole purpose of her work was to ensure that mothers rested during the lying in period, 'the monthly nurse should be a dragon of watchfulness keeping away small bothers which men cannot refrain from bringing to their wives' (Flanders, 2003) Good monthly nurses were tremendously in demand, and Anne Verrall may have had a hand in engaging one.

Despite the excitement there would have been anxiety. Maternal mortality was still very high. By 1899, sixteen percent of children did not survive until their first birthday. Perhaps, not surprisingly, pregnancy began to be medicalised. The middle classes used a doctor rather than a midwife. Rest and seclusion was the extent of Victorian antenatal care, so it is unlikely that Anna would have travelled to see her parents. Her one liberation would have been to leave off her corsets as the baby grew. John and Julia Hodgson probably came to visit Anna, perhaps with some of the 'little aunts' as Anna called them. This visit would have generated complex social ripples. Julia would have been longing to give helpful advice to Anna, but the evidence of Anna's diary suggests that there were tensions between Anna and her mother. Anna's long period as a governess may have been partly a way of leaving home. The tensions between Anna and Julia were mirrored later when Joan became a mother.

The Verralls viewed the Hodgsons as socially inferior, which led to difficulties when Hugh and Anna chose Joan's names. The Verralls were financially better off, and a clergyman who took in boarders would have been considered inferior to a successful professional man. Ironically, it was Joan's birth and Hugh's temporary desertion which drove Anna back into the arms of her family. However, when the first baby was born, Anna was firmly embedded among the Verralls. The doctor was called, and Anna may have been offered chloroform. In 1857 Queen Victoria had chloroform during childbirth. However it was slow to gain popularity and Charles Darwin administered it to his wife Emma himself. At first there was excitement, the baby was a boy. He was put into Anna's arms, but then came a terrible anti-climax: he died a little while later. The fact that infant mortality was high does not mean that the loss was not keenly felt by the parents. A popular pair of pictures by Frank Holl painted in 1877 shows a mother with a baby in a cradle telling an older child to 'hush'. The second picture, *Hushed*, shows the mother doubled up with grief and a dead baby in the cradle.

Hugh and Anna's baby was baptised. Anna's diary says that she was almost alone in the church. The loss of this baby mirrored Henry and Anne's loss of their first baby. Even if Hugh was there, 'almost alone' probably describes Anna's feeling of no one to turn to. Her pride may have made her a difficult person to comfort. By modern standards, Anna did the right things, holding her baby, giving it a name and a grave. A few months later Anna was pregnant again. A pregnancy which follows rapidly on a miscarriage or a stillbirth is now thought to interfere with mourning, but Anna kept her dead baby in mind (Reid, 2007). Twenty-seven years later, as Hugh was dying, Anna remembered the death of the baby. Elizabeth Gaskell, the novelist, had a similar experience to Anna, a stillborn baby followed by a live one. Three years later, after her daughter Marianne was born, she visited the baby's grave and wrote this sonnet:

> On visiting the Grave of my stillborn little girl. Sunday July 4th 1836
>
> I made a vow within my soul, O child,
> When thou were laid beside my weary heart,
> With marks of death of every tender part
> That, if in times a living infant smiled
> Winning my ear with gentle sounds of love
> In sunshine of such joy, I still would save
> A green rest for the memory, O Dove!
> And oft times visit thy small, nameless grave
> Thee I have not forgot …

Although Gaskell did not forget her baby, she accepted that the birth of the new live baby had a healing effect (Uglow, 1993). Gaskell's recovery is all the more remarkable as her own mother had died when she was a year old. Both Anna and Mrs Gaskell kept diaries of the early months of their first live babies, and as we shall see, it is possible to trace the impact of these losses on the subsequent baby.

Anna's new pregnancy galvanised Hugh into finding a house of their own. In 1883 they moved into 12 Buckingham Place. This is a handsome street of white stucco Regency houses which soars above Brighton station with a view over the town. A curious feature of this move is that the house is just a few doors down from the one that Anna grew up in. This could have been a comfort to Anna at a time when she must have been anxious. As she confided to her diary, she dreaded a repeat of the previous year's experience. Even more curiously than the move to No. 12, in 1885 Anna and Hugh moved to No. 18, the house that Anna grew up in. This was a strange move because No.18 was an enormous house, occupied by a boy's school after the Hodgson's left. Did this house belong to John Hodgson? The effect of this move meant that Joan's childhood was spent in the house her mother grew up in.

Anna was passionately interested in appearances, so she must have enjoyed furnishing and decorating these houses. It was the height of the aesthetic movement, Morris fabrics and tall vases of flowers were all the rage, 'number 31 Kensington Square, where they lived, was full of Morris wallpapers, and Morris curtains and blue china, and peacock feathers, and Arundel prints, and all that sort of thing' (Raverat, 1952). An indication of Anna's attachment to her furniture is given in a story told by Diana Riviere, Joan's daughter, who says that Anna prevented Joan and her sister Molly from going to a ball because they had spilt a drop of candle wax on the table. After Hugh Verrall died, Anna wrote in her diary a little hymn of admiration for the beauty of the bedroom he had died in.

The beauty of the rooms was not achieved by Anna's work alone. The move to their own house meant that Anna had to engage servants. Hugh would have been earning enough to pay a cook at £20 a year and a housemaid at £18 a year. Anna would have had to decide whether to employ a monthly nurse again. Mrs Beeton's description of a good monthly nurse describes someone rather like a good mother – good tempered and with a kind and gentle disposition (Beeton, 1861). Anna may have decided that she wanted that sort of care again after her traumatic first experience of childbirth. At some point she must also have employed Marsh, their gentle nursemaid. Anna's arrangements with her servants seem to have mostly run smoothly and she occasionally speaks warmly of them.

> Our sweet little daughter was born on June 28th 1883, a Thursday at five o'clock in the afternoon. I had been dreading it inexpressibly after my terrible experience last year … I was spared a repetition of that and had a decidedly good time!

Having a decidedly good time is a robust response to childbirth, and maybe an attitude Anna had inherited from her mother. However, there are some hints that Anna initially found her baby difficult. Her diary records that on 17th September Anna weaned Joan, though in fact she had been giving Joan supplements since she was a month old, 'My meals were certainly of very little use to her and it is hoped my inflamed eyelids might benefit by giving it up'. Perhaps Joan's large size, 9¼ lbs – which Anna proudly comments on a number of times – may have worried Anna as to whether she was getting enough food. However, the reference to inflamed eyelids is more like folklore. The psychotherapist Alexis Brook (1995) points out that apart from the mouth, the eyes are the most important organs through which we experience the world. This is reflected in figures of speech like 'turning a blind eye', or 'to be hit in the eye'. Brook's research shows that a range of eye disorders are linked to difficulties in mourning. We shall see later that Joan had difficulties with styes during periods when she was depressed. It is possible that Anna's rapid conception after the death of her first child interfered with mourning her loss. Mrs Gaskell's 'green nest for thy memory' is benign but sad. At Joan's christening Anna wrote in her diary: 'I was so glad to be able to be present at our darling's baptism but it reminded me very sadly of that other baptism when I was almost alone'.

Anna was not only proud of her baby's size, but also of her 'beautiful hands' like 'her father's'. To her relief, the baby was not only pretty but remarkably good. By this Anna meant that she did not cry. When Joan's routine was disrupted and she began to cry 'more than I would like' when being dressed, Anna recorded thankfully that she never cried during the night. Quite an achievement for a baby.

This picture of a rather distant mother, preoccupied with appearances is echoed by Gwen Raverat, Charles Darwin's granddaughter. Raverat was born two years after Joan to a wealthier family.

> I can never remember being bathed by my mother, or even having my hair brushed by her, and I should not have liked it if she had done anything of the kind. We did not feel it was her place to do such things.
>
> (Raverat, 1952)

It could be said that Raverat and Joan were born at a point when the move from a parent-centred to a child-centred world was not yet complete. However Mrs Gaskell, whose baby was born fifty years earlier than Joan, kept a diary which gives a very different picture of the mother/child relationship:

> I had no idea the journal of my own disposition and feelings were intimately connected with that of my little baby, whose regular breathing has been the music of my thoughts all the time I had been writing. God bless her.
>
> (Quoted in Maroni, 2004)

Mrs Gaskell was not afraid of her baby crying, 'we must consider that a child's cry is a child's only language for expressing its wants'. She also confesses to feeling jealousy when Marianne expresses a preference for her nurse Betsy, but 'I believe Betsy fully deserves and returns her love'. Both Mrs Gaskell and Anna lost their first baby, but there are obviously crucial differences between them. Mrs Gaskell had the capacity to bear emotional pain and guilt. She hoped Marianne would forgive her for any failings as a mother.

When Anna felt supported she was able to make astute observations about Joan's character. She and Hugh noticed that from very early on Joan could grasp firmly with her fingers and linked this with her intelligence. Many years later, Joan's first psychoanalyst, Ernest Jones, commented on Joan's powerful intellectual grasp of psychoanalytic theory. Anna was also aware of a more vulnerable aspect of Joan's character: 'I am sorry to find that she is very nervous and easily frightened by sudden noises and movements – she will require very gentle treatment I am sure'. These words were uncannily like those of Freud at the end of Joan's analysis in 1922: 'I fear she will require special care and regard indefinitely'.

Although Anna was aware of a more fragile aspect of Joan, in general she looked to Joan to dispel the ghost of the baby who died, and Joan seems to have picked up that it was her role to reassure her parents. When Joan was six months old Anna writes: 'So far our sweet maid has not given us a moment's anxiety – her only ailment being a slight cold once or twice'. However, a close examination of Anna's diary reveals a more complex picture.

On 27th July 1883, Joan was baptised in St. Martin's Church. Joan looked delightful and behaved well, but under the smooth surface there were family tensions and rivalries. Anna wrote 'The little maid was exceedingly good and looks very sweet in a lovely robe which was *our* present – her handsome cloak and hood being her grandmother Verrall's present.' However, the older Verralls were not keen on Joan's name, Joan Hodgson. Hugh and Anna stood firm on this. It is not clear whether it was Joan that the Verralls objected to or whether there was a more hidden dislike of Joan carrying her mother's family name. However, Hugh and his siblings all carried Anne Verrall's family name Woolgar, so Hugh and Anna were carrying on a family tradition. Joan's godparents were Ethel Weir, who had supported Anna after Joan's birth, Willoughby Hodgson and Annette Verrall, so both sides of the family were taken account of. Anna herself was very sensitive about family involvement. Her diary records that all the Verralls were at the christening 'except Arthur and May'. Arthur and May (Margaret) were now both lecturers in classics at Cambridge. They were probably absent because of the birth of their own child, Helen. Apart from this early absence Arthur and May were to become a second family and formative influence on Joan.

After the enjoyable fuss of the christening, and the sadder thoughts about the lost baby, Anna's next diary entry betrays a sense of shock. On 18th August, less than two months after Joan's birth, Hugh set off with his friend Mr Jennings for a three-week holiday in Switzerland. Although Anna says that Hugh needs a holiday, she conveys a sense of being abruptly dropped at a vulnerable time. As one of the older children in a family of thirteen children, Anna must have had the repeated experience of being emotionally dropped when her mother's attention turned to the new baby. When I first read this in Anna's diary I assumed it was the early signs of Hugh's rheumatic fever. However, this was not diagnosed until Joan was three. My view now is that whatever the state of Hugh's health, he found it hard to cope with the demands of a new baby. When Anna notes in her diary that Hugh will see a great improvement in Joan when he returns, there is a hint that he found the baby difficult. Perhaps Hugh's response to Joan was similar to his contemporary George Darwin's response to the birth of his daughter Gwen. This was recorded by his wife's cousin Ella:

> George looked at the baby with a good deal of pride last night – but from a distance, I could not induce him to touch it. He went into Maud (Darwin) for a minute and came out very meekly ... Having had his orders to hold it and kiss it, which he did with good grace, only showing a great deal of horror when it cried.
>
> (Raverat, 1952)

New babies do cry a lot, however well-managed they are. Hugh took refuge in Switzerland, and Anna took refuge from her sense of abandonment with her family in Chalgrave.

The family at Chalgrave gave Anna the support and admiration she needed. The little aunts loved to nurse Joan, and her father 'delights in her and constantly goes into raptures over her clear warm complexion and soft skin and healthy looks'. A photograph of Joan as a toddler shows a child who is both beautiful and full of vitality. This may have been intensely important to Anna to offset the image of the dead baby whose unmourned shadow seems to have haunted her mind. The person who is missing in Anna's account of family support is her mother. It certainly seems to have been the case that Anna did not have a figure in her mind who could respond to emotional distress. The change in routine, and perhaps Joan's sensitivity to her mother's distress made itself felt, and she began to cry more often. Anna was aware this was not a reflection on her gentle nursemaid Marsh, but did not seem to consider that Joan might be upset by a change of place and the sudden absence of her father. Within a couple of weeks Joan seemed to have settled and reassured her mother by laughing and cooing often – 'her father will see a great deal of improvement I feel sure'. This comment seems to indicate a continuing anxiety that Hugh will find Joan a problem.

While Hugh was away, Anna seems to have found it impossible to return home, and moved on to stay with friends in Beckenham. These moves so soon after her baby was born must have been a strain on Anna, although Joan behaved immaculately on the train. Finally, on 12th September, Hugh returned and joined them at Beckenham. To Anna's relief he was 'delighted' with Joan. On the way back to Brighton they called in at Redhill to visit Hugh's aunts. Anna was pleased to discover that, unlike Joan, cousin Helen (Arthur and May's daughter) was 'always crying'. A few days after their return home Joan was weaned.

Anna's diary on 10th October illustrates the extent to which Anna expected Joan to cope with even distressing events without making any demands on her. In the morning Joan went out for the first time in the new carriage bought for her by her grandfather Verrall, 'She lies down in it and is very happy'. Late in the day 'Uncle Fred' came to vaccinate Joan. It is very interesting that the presence of a supportive man enabled Anna to help Joan through the ordeal by 'holding her myself'. Characteristically, Joan was not cross or fretful even when her 'whole system seemed upset' on the 9th, and she had sickness and diarrhoea. After this upset, Anna records with satisfaction that Joan is now in a regular routine. She went to her parents between seven and eight in the morning. Anna had her for an hour after lunch while Marsh got her meal, and on Monday and Tuesday Anna had Joan for half a day so that Marsh could do the washing and turn out the nursery. Sometimes Joan was taken down at teatime to entertain guests, but this tended to make her over-excited. This collaborative routine was soon to be disrupted.

December 1883 was Joan's first Christmas, but on 21st December Anna and Hugh went to Chalgrave, and Joan was sent with Marsh to 'Uncle Tom's', Hugh's middle brother, for a week. This seems an extraordinary thing to do. Joan was sent to a family she would hardly know instead of a family where she would be petted and welcomed. Maybe Anna was worried that Hugh could not cope with a more prolonged contact with a small baby. In view of later developments this seems a possible explanation. As usual, Anna reports how pleased the relatives are with Joan. However, she discovers that cousin Helen is much improved in looks and has two teeth! 'A degree of precocity I do not long for in my baby!' Despite the apparent success of the visit, Joan had a succession of colds the whole of the next month, which may have been a response to the temporary loss of her mother, and the beginnings of her psychosomatic responses to emotional distress. After Hugh abruptly left Anna when Joan was tiny, Anna seems to have accepted that Hugh was to be her priority, to be looked after by her, even if was at Joan's expense.

'I measured her today – 29½ inches!' Joan was certainly a tall baby for nine months old. Anna comments repeatedly what a healthy baby she is, as if to reassure herself. By now Joan was pulling herself to her feet and crawling, Anna was having to adapt to a more mobile baby. This mobility had shocking consequences on 29th March when Joan fell off her parent's bed and onto her head, 'Her screams were so instantaneous and violent poor little wee she was frightened of course – but I felt sure she could not be seriously hurt!' Joan already seems to have been sensitive to her parents' needs in this situation, 'After the first she was wonderfully good and brave and tried to smile through her tears at her daddy!' Uncle Fred, the doctor, was downstairs and reassured Anna and Hugh, although there was no suggestion that he should examine Joan. The following day Joan amused her parents by crawling up to the mirror in her mother's wardrobe, and licking and patting the reflection of her own face. She seems to have been kissing herself better and may even have reflected Marsh's response to her bruise. A few days later Joan narrowly missed an even worse accident. Marsh fell downstairs while carrying her. Fortunately, Anna was standing at the bottom and caught Joan, 'It was very frightful to see even for that moment her peril and I cannot be sufficiently thankful that I was there'. Anna recorded that Joan was not even frightened and 'laughed heartlessly at her poor sobbing nurse who was very much bruised and shaken'. Once again, it seems as if Joan knew she should not show distress, and Anna could not see the shock behind the laughter.

A day or two later, Anna and Hugh went away for a few days. While they were away Joan went to her Verrall grandparents every day for dinner. This might also have been a support to Marsh, who could easily have been as young as sixteen or seventeen. These sorts of intense contacts with nursemaids often created very firm ties of affection. We have already heard of Marianne Gaskell's attachment to her nursemaid Betsy, although it was clear that she had not given up the intimacy with her mother. A more extreme example is given by Gwen Raverat:

> Nana [a name that sounds like mamma] hardly ever went out, and if she did the housemaid or nursery maid was left in charge of us. About once in two or three years there was an appalling calamity, and Nana left us poor little orphans while she went away for a week's holiday ... My mother did nothing extra herself!
>
> (Raverat, 1952)

When Anna came back from her few days away she was delighted that Joan had at last cut her first tooth. She did not consider the effect of her absence on Joan. The Verralls were not heartless, but they seemed to have a lack of imagination where their children were concerned. This may have been partly their period and class, but Mrs Gaskell displayed a very different attitude, and even aristocratic families could be sensitive about separations. In 1825 the Countess of Gower went abroad with her husband and wrote to her sister:

> My dearest Caroline, the parting with one's child is most dreadful ... You have no idea of the treasure of her little likeness is to us; we have it out and look at it constantly when by ourselves. I tell you all these things because I know you will not think them affected and would feel them very much the same à ma place.

Joan's second major separation (if one includes the week at Uncle Tom's) was three and a half months while her parents were travelling in Europe. She was about a year old. On their return Anna was pregnant with Joan's younger sister Molly, who was born on 18th April 1885. Two weeks before Molly's birth, Joan fell and cut her eyelid so badly it had to be stitched. It is interesting that there is a problem with eyes again. Anna's sore eyes and Joan's styes. Joan may have felt 'hit in the eye' by her mother's pregnancy. When Molly was three months old, Hugh and Anna went abroad again. Athol Hughes considers this an 'example of extreme denial of infantile need' (personal communication, 2015). The reason again is Hugh Verrall's health, but perhaps it was not a coincidence that it broke down when there was a very young baby in the house. Anna may have been determined not to be left on her own again with Joan. Hanna Segal, Joan's psychoanalytic supervisee, remarked to me that Joan 'did not like children'. Perhaps this was not surprising when babies were linked with a separation from one or both parents.

Chapter 3

Other worlds

London, 1874

A darkened room in the house of William Crookes. A group of ladies and gentlemen are sitting round a large mahogany table. The Medium, Florence Cook, an attractive young woman, is sitting in a sort of cupboard cut off from the table by curtains. Florence is tied to her chair with strings whose knots are sealed with wax. The guests sing spiritualist hymns. At last the pale face of the spirit of 'Katie Price' appears above the curtains. After answering various questions she graciously agrees to promenade around the room on the arm of William Crookes. Crookes was a talented scientist, the discoverer of the element Thallium, and a president of the Royal Society. Did he not suspect any fakery? A rumour went round that Florence was his mistress. Florence was conclusively unmasked in 1880 by Sir George Sitwell, who detected a most unspiritual corset. Her boots and strings lay inside the cupboard. Her robe had apparently been concealed in her drawers. Interestingly, Crookes's reputation did not suffer. In due course he received a knighthood (Oppenheim, 1985).

Spiritualism may seem a long way from psychoanalysis but Joan could not have got to it by a quicker route. By the 1870s there was a groundswell of scepticism about the phenomenon of spiritualism. The hard core of convinced spiritualists, which included Arthur Conan Doyle, separated from another group who wanted to believe in the hitherto unknown aspects of the mind, but felt they should be investigated in a scientific manner, although the gap between these two groups was not as clear cut as it appeared. In 1874, Henry Sidgwick, Knightsbridge Professor of Moral Philosophy, and two of his former pupils, Frederick Myers and Edward Gurney, formed the Society for Psychical Research. Some of the initial seances were carried out in the house of Arthur Balfour, the future prime minister, and included his sister Elinor. This was a satisfactory arrangement for Sidgwick, who was courting Elinor. In due course, the two married. Elinor eventually became the principal of Newnham College and later on the president of the Society for Psychical Research (SPR). As time went on the SPR conducted fewer seances and concentrated on telepathy, automatic writing and table turning, as these were thought more suitable for experiments.

It was not surprising that Cambridge was a seedbed for psychical research, as there were men and women who experienced a gap which had been previously filled by religion. Sidgwick himself had given up his Trinity fellowship because he could not subscribe to the 39 Articles. That this did not impede his academic career, was a reflection of the changing climate of opinion within the university. For those who no longer had the comforts of religion, the idea that parts of the mind could be in touch with other minds, even if those people were dead, was very appealing. The SPR set itself up as a respectable scientific society with a dazzling list of members, a journal – the *Proceedings* – and a library. By 1916 the links with psychoanalysis were so well established that Joan consulted the library when she was looking for a psychoanalyst. The SPR still exists, and without any apparent irony shares its premises in Kensington with a funeral parlour. The library derives gravitas from bound copies of the *Proceedings*. Looking through these I was struck by their similarity to the *British Journal of Psychotherapy*. There are papers on hysteria, multiple personality, the unconscious, the Liverpool Psychotherapy Clinic and reviews (favourable) of books by Freud. For a while the SPR ran in tandem with mainstream psychology. During the 1870s and 1880s, Sidgwick played a significant role in getting Psychology accepted as part of the Cambridge curriculum. This was no mean feat, as Physics and Chemistry had only been introduced twenty years before. Some of the Cambridge scientists became members of the SPR and added credibility to its work. Prominent among those was Lord Rayleigh, who was married to Elinor Sidgwick's sister Evelyn. Elinor, who was a talented mathematician, helped with some of the calculations for Rayleigh's experiments.

In 1892 Henry Sidgwick presided over the Second International Congress of Experimental Psychology. Most of the English delegates were SPR members. Sidgwick and Myers read a paper on hallucinations and Elinor Sidgwick read one on thought transference. Such was the respectability of the SPR, that William James, the distinguished American psychologist, was briefly president. Jean Charcot, whose work on hysteria at the Salpêtriere in Paris won him an international reputation, also expressed an interest, as shown by a letter from the archives of Trinity College, Cambridge:

> 5th November 1886
>
> Dear Sir
>
> I have just received the books you were kind enough to send me. Thank you many times for your kindness and I am sure that I will acquire by reading the Proceedings of the SPR a great deal of new scientific knowledge – I had the extreme pleasure of dining last Wednesday with Dr Myers and Mister Gurney and my only regret was that you had already crossed back to England.
>
> Yours most gratefully,
> Jean Charcot

Charcot may or may not have been a convert to the SPR in the long run, but his initial response was positive nonetheless.

1893–1895, Selwyn Gardens, Cambridge

Joan has come to stay with her cousin Helen Verrall, daughter of her Uncle Arthur and Aunt Margaret. Despite some tensions between the two sets of parents, Joan is a regular visitor to Cambridge. On this occasion the adults are having a dinner party. The two little girls are standing on the stairs watching a line of guests snaking into the dining room for what Margaret's friend, Jane Harrison, calls a 'small but not informal dinner party with the university order of precedence strictly observed' (Harrison, 1925). The guests are Henry and Elinor Sidgwick, Frederick Myers and his wife Evelyn, Edward Gurney and Jane Harrison. The servants, who have been with Margaret for years scurry round, are carrying coats and getting the first course ready to bring in. Gwen Raverat, whose parents George and Maud Darwin were friends of the Verralls, describes an informal menu:

> Tomato Soup
> Fried Smelts of Drawn Butter Sauce
> Mushrooms on Toast
> Roast Beef, Cauliflower and Potatoes
> Apple Charlotte
> Toasted Cheese
> Dessert: Candied peel oranges, peanuts, raisins, or ginger.
> (Raverat, 1952)

Frederick Myers, a great enthusiast, regaled his fellow guests with his latest discovery: two Viennese doctors, Josef Breuer and Sigmund Freud, who had been treating patients suffering from hysteria. The significance of this for the SPR members was the idea of an unconscious part of the mind, not available to conscious thought. Elinor Sidgwick and Arthur Verrall, the resident sceptics were dubious, but a decision was made to invite Freud to join the SPR and contribute to its *Proceedings*. Myers wrote a report on Freud's work in 1893 for the *Proceedings* and Freud contributed an important paper, 'A note on the unconscious in Psychoanalysis' in 1912. Both these papers were Joan's first encounter with psychoanalysis. We know from a letter to a Herr Bode in Gotha that she was also interested in psychological novels.

Margaret really belonged to the more mystical wing of the SPR. One of her papers in the *Proceedings* describes some table tilting by Joan and Helen after Joan's marriage to Evelyn Riviere. The party were waiting for Evelyn to arrive from London. The words tilted by Joan and Helen were: 'E Fontaine, I demur to your plea your claim is void'. Helen suggested that E Fontaine was 'Evelyn Riviere'. Further tilting produced: 'Simpkinsons is claimant, water rights'. When Evelyn arrived he confirmed that had been working on a water rights case, which suggested to Margaret that there was thought transmission.

The amount of work Margaret did for the SPR suggests a desperation to believe. One reason, perhaps, was that she had lost two little girls, one with spina bifida, and the other was stillborn. In some ways, she and Arthur treated Joan like a surrogate child. Joan carried on working for the SPR into her twenties. In 1957, when Joan had many years' experience as an analyst, she wrote to Ernest Jones (her former analyst):

> The apparent telepathy which occurs between (*some*) patients and their analysts is amazing, but it is not recorded and studied. As a psychoanalyst I have also experienced this sort of telepathy, and there still seems to be a reluctance to study it.

Although the SPR was important to Joan, her introduction to Freud and psychoanalysis would affect the rest of her life.

Joan's relationship to Margaret was closer and more affectionate than that with her own mother. Margaret's family were forward-looking, although her early education was conservative – that is 'at home' as the Newnham College register put it. However, through the Merrifields' involvement with women's suffrage, they met Millicent Garrett Fawcett, the leader of the movement. In 1875 she wrote to Margaret's mother, Maria Angelique de Gaudrion, urging her to send Margaret to Cambridge: 'she would make a success and further the cause of women's eduction'. The Merrifields were willing to be persuaded, and as Mrs Fawcett was one of the founders of Newnham, Margaret went there.

Margaret thrived at Newnham, in 1875 she was awarded a college scholarship, in 1876 she was a Goldsmith's Scholar, and in 1878 she was a college scholar. Margaret had intended to study Political Economy and Moral Sciences. However, she came under the influence of an older student, Jane Harrison, who persuaded her to study classics instead. Jane was very persuasive, and she was also the epitome of intellectual brilliance and fashionable style (Robinson, 2002). She was tall, and wore her hair coiled around her head. She dressed in Pre-Raphaelite clothes. Her room was papered with William Morris wallpaper. One of the issues facing the early women students at Cambridge was how to present their femininity. Judging by contemporary photographs they decided to flaunt it. Henry Sidgwick, the founder of Newnham, was worried by their beautiful faces and fashionable tied-back dresses. Jane Harrison, as always, went further. She claimed the ruffles she sewed on her friend Mary Paley's blouse brought about her engagement to Alfred Marshall. In 1926, when the adult Joan appeared at a congress with Melanie Klein, they were both exquisitely dressed – their outfits possibly made by Joan.

The friendship between Jane and Margaret faced an early challenge. When the results came out, brilliant sparkling Jane got a Class II, like Margaret. Not only this, but Margaret was offered the college lectureship which Jane expected for herself. By the time the offer was made to Margaret, Jane had taken flight to London. Margaret took a train to London and gratified her friend by stomping round the room and offering to give the lectureship to her. Jane persuaded Margaret that this would be quixotic. Margaret returned to Cambridge and settled gracefully into her new post. She proved to be a precise and scholarly lecturer, and she was soon in demand to mark the scholarship papers. In 1882 she married Arthur Verrall, Fellow of Trinity and Joan's uncle. After her marriage, she carried on working and dined at the college several times a week. Her attachment to Newnham was demonstrated when she had her (very large) new home designed by Basil Champneys, architect of Newnham. It was built only a few minutes' walk away from the college. In modern terms, Margaret was a woman who had it all. A supportive husband, a daughter following in her footsteps, a career and an absorbing interest (the SPR). She also had a beautiful home and her servants stayed for years. On her regular visits, Joan could not fail to be aware of these things.

Jane Harrison lived in London and supported herself with fees from lecturing on the ancient world. She treated it like theatre and dressed in spangly shawls and feathers in her hair. Although Jane took her clothes seriously she was prepared to be amused. On one occasion a boy at Winchester was asked if he enjoyed her lecture. 'Not the lecture', he replied, 'but I liked the lady; she was like a beautiful green beetle'. As well as the lectures, Jane studied with a purpose. She examined the notes in the British Museum and travelled abroad to study archaeology and anthropology. Gradually she laid the foundations of what would be the Myth and Ritual School. The essence of this approach is summarised by Mary Beard: 'the basic method of her work – that somewhere underneath the calm, shining, rational exterior of the classical world is a mass of seething irrationality' (Beard, 2000). Not surprisingly, Jane admired Freud, whose ideas she must have encountered through the SPR. Eventually, Jane's scholarship was acknowledged by Newnham and she returned as a Research Fellow in 1898. She was spared most of the drudgery of teaching and marking, but the students she did teach got something else. Frances Darwin described Jane coming to Sunday lunch: 'Even as a child I felt she gave roast beef and Yorkshire pudding a particular glow and she went to the head of any intellectual adolescent like champagne' (Peacock, 1988). It would be twenty-five years before Joan met another woman like Jane, and she recognised her importance immediately. That woman was Melanie Klein.

In this sort of climate it would be expected that Cambridge would be a hotbed of women's suffrage. Margaret was quick to defend the cause. When she heard of a woman who had given up her job to support her husband's career, Margaret exclaimed 'I call that simply squalid!'. With surprising restraint Jane said she would like the vote as a gift, but was not sure what she would do with it. Perhaps it was enough for them to live the life of emancipated women. However, Newnham and Girton became centres of suffragist campaigning. There was a suffrage caravan, pulled by a horse which wended its way north to spread the word. Despite this, women at Cambridge were not allowed to receive degrees until 1945.

In contrast to the lively, fiery women visiting the Verrall household, Arthur was calm and humorous. As a boy he was close to his mother, who had a talent for music and languages, something Joan also inherited. Ironically, in view of Hugh's poor health, it was Arthur who was considered too fragile to go to prep school. When Arthur was nine he was sent to the Reverend Blaker, Vicar of Ifield, who thought that he showed academic promise. By 1863 he was well enough to go to Twyford, the prep school for Winchester. However, his health remained poor. It is not clear what illness he was suffering from but there may have been psychological factors, as there were for Joan as a young adult. Arthur failed the Winchester scholarship exam, but got a scholarship to Wellington College. He was not well suited by the harsh regime of the school. However, Arthur was an attractive young man, and a contemporary described him as 'talkative and vivacious, his eyes kindling with life'.

In 1869 Arthur got a minor scholarship to Trinity College Cambridge. The following year he got a foundation scholarship. Arthur's brilliance was also recognised by the talent spotters of the Apostles, 'a private but not obscure society' as one contemporary coyly put it. In fact, the Apostles were one of the most prestigious groups at the university. Membership was for life, and they met regularly, taking it in turns to present a paper. The rule was absolute truth and frankness. Lytton Strachey took this to an extreme when he presented a paper on the joys of defecation. Not surprisingly, Strachey was also an admirer of Freud. According to Arthur he owed more to the Apostles than any other influence. It is not clear what he meant by this, but his best-known book *Euripides the Rationalist* is a search for truth of Euripides's beliefs beneath the surface of his plays. Where Margaret and Jane looked for the otherworldly and irrational beneath the surface, Arthur looked for reality. As a psychoanalyst, Joan followed Jane Harrison and her uncle in her search for the truth and the seething irrationality beneath the surface of the mind.

Before Arthur settled down for good in Cambridge he spent three years reading for the bar – perhaps to satisfy his father. In 1875 he was awarded the Whewell Scholarship in International Law. In 1877 he was called to the bar and even took one or two briefs. The bar did not suit his pacific nature, his contemporaries noticed his avoidance of controversy. It is interesting that this vulnerability runs through the men in Joan's life, Hugh, Cuthbert, Arthur, and later her husband Evelyn. In 1898 Arthur became one of four university tutors. This more pastoral role suited him well. He used his position to get to know 'the men' in a more human and personal way. With fifty students to get to know, he and Margaret held dinner parties two or three times a week in the autumn term. There were croquet and tennis parties in the May term. It was at a Sunday afternoon party that Joan first met the undergraduate who would become her colleague and rival as Freud's translator. James Strachey was the younger brother of Lytton Strachey, the author of *Eminent Victorians*. In an obituary of Joan, written in 1963, James described Arthur in glowing terms:

> He was a truly remarkable person. He had a mind which cut through conventional attitudes and superficial shams in a way which always seemed to me strangely reminiscent of Freud's, and I was amused to find not long ago that Joan had had the same feelings.
>
> (Strachey, 1963)

This quality of speaking the truth regardless is useful in a psychoanalyst, but uncomfortable in everyday life, and James acknowledged that he was afraid of Joan. Arthur was not only an iconoclast, his students found him sympathetic, and 'he was an extraordinary sound, just and sympathetic judge of character', qualities that must also have been very valuable in an uncle.

There does seem to have been something in the ethos of Cambridge that was conducive to the development of psychoanalytic thinking long before it was widely known. The SPR played an important role, as we have seen, and also the Apostles with their creed of truth and frankness. However, it was not only men who were preoccupied by the truth. Jane Harrison gave an entertaining account of a disagreement with Elinor Sidgwick after dinner in Newnham.

> We were talking in hall about some of the odd words that shops and businesses invent. I cited *Alight* for the Albert Memorial, whoever says alight? I always say 'alight' remarked Mrs Sidgwick … Forgive me said I, I am sure you don't. A few minutes later she joined me in the corridor, 'you are quite right, I find I don't always say alight'.

There has been speculation about whether Joan acquired her passion for literature from her father. However, there is no evidence that he was interested in anything except the Volunteer Rifle Brigade, shooting with Lord Sheffield, and perhaps local affairs. Arthur Verrall became a professor of English Literature, and it seems more likely that he and Margaret influenced Joan's intellectual tastes.

Chapter 4

Education

> She despises all of us, especially the women.
>
> Ernest Jones

Early in 2013, Mrs Cunningham's little car bumped up the track to the remote building which housed the Wycombe Abbey archive. We started off by looking at the school register. Joan arrived in May 1897 when she was fourteen and left in April 1900 when she was seventeen. Leaving in April was obviously unusual; in fact the school prospectus described it as 'inconvenient and undesirable'. It was not likely to have been for financial reasons, because quite a lot of money was subsequently spent on Joan. As she spent three years at the school some things must have gone well. Mrs Cunningham found a photograph from Joan's house. It was a small group of girls and I wondered if I would recognise her. She stood out immediately partly because of her height but also because of an indefinable impression that she was somehow separate from the group, although she was in the middle of the row. Some of the girls are smiling, Joan has a faint smile, but she looks uneasy and strained. Was the problem in the school?

Objectively, Joan was lucky to be at Wycombe Abbey. It was the cutting edge of girls' education at a time when education for middle-class girls was evolving rapidly. The traditional approach was for boys and girls to be educated together by their mother or a governess until they were eight or nine. Then boys went on to a day school or boarding school. Girls remained at home, perhaps with some visiting teachers. There had been boarding schools for girls since the eighteenth century. Harriet Smith in *Emma* attends a benign version of one such establishment. More often these 'Academies' were for girls who needed 'warehousing' until they could be married off. They taught skills that might increase a girl's value in the marriage market. Jane Frances Dove, the future headmistress at Wycombe Abbey spent a year at one such school when the girls slept two to a bed and the education was correspondingly inadequate. Paradoxically the thing that moved on girls' education was the changes for middle-class boys. The Victorians were gradually formalising the professions – medicine, law, engineering and civil service. There was a requirement to prove what had been learned by taking exams. Oxford and Cambridge introduced the 'locals' – pre-university exams. Getting permission for girls to enter these exams became a goal for the early feminists.

In 1862, Emily Davis, Barbara Bodichon and other colleagues obtained permission for a group of girls to take the Cambridge Local Examinations. The experience of taking these examinations was an invigorating one for the girls, who enjoyed meeting other young women from around the country. However, it drew attention to the deficiencies of current female education:

> Experience has taught these young women that knowledge acquired in the desultory, unstructured fashion thought suitable for girls taught at home by a mother or governess, or in schools run by women who themselves had no professional training, would not advance them in the world outside home.
>
> (Crawford, 2002)

Despite these important battles fought over twenty years before, Joan started her education in the traditional way. It is likely that Anna and Hugh thought that Anna's experience as a governess would have made her particularly well-fitted to teaching their children. Family tradition had it that Anna spent seven or eight years with one family. If this was true, then she would have been a particularly successful governess, as the turnover was high, often owing to disappointed expectations on both sides. However, the standard of teaching was often very low. Gwen Raverat put the problem very trenchantly:

> They were all kind, good, dull women; but even interesting lessons can be made incredibly stupid when they are taught by people who are bored to death with them, and who do not care for the art of teaching either.
>
> (Raverat, 1952)

The problem with governesses was that they were often not very well educated themselves. Elizabeth Garrett Anderson's cousin Rhoda could only offer English and the rudiments of French and Music, when she became a governess, and this was a family interested in women's education! Rhoda later redeemed herself by training in an architect's office as an interior decorator. However, one wonders how she managed the more technical aspects, as most girls were only taught enough arithmetic to do the household accounts when they were married. Although Rhoda's choice was unusual, the professions were slowly opening up to women, and teaching, a career accepted for women, was becoming professionalised (Crawford, 2002).

The Governesses Benevolent Fund were aware of the problem of the education of governesses themselves. In 1848 they founded Queen's College, Harley

Street, to provide governesses with an education and teach them how to teach. Classes were held in the evenings so the students could come after work. After a while the college began taking girls from the age of twelve, becoming in effect one of the early girls' day schools. It seems very unlikely that Anna had the benefits of an education like this, but there were some advantages to growing up in the Hodgson family. As one of the older children she would have had more of her mother's attention, and probably learned to read and write from her. The flowing, confident hand in her diary suggests that she was well taught. Girls in large clerical families had certain advantages. They learned to run a complex home and probably took on some of the teaching of their younger siblings:

> Only those girls who were lucky enough to have fathers, frequently clergymen, who kept large libraries found themselves embarking on an education, sometimes shared with her brothers, which was both wide-ranging and rigorous. Such was the experience of Emily Shone, who was taught Latin and Greek by her clergyman father and English and History by her mother.
>
> (Hughes, M., 1991)

Two of the Hodgson boys went to Cambridge and John Hodgson also took on pupils, so it is not impossible that Anna obtained some of her education from her father. In her diary she speaks of her father with warmth while her mother hardly gets a mention, suggesting she may have had more of what we would call quality time with her father.

Whatever the extent of Anna's learning, she seems to have been an effective teacher for Joan and her sister Molly. Joan learned to read by the time she was four. One unspoken aspect of being taught by your mother was the physical closeness which Anna had delegated to the gentle Marsh. Contemporary pictures show exquisitely turned-out children poring over books with their mothers.

While this scenario might have been true of Joan and Molly, Cuthbert was another story. Anna complained that he was better at arguing than learning, although she appreciated his affectionate nature. He comes across in Anna's diary as clumsy and not very bright. A number of schools were tried for him without much success. 'We think he seems to be doing much better at Weldon and we hope much for the future'. This proved to be a vain hope and eventually Cuthbert was encouraged by his parents to emigrate to Canada.

> We know our dear boy has a splendid chance for his future – we feel absolute confidence in his being under the influence and example of a man like Lewis – and he seemed so happy and ready to go.

It may have been that Cuthbert was under the shadow of his dead elder brother and delicate father. These ghosts were to haunt Joan's life and writing. Cuthbert seems to have kept some contact with his family, but gradually he drifted away. Despite the family's conventional Victorian facade it was the two daughters who went on to have careers – Joan as a psychoanalyst and Molly as an Almoner at St Thomas's Hospital.

Joan's daughter Diana told Athol Hughes that when Joan was eight she went to an 'academy' for drawing lessons and when she was nine she started the violin. These specialist teachers were often more stimulating than the regular lesson at home. There was a chance of someone who loved their subject and was keen to convey this. Like Joan, Gwen Raverat was sent to a specialist drawing teacher.

> There was always Miss Mary Greene's Wednesday Drawing Class, which was the centre of [my] youthful existence ... for it was not only that the drawing was an ecstasy, but Miss Greene's warm, generous, appreciative nature was a great release and encouragement to me.
>
> (Raverat, 1952)

We do not know what Joan felt about her drawing lessons, but she had a lifelong love of beautiful things, perhaps also influenced by her mother. In 1922, Joan visited the psychoanalyst Max Eitingon's house in Berlin and wrote an ecstatic description for her mother. 'Wonderful paintings, panelling, Chinese Wallpaper and influence on furniture, beautiful bookshelves, and marvellous *food*' (Hughes, A., 1991). All her life Joan appreciated food. The Wycombe Abbey prospectus emphasised the quality and quantity of the food.

It is not clear how Joan was educated between the ages of nine and fourteen. The *Dictionary of National Biography* says that she was at St Michael's Hall School, but I have not been able to find a school of this name. There was a St Mary's Hall School in Brighton, but there was no record of Joan or Molly there. Roedean would have been geographically convenient, but there is no record of Joan there either. Perhaps the Verralls were put off by its reputation for strenuous sports. Fathers sometimes became involved in the education of older girls – especially if they had intellectual interests of their own. Viginia Woolf and her sister Vanessa were both taught by their mother and father, as well as visiting teachers for Latin and Greek. As well as practical teaching, Virginia got something equally precious from her father – his belief that she would one day become a writer, and from an early age she had the run of his library (Lee, 1996). Hugh Verrall supposedly had literary tastes, and it is tempting to assume that he nurtured Joan's taste in literature and lent her his books, but there is no evidence for this. As an adult Joan's beautiful writing style was commented on by many who read her papers (and also deployed in her translations of Freud).

It is possible that Joan and Molly went to day schools, but these were frowned on by the middle classes as places where tradesmen's daughters might go and social mixing could take place. North London Collegiate, an early day school, was founded in 1850 by Mary Frances Buss, a graduate of Queen's College in Harley Street. One pupil, Molly Hughes, remarked: 'No one asked you where you lived, how much pocket money you had, or what your father was – he might be a bishop or a rat catcher' (Hughes, M., 1991). This sort of egalitarian atmosphere was not likely to appeal to Anna Verrall. The new boarding schools catered for a more upper-class group of parents. Dorothea Beale (another Queen's College graduate) became the principal of Cheltenham Ladies College in 1858 and refused to take girls whose parents were in trade. Although, the education the school provided was known to be excellent, and Miss Beale insisted it was to prepare girls for the roles of wife and mother.

> An education based in religious principles which, preserving the modesty and gentleness of the female character, should so far cultivate [a girl's] intellectual powers as to fit her for the discharge of those responsible duties which devolve upon her as a wife, mother, mistress and friend, the natural companion and helpmate for men.
>
> (Steinbach, 2004)

Despite this nod to the Angel in the House, those early educational pioneers were involved in a range of feminist causes. Miss Buss gave evidence to the 1856 School's Enquiry Commission on gender inequalities in education and worked with Emily Davies to open the Oxford and Cambridge examinations to women. Miss Beale was active in bringing the suffrage movement to women outside London and bought the house that would become St Hilda's College, Oxford, one of the first women's colleges. Although the suffragette movement was (for us) the visible face of early feminism, in reality there were a wide range of activities which changed the quality of some women's lives.

By the time Joan went to boarding school there were a number of schools modelled on the boys' public schools. Just as importantly there was now a trickle of women who had been to university or trained as teachers ready to teach them. In 1897, aged fourteen, Joan sat the entrance exams for Wycombe Abbey – English, Latin, French and Arithmetic. The school prospectus promised an education 'complete on all sides as that given to boys at the great public schools'. This move into a masculine world was coupled in some respects with an insistence on femininity. The first students at Newnham College, Cambridge, were so beautiful and fashionable that the college founder Henry Sidgwick despaired of them being taken seriously. A photograph of Dame Jane Frances Dove, founder and first headmistress of Wycombe Abbey taken in 1898 shows a formidably elegant woman. Her silk dress is ruched and pleated and her silver hair is piled high on her head.

She was not just a woman with good dress sense, she was supremely practical too. Initially, this was put to the service of her large clerical family. A photograph of the family taken in 1870 shows all ten members of the family, including the men, wearing clothes made by Jane Frances. The girls at Wycombe Abbey learned carpentry and cricket, but they also learned needlework and took the exams of the London Institute for the advancement of plain needlework. These needlework skills would be unexpectedly valuable to Joan in a few years time.

Jane Frances's own professional trajectory showed the importance of family support and the rapidly developing old girls network. Jane Frances began her education with her brothers Horace and Arthur, all three being taught by their father. She then spent three years at Queen's College, Harley Street. The family then moved to a remote rectory in Lincolnshire. However, Jane Frances's father was a friend of the Reverend Llewellyn Davies, brother of Emily Davies, founder of Girton College, Cambridge. In 1871, Jane Frances passed the entrance exam to Girton, and although she did not get a scholarship she was first in mathematics. This was the period where Girton moved from its early base in Hitchin to the newly-built college just outside Cambridge. The ethos of Girton was that the girls should take exactly the same exams as the men even if they had not the same preparation. In 1875, Jane Frances sat the Natural Sciences Tripos and obtained the equivalent of an ordinary BA degree. She was then snapped up by Cheltenham College to teach physiology at a salary of £130 per year.

Miss Louisa Lumsden, the headmistress of St Leonard's School in Scotland and another old Girton girl invited Miss Dove to join the staff of the school. When Miss Lumsden had to retire owing to ill health Miss Dove took over. Once in charge she showed her genius for organisation and publicity. The school doubled in size and a junior house was opened. Following the English public school pattern the school was divided into houses, in the charge of house mistresses. This structure created a training in service and community life, which Miss Dove took with her to Wycombe Abbey. In 1895, Miss Dove announced to the astonished council in St Leonard's that she planned to leave and found a sister school in England.

> This was indeed a thunderclap, but to all who knew Miss Dove it did not come entirely as a surprise. Her courage and enterprise had no limit, while her vision and faith were deep and strong.
>
> (Bowerman, 1965)

Winifred Peck, a contemporary of Joan put it in a less flattering light: 'She got her way because … she felt so clearly the pulse of the educational market' (Peck, 1952). There were women who wanted to engage in social work, church work and suffragette activities, who wanted their daughters looked after and imbued with a sense of public service. This ethos must have affected Joan, who in the period before she discovered psychoanalysis tried one worthy cause after another.

With the help of her cousin, solicitor Francis Larken, Miss Dove set up The Girls Education Company, and following this a Council and offices. Gradually, with the help of Miss Dove's many friends and contacts, enough people were found to take up the first thousand shares. A prospectus was written, and Miss Dove – with Francis Larken and her father – searched for suitable houses. Eventually they bought Lord Carrington's house, Wycombe Abbey, for £20,000. This was an attractive neo-Gothic house with a ballroom, which was initially used for lessons, and a lake. In the days before health and safety, the girls were allowed to build punts and go boating on the lake. It is easy to imagine the screams and splashes. On the 26th September 1896, just a year after Miss Dove's cataclysmic announcement the new school opened with forty pupils.

A contemporary of Joan's at Wycombe Abbey wrote in her memoires:

> 'This is a wholly new type of school to you,' said the housemistress firmly. 'It is modelled on the schools which your brothers attend. There are no petty rules and regulations ... but' – her voice wavered – 'you are not of course allowed to eat butter and jam *together* with your bread as some of you did tonight'.
>
> (Peck, 1952)

This announcement embodied the mixture of freedom and austerity which characterised Miss Dove's regime. The freezing cold dormitories had Liberty curtains with Morris patterns. Each girl had a hip bath under her bed which was filled by a maid in a print dress in the mornings. On winter mornings the girls sometimes had to break the ice in their baths. At first there was no electric light and the carpentry mistress got the girls making candelabras. It says something about the changing times that there was not only a carpentry mistress but also a gardening teacher, Miss Agar, who helped the girls tend to their individual plots. The days were packed with activity, although Miss Dove decreed that the younger pupils should not do more than three or four hours of brainwork, rising to five hours when they were fourteen. Initially, the girls were taught Scripture, Arithmetic, Literature, History, Latin or German, French, Gymnastics and Part Singing. Later Maths, Natural Science, Greek and Italian were added. Miss Dove aimed to appoint the best teachers; many were graduates of Girton, and the music mistress had been a pupil of Clara Schumann. It would have been interesting to know if Joan had chosen German in preference to Latin.

Games were another thing. In keeping with the public school ethos competitive games were compulsory. The girls played hockey, lacrosse and cricket depending on the season. Some, like Winifred Peck, loved the freedom and sense of belonging.

> [W]hat freedom, what glory, to scamper about after one ball or another in sun or rain or wind as one of a team, as part of the school, on an equality, I felt, with my brothers at last.
>
> (Peck, 1952)

Judging by Joan's adult personality it is hard to imagine her enjoying running round on a muddy games pitch, and it is unlikely that she felt respect and envy of her brother. Winifred Peck was chosen for the first eleven, but Joan was chosen to be head of her house. Initially she belonged to Cloister House. Later she moved to Campbell to follow her housemistress. A position like this is usually given to someone who fits in with girls and teachers. In a boarding school, girls and staff get to know each other very well and it is likely that Joan showed that she could be depended upon.

Mrs Cunningham showed me a copy of the *Wycombe Abbey Gazette* of November 1899. Twenty-five girls entered for the Oxford and Cambridge Higher Certificate. Six gained certificates and fifteen, including Joan, gained 'letters'. On the results of the examination some girls, including Joan 'are excused the additional subjects of the Cambridge Previous Exam'. This contradicts the hypothesis that Joan did not go on to university because she did not have the right qualifications. Even if Joan did not have the qualifications someone of her ability could have acquired them. James and Lytton Strachey's sister, Pernel, was coached by her older sister, Dorothy, for the Cambridge Little-Go exam – which included Latin, Greek, Mathematics and Logic. Pernel not only passed, she did well. Their father wrote to Pernel:

> I do not know which to admire most: the diligence displayed by you and Dorothy in preparing you for your battle with the giant Little-Go – or the wonderful stupidity of the system of education of the other sex which hardly accomplished in eight or nine years what you did in as many weeks.
>
> (Caine, 2005)

In 1898 Anna visited the school on speech day:

> I went with Mrs Percy Willetts to see the Speech Day at Wycombe Abbey – a very nice day. The girls in their white frocks and long blue cloaks thrown over looked very picturesque and happy. Joan recited a scene from Macbeth and did well.

It is characteristic of Anna that she would be pleased by the aesthetic aspect of the event, but she could be aware of Joan's moods and she makes no mention of any unhappiness. On this occasion Joan seems well-integrated in school life. The archives yielded another perspective on Joan's presence at the school. There was a letter from 'Mrs. Verrall'. It was not from Anna, but from Margaret Verrall. The letter is addressed to Miss Dove and queries the school's policy of strict Anglicanism. A more careful look at the register showed that Arthur Verrall was a shareholder in the school and was Joan's sponsor when she applied. Although Anna was happy with the school it seems likely that the impetus to send Joan there came from her uncle and aunt.

This would not be the first time that Arthur and Margaret influenced Joan's life. In this case it is likely they wanted Joan to be prepared for coming to Newnham where Margaret was a lecturer and Joan's cousin, Helen, was about to become a student. This was such an obviously happy arrangement for Joan that something dramatic must have happened to prevent her from taking this up. What was the reason for abrupt withdrawal from the school? The most obvious reason is that she was unhappy.

Winifred Peck gives two main reasons why a girl might be unhappy there. There were those who rebelled against the innocent, hearty atmosphere of the school and who were 'persistently and obstinately feminine in spite of Miss Dove and the prefect system!' These girls lived for parties and dresses and the holidays. This might have been true of Joan a year or so later, but was probably not a pressing issue at the time. Peck's second reason sounds more like Joan: girls who were artistic, sensitive, introspective and hard working. The Wycombe Abbey way of life made introspection virtually impossible, each day was crammed with activity and so tightly timetabled that the girls often had to sprint to get to the next activity on time. As an adult, Joan was hard working and obsessively meticulous over her translations. As the translations editor of the *International Journal of Psychoanalysis* she did a huge amount of unpaid work. With this personality it would not be surprising if she felt under strain, as she appears in her photograph.

But Joan's time at Wycombe Abbey was not a failure, although she may have felt it. She did well in her academic work and had a position of responsibility. Freud commented on her ferocious superego, but more subtly he said that she could not tolerate success. Whatever the reason, Joan came home from school early and the Verralls had to decide what to do with their brilliant, beautiful and unhappy daughter.

Whatever the cause of Joan's unhappiness at school, it must have been considerable for her parents to remove her in the middle of the year. A misfit between Joan's character and the school ethos was, of course, possible, but Joan had been there three years and become head of her house. Another possibility which gains substance from the pattern of Joan's later relationships is a passion for another girl or member of staff. In the hothouse world of early boarding schools this sort of occurrence was so common as to have a special name – a 'rave' or a 'gonage' – as in 'gone on'. Some schools went to great lengths to break these up. At Girton the cool Miss Dove had a passion for brilliant, aristocratic Louisa Lumsden, making her bed and leaving her flowers. It is unlikely she would have excluded a pupil for this reason. Prior to her analytic training, Joan had a close friendship with someone called 'IEE'. I think this is likely to have been a woman, partly because they went to stay together at one of Anna's cottages, and partly because they had a pattern of rows and making up, which Joan had with her mother. Joan also had a pattern of intense relations with other women. As we shall see later, Joan's paper 'Womanliness as a Masquerade' describes a certain sort of feminine woman who has a fantasy of possessing a penis.

The idea of sending Joan to Germany for a year probably came from Margaret and Arthur Verrall. It was a common practice among Cambridge intellectual families. The experiences of the young people were very variable. However, in the period before the First World War, Germany was seen as a place of culture, Goethe and Beethoven. Besides, it had links to the Royal Family. With her genius for making contacts, Anna planned to send Joan to a Frau Mezeroth. This may have been a family or it may have been a small boarding school. When Joan was told she was going to Gotha she does not seem to have made any fuss. Perhaps she was glad to be leaving home. Anna commented on Joan's bravery as they took her to Victoria Station, and consoled herself with the idea that Joan had a good supply of clothes from a Brighton dressmaker. Joan hated these clothes.

In 1913, my husband's grandmother, Mary Solomon, was sent to Hanover for a year. Her letters home give an idea what the experience was like. She was only fourteen and travelled with an older woman. Where she stayed was more like a small boarding school. On arrival, Mary developed a strategic stomach ache, which enabled her to retreat from the group of unknown girls and lie on her bed in the dormitory. Teaching seemed to concentrate on arts subjects. Mary learned the piano, which she disliked because she thought the teacher was anti-Semitic, we see this in letters to her family. Homesickness was assuaged by admiring the beauties of nature. On the Kaiser's birthday, the girls strewed cornflowers in his path. The school did not neglect the girls' social needs. Older girls had boyfriends, usually army officers. Joan seems to have developed a crush on an older man, Herr Bode. Among her papers were two letters to Herr Bode. These were presumably drafts. They are written in German. A German friend told me that her German, even at this stage, was very fluent. Joan seems to have regarded Herr Bode as rather an intellectual, and is apologetic for the frivolous nature of her activities at home, such as playing ping-pong or the piano. However, she hopes to impress Herr Bode with her reading:

> I cannot really say that I love the whole great humankind as so many admirable men have done, but I am extraordinarily interested … Also

> recently I read three or four of the 'Novellas' by Paul Heyse which I found charming. He has this modern tendency in histories that we call Psychological Development.

Considering that Joan was only eighteen or nineteen this was very prescient.

A number of years later, when Joan was married, she and Helen made a trip to Gotha together. Presumably Joan must have enjoyed her time there, or perhaps she hoped to encounter Herr Bode again!

Chapter 5

Apprenticeship and marriage

On 26th February 1901, Hugh and Anna invited Margaret and Arthur Verrall to dinner with Mr Kidd. The two couples rarely met, and inevitably the talk would have turned to the question of what Joan planned to do after her time in Gotha. The news that Joan was to be apprenticed to a dressmaker, Mrs Nettleship, would have come as a bombshell. Anna got Mrs Nettleship's details from a novelist friend, Mrs Flora Annie Steele. Arthur and Margaret had been expecting Joan to join Helen at Newnham. Was dressmaking a suitable occupation for an intellectual girl with a fondness for psychological novels? The problem with dressmaking was that this had unfortunate connotations. Along with being a governess, being a dressmaker was what a woman did when she had no husband or father to support her. Dressmakers at the lower end of the scale often resorted to prostitution to make ends meet. Did Anna worry that Hugh, with his persistent ill health, might not be able to support his daughters?

The idea that Anna was forcing Joan into the same mould as herself does not bear closer examination. Joan's diary is mostly laconic single-line entries, but she takes the trouble to say that she has been dressmaking and what she was working on. 'Working on my silk dress'. She *loved* dressmaking. When Joan was comfortably married to Evelyn Riviere she rented rooms in Manchester Street, Marylebone, apparently with the intention of setting herself up commercially, though the enterprise later fell through.

Mrs Nettleship was a different species from the Brighton dressmaker whose clothes Joan had hated. The Nettleship family were middle-class in origin, and all artistically talented. John Trivett Nettleship was the son of a solicitor and was trained as a solicitor himself. However, this life did not satisfy him, and he trained at Heatherly and the Slade. He was strongly influenced by Blake, and had some success, exhibiting at the Grosvenor Gallery, which was the fashionable art gallery at the time. There was something raffish and eccentric about John. He took up boxing and walked from London to Brighton. He held his alcoholism at bay by taking constant sips from a large jar of cocoa. By the time Joan arrived he had lost confidence in his work and was reduced to drawing lions and tigers for the *Boys Own Paper*. Ada Nettleship was the daughter of an otologist, a new disease specialist, and worked hard to keep the family respectable. The Nettleships had three talented daughters. Ida won a scholarship to the Slade. Ida's marriage to Augustus John cost her her life. She had five children in quick succession and died in childbirth. Even before this Augustus had taken a mistress. Ethel was a cellist who drove an ambulance in the First World War. Afterwards she took up lacemaking to calm her nerves. Ursula was an adventurous mountaineer and skier – presumably dressed by the rational dress movement. Later she became a singer, and Benjamin Britten dedicated his *Ceremony of Carols* to her.

Anna Verrall travelled to London to meet Mrs Nettleship at her business in Wigmore Street. She would have found a very conventional-looking woman dressed from head to toe in heavy black brocade, with a white lace jabot at her neck. They would have agreed the conditions for Joan's apprenticeship and decided that Joan would live in lodgings. In Mrs Nettleship's plump and capable hands her business was flourishing. The demand for dressmakers in London at that time was enormous. At one point there were 2,000 dressmakers in the city. Four hundred of these were 'court dressmakers', who were familiar with the needs and customs of young women who were going to be presented at court. The number of young people acceptable in 'Society' was increasing as professional men and some businessmen were increasingly joining its ranks. It was not just that there were more people in Society, but also that women wore an enormous number of clothes. A woman going on a visit to a country house would change her clothes four or five times a day. Underneath these clothes underwear proliferated. Gwen Raverat gives and astonishing description of what one young lady put on in the morning:

1. Thick, long-legged, long-sleeved woollen combinations.
2. Over them white cotton combinations with plenty of buttons and frills.
3. Very serious, bony, grey stays with suspenders.
4. Black woollen stockings.
5. White cotton drawers with buttons and frills.
6. White cotton petticoat-bodice.
7. Rather short white flannel petticoat.
8. Long alpaca petticoat, with a flounce around the bottom.
9. Pink flannel blouse.
10. High starched white collar fastened with studs.
11. Navy blue tie.
12. Blue skirt touching the ground, fastened tightly to the blouse with a safety pin behind.
13. Leather belt – very tight.
14. High button boots.

(Raverat, 1952)

Underclothes were so important that one of Mrs Nettleship's rivals Lady Lucy Christiana Duff Gordon, who traded as 'Lucile', had a room in her shop, 'the Rose Room', entirely devoted to underwear. The fact that a titled woman made dresses *and* sold underwear showed how much dressmaking – and customers – had changed.

Mrs Nettleship had a weakness for her titled customers, for whom she made exquisite but conventional dresses. Unfortunately, some of these customers failed to pay their bills. However, there was another class of customer from the arts and theatre for whom she created 'unique dramatic and sometimes consciously bizarre outfits that were considered to represent the most outrageous and expensive end of the dress market'. One of Mrs Nettleship's most faithful customers was Mrs Oscar Wilde, who belonged to the bohemian end of the spectrum, and whose clothes scandalised the conservative press. At a preview of the Grosvenor Gallery's open day in 1885, *The Hampshire Telegraph and Chronicle* reported that:

> aestheticism culminated in Mrs Oscar Wilde's costume of a woollen stuff in dull reseda trimmed with pink, and a kind of Kate Greenaway dress, tied at the waist by a drooping pink sash. Round the neck she wore a wide Toby frill of two rows of ficelle lace with vari-coloured beads, and a large pink bow fastening on a bunch of yellow Marguerites; on her head a small Tam O'Shanter cap of the same greenish-grey material.
>
> (Moyle, 2012)

The following year, at the same event, Mrs Nettleship and Mrs Wilde excelled themselves with a dress 'in every shade of green from the palest lichen to the fullest summer foliage – a lizard trimmed with beetles'. The 'beetles' were the iridescent wings of the jewel beetle. The beetle effect seems to have been fashionable.

How would Joan have felt about working with Mrs Nettleship, her eccentric family, and her working girls? In many ways Joan had a very sheltered upbringing: lessons at home, an elite girls' boarding school, 'finishing' at Gotha and high-minded gatherings in Cambridge. The gap between the Nettleships and their workers could be tenuous. There was the occasion when Ida crept down to one of her mother's employees (Elspeth Phelps) and announced in a trembling voice that she had married Augustus John. As we will see, Joan could be a snob and anti-Semite, but she was deeply curious about people and respected those who were good at their job. There is a possibility that one of Mrs Nettleship's working girls got into Joan's first psychoanalytic vignette, written in 1920. In it she describes a young woman working in a business who has been sexually abused. Perhaps the hardest thing for Joan was loneliness. However, Hugh and Anna had friends in London who invited her round and chaperoned her to balls. London was an increasingly friendly place for working women. There were women-only blocks of flats and women-only restaurants where Joan could eat and observe the other diners.

By an extraordinary piece of good luck one of Mrs Nettleship's apprentices, Elspeth Phelps, who was Ida's confidante, kept a record of her time there. It is a reflection of Mrs Nettleship's artistic reputation that the diary is now kept in Tate Britain. It records the mind-numbingly hard work for the apprentices and working girls. The diary opens with a group of ladies examining different types of brocade. Finally they confess that they are only sheltering from the rain. The sales girl ticks them off: 'time is valuable for a working girl'. In the private and sensuous atmosphere of a fitting some customers whispered confidences. One woman confesses, in a flood of tears, that she does not want to marry her fiancé. However, some of the work was physically back-breaking. Grecian pleats were made by tightly twisting muslin. It made the girls' hands raw, but it looked artistic. Each dress was made under the direct supervision of Mrs Nettleship, and each dress was individual, 'a carefully thought-out work of art, studied in every detail to suit the client'. She went to Paris each season, but much of her inspiration came from the museums and galleries closer to home:

> She found inspirations in pictures, engravings on old china ... she used to spend hours in picture galleries looking out attractive ideas for details in dress. Nothing came amiss from the primitive designs on savage weapons in the British Museum and the elaborate ruffles and frills in the Watteau pictures at the Wallace Collection.
>
> (Phelps, n.d.)

Apprentices were sent out to look at a picture and bring back a sketch. Or they might have to paint flowers onto chiffon. A 'picture dress' might be dyed. The regular seamstresses worked enormously long hours. Hopefully the apprentices less so. However, there were consolations, particularly when Mrs Nettleship designed for the theatre. When George Edwards wanted costumes for *The Country Girl* everyone worked fourteen-hour days, but they got tickets for the shows. The same applied to the more serious theatre at the Lyceum, when Ellen Terry and Henry Irving were playing.

The atmosphere in the showroom in Wigmore Street was not entirely innocent and female. Augustus John came to visit Ida Nettleship with his ringlets and earrings and general air of not having washed. Maud Allen, the scandalous American dancer, came for a Botticelli dress. However, she is usually remembered for her portrayal of Salomé, wearing very little, in Oscar Wilde's play. Elsbeth innocently admired the muscles in her arms, perhaps an unconscious reference to her sexual orientation. However, a dressmaker could not help being aware of the architecture of the bodies she was covering. Perhaps some of this matter-of-factness about the female body rubbed off on Joan, when she gave a vivid description of the female orgasm at the Institute of Psychoanalysis.

Despite the demand for dressmakers the competition for customers was fierce. Both Mrs Nettleship and 'Lucile' diversified into designing costumes for the theatre. Lady Duff Gordon eventually set-up shops in Paris, New York and Chicago, a precursor of our modern, international brands. Mrs Nettleship became the dressmaker for the Lyceum Theatre, the home of Henry Irving and Ellen Terry. Terry's letters to Ada show that a close and affectionate relationship developed between the two women.

> Sweet Nettle
>
> Cld you have a little dress run up for tonights wear for Miss Gibson ... I want a *cheap* cloak for Wednesday looking like Ermine, but *really* the innocent bunny rabbit – and unlined ... Mr Irving's tent scene dress is *very* dirty so will you wire it and make a new one as soon as possible.

In June 1900, Terry offered one of Mrs Nettleship's assistants a rest cure at Vine Cottage:

> I will expect Miss Tyrell at any time will she go on her bike or *take* it [on the train] ... I expect her to get quite well at VC. The fish hook was an improvement thanks, the red dress looks lovely.

Miss Tyrell sounds rather vigorous, cycling to stay with Ellen Terry. Perhaps she wore a new divided skirt, a precursor to trousers for women. Paradoxically, Mrs Nettleship supported the rational dress movement. She contributed an outfit to the Rational Dress exhibition. Basically, the rational dress movement advocated clothes that were comfortable and practical. Precursors of these clothes were worn by the Pre-Raphaelite women – long, flowing dresses work without corsets. As well as flowing corset-free dresses there were clothes designed for active women, including outfits for mountaineering, fencing and cycling.

Perhaps the most spectacular dress that Ellen Terry wore was when she played Lady Macbeth for one of Henry Irving's lavish productions. The entire dress was covered in jewel beetle wings and gave the impression of iridescent scales. It was in this dress that Terry was painted by John Singer Sargent. Alice Comyns Carr, who designed some of Terry's dresses is credited with designing it, but the manufacture must have been Mrs Nettleship. Only a workshop of women could have fixed so many tiny wings. The dress must have been important to Ellen Terry as she kept it, and it has recently been restored. Perhaps Joan's immersion in exotic costumes played a part in her later passion for the Ballets Russes.

In 1902, Joan came home for Christmas, and in the new year Hugh and Anna took her to the South Down Hunt Ball at Lewes, 'A pretty ball with so many "pink" coats. As usual she had plenty of partners. We drove there and back and I was not in bed until 5 o'clock in the morning'. The following year Molly was 'out' and both girls went to Mrs Blake's dance together, 'The girls danced everything and were immensely admired. I was repeatedly told they were quite the belles of the ball'. Anna seems to have enjoyed the balls herself, and had a Mrs Bennett-like pleasure in hearing compliments about her daughters' beauty. Photographs of Joan and Molly show that their beauty was not imagined by Anna. In contrast to these jolly scenes Anna was worried about Joan's health: 'Joan went back to work. She does not seem nearly so well or strong as I could wish and I shall certainly take her again to Dr. Griffith'. This seems a strange anxiety about a girl who could dance until the early hours of the morning. There is something morbid about Anna's preoccupation with health, a miasma of ill-health hangs over parts of her diaries: 'Another bad cold', 'Had a wretched week – could do nothing', 'Had my eyes examined by Dr Griffiths, chose glasses', 'Hugh very seedy – in several days – also Molly'. While there was real illness in the case of Hugh it often seems that illness substituted for the expression of feelings, like Cuthbert's 'congested kidneys' when he had to return to the hated school. Joan handed her body over meekly to her mother and Anna came up to London to take her to Dr Griffiths, 'I made all arrangements for a small operation to be done. Dr G thinks she will never be well without it'. Whatever the operation was, it certainly did not improve Joan's health, and as we shall see, she was plagued with physical and psychological illness until her psychoanalysis with Freud.

Despite Dr Griffiths' ministrations, Joan continued to work with Mrs Nettleship and to attend balls in Sussex and in London. As an older woman, people found Joan intimidating. Joan was a misleading person. The intimidating manner covered her shyness. Once this was overcome, she could be artlessly friendly. James Strachey describes her at an evening party – probably before her marriage:

> I still have a vivid picture of her standing by the fireplace at an evening party, tall, strikingly handsome, distinguished looking and somehow impressive.
>
> (Strachey, 1963)

Perhaps James would have felt less intimidated if he had read the letter that Joan wrote in 1902 to Herr Bode in Gotha:

> balls, concerts, theatre parties, ping pong parties … dinners and all kinds of entertainments would be of little interest to you – but I have not done anything else, only politely enjoyed myself throughout the whole winter … Admittedly the first season in the world of society brings up many thoughts: one starts to observe people and understand them – which I find to be the most surprising of occupations.
>
> [trans. Carola Gross]

One of the people that Joan was observing was Mrs Nettleship. Her powerful character was a mass of contradictions. She was happy to dress her artistic clients in outrageous clothes which suited their character, but she had the most conventional aspirations for her children and was not afraid to appear ridiculous in the pursuit of them. When Ida died tragically giving birth to her fifth child, Mrs Nettleship did not want her grandchildren brought up by Augustus John and his mistress Dorelia. After an undignified chase round London Zoo, Mrs Nettleship had to content herself with bringing up the baby. Ida's experience of marriage had been so traumatic that both her sisters vowed not to marry. This relationship with a powerful and creative woman was a precursor of Joan's later relationship with Melanie Klein. Alix Strachey, James Strachey's wife, painted a cruel and snobbish picture of Klein on the eve of Klein's first trip to England to present her work:

> Melanie showed me a hat she's brought to lecture in London and knock her audience ... It's a vasty, voluminous affair in bright yellow, with a huge brim and an enormous cluster, a whole garden of mixed flowers somewhere up the back, side or front – The total effect is that of an over-blown tea rose with a slightly rouge'd core (her phiz) ... through it all there is something very handsome and attractive in her face ... But there's no doubt whatever is stored with things of thrilling interest.
>
> (Meisel and Kendrick, 1986)

Like Alix, Joan recognised immediately the importance of Klein's ideas, but unlike Alix she also shared Klein's taste for clothes. A photograph shows Joan and Klein together in fashionable beach pyjamas and floppy hats. Both look very pleased with themselves.

Some time in 1904, Joan met Evelyn Riviere. How and where is a mystery. As Evelyn was a Chancery barrister it could have been through the Merrifields or Arthur Verrall. Anna's diary makes it clear that she and Hugh had friends in London, who probably chaperoned Joan to some of the London balls. A meeting may have taken place through them or at a ball – which after all is what a ball is for. They must have been very conspicuous figures, Joan was very tall and beautiful, Evelyn was a very good-looking man with an air of refinement. He was noted among his colleagues for being well-dressed without any affectation. There was also an aspect of his character which may have particularly attracted Joan, and that was his air of fragility, which may have reminded Joan of her father. This fragility was reflected in the type of law work he had chosen: he was an equity draughtsman and conveyancer. This was a specialist type of barrister engaged in the technical business of drafting the complex written proceedings in a court action in the chancery division of the High Court. He was very successful at his work and wrote two books on the subject. Evelyn also had interests in common with Joan, in painting, music and literature. In his obituary his colleagues commented on his subtle conversation and sense of humour. Anna fell for him immediately: 'Joan's engagement is a great source of happiness to us and we feel that Evelyn is almost like a son already!' There is evidence that Joan had fallen for Evelyn too. Her diary begins after their meeting and although it only contains laconic single sentences for each day it communicates a sense of her world opening up.

In 1904, Evelyn took Joan home for a few days over Christmas to meet his family. The atmosphere was very different to the quiet family gatherings in Brighton. The Rivieres lived in a huge house, Flaxley, in Finchley Road, London. Briton Riviere, Evelyn's father, had it rebuilt to meet the family's needs including a studio for himself and his wife Mary Alice. Briton Riviere came from a family of painters. His father, William, was the drawing master of Cheltenham College. Briton was educated there from 1851 until 1859. From an early age, Briton was fascinated by animals and spent many hours at London Zoo observing them. In 1859 Briton went to St Mary's Hall, Oxford, where he studied for a BA and an MA, while spending much of his time painting. Briton came under the influence of Clarence Dobell, who introduced him to the outer circle of the Pre-Raphaelites, particularly John Evrett Millais. Although Briton's paintings were realistic, they do not have the hyper-realism of the Pre-Raphaelites. They show the influence of the more popular and conventional Landseer. Briton made his reputation by a sequence of animal paintings displayed at the Royal Academy. One of his best known pictures is *Sympathy* painted in 1878. In the picture a little girl, based on his daughter Millicent, is sitting on the stairs, evidently as a punishment, and comforted by an exquisitely painted white dog. The precision and realism of the painting lift it out of bathos, although it stimulated John Ruskin to a sugary outpouring of emotion:

> It is a long time since I have been so pleased in the Royal Academy … as I was by Mr Briton Riviere's picture Sympathy. The dog is uncaricatured doggedness, divine as Anubis … the child entirely childish and lovely, the carpet might have been laid by Veronese … not one for a museum. Everyone would only think of the story in it, everyone would be wondering what the little girl had done, and how she would be forgiven, and if she wasn't how soon she would stop crying and give the doggie and kiss, and comfort his heart.
>
> (Maas, 1969)

The painting was bought by Charles Holloway, the founder of Holloway College for Women.

In the Riviere family the little girl in the picture would soon have been forgiven. The family were warm and easy-going. It was probably significant that Briton Riviere had most success with his animal pictures, laced with pathos and humour, and his portraits. Mary Alice Riviere was also a painter in her own right, adding to Joan's experience of women with a profession. Joan's diary records tennis parties and 'At Homes' where the seven children could bring their friends, and where Evelyn could occasionally retreat at times of difficulty. The census of 1910 showed that Joan's daughter, Diana, and a nursemaid were living with the Rivieres. This must have been during one of the periods of mental and physical ill-health which dogged Joan's life in her twenties.

Joan's engagement did not cramp her social life. She continued to go to balls and dances. Her diary of 1905 records the Ionides's dance at the Empress Rooms, the Morse's Dance, the Josephs's Dance and the Lincoln's Inn Ball. The Lincoln's Inn Ball was on a huge scale and was organised by a committee. Perhaps because they were lawyers the committee kept a careful record of their plans, and this reveals the level of organisation beneath the glittering surface. The committee was chaired by the Right Honourable Lord Alverstone. Nearly 1,000 guests were expected, and the committee worried about a human traffic jam leading to the supper room. Should they have the terrace tented? Messrs, Searcy and Tarsley were contacted to provide the supper, which consisted of:

> Consommé glacé en tasse
> Saumon d'Ecosse Norvegienne
> Chavelfraide de cailes à la perigeux
> Pyramide de bouef epicé
> Gelee aux liqueurs Byzantine
> Corbeilles des fruits

The menu card would have a crest and there would be a smaller menu card for the puddings:

> The et cafe
> Hock cup/claret cup
> Gateaux Francais
> Marrons glaces
> Glaces

The caterers recommended Iff's band, but even then nothing was left to chance. Iff was provided with a contract:

> I William Iff hereby agree to provide an orchestra of 30 persons to play up to date dance music ... and to personally conduct the same during the whole of the evening for the sum of £45.

The dance card had tassels and pencils and the Lincoln's Inn crest. There were eighteen dances and four extras – including waltzes, lancers and two-steps.

Two-steps included 'Mumblin Mass', 'Mosquito's Parade' and 'Kunnin Kaffirs'. The dance cards were for women to write down their partners. As usual Joan's card would have been full. After the ball was over the cost was reviewed: £1103:0:10. This included £3:4:6 for extra wiring for the electric lights, and the police. It is not clear what the police were for, perhaps to prevent gatecrashers or theft, but there were also stewards with blue and white badges to keep the guests in order.

Joan was no longer an ingénue in her first season. She moved into the world of the wealthy and sophisticated as well as the world of haute bohemia. She also had experience of being a working woman. After her engagement to Evelyn it seemed appropriate for her to have a place of her own to live. There was an increasing acceptance that women who worked, particularly if they earned a reasonable salary, might want to live separately from their families. Living separately was part of a bid for independence. H. G. Wells' eponymous heroine, Ann Veronica, takes flight into London from her stuffy father who refuses her permission to attend an art students' ball. After an anxious hunt through the streets of North London,

> she hit upon a room that had an exceptional quality of space and order, and a tall woman with a kindly face to show it ... The room was papered with green large patterned paper ... and the armchair and the seas of the other chairs were covered with the unusual brightness of a large patterned chintz which also supplied the window curtain. There was a round table covered not with the usual 'tapestry' cover but with plain green cloth that went passably with the wallpaper. In the recess beside the fireplace were some open bookshelves.

There is an implication that Ann Veronica will soon fill them. The kindly landlady gives Ann Veronica a boiled egg and tinned peaches for her tea. It was widely known that Ann Veronica was based on Amber Reeves, a Newnham graduate with whom H. G. Wells had an affair and a child. By a nice coincidence, Joan became friends with Amber Reeves in her married incarnation of Amber Blanco White.

Wells wrote *Ann Veronica* in 1904. In 1905 Joan's diary records that she has moved into Miss Chattaways at 43 Belsize Road. The house no longer exists, but it would have been part of a handsome white stucco terrace. One of the great advantages of its location was that it was close to Evelyn in Finchley Road. For Joan and Evelyn this relative freedom led to a joyous burst of shared activity. They wanted to show each other people and places which were important to them. Evelyn bought a car called 'Daisy' and they visited people and places in easy reach of London. There were two trips to Oxford where Evelyn had been at Balliol. One of these visits involved an overnight stay. In view of the rigorous rules about chaperonage at the time, Joan's freedom to come and go with Evelyn seems remarkable.

Naturally, one of the places they visited together was Cambridge. Like Jane Austen's Elizabeth Bennett, Joan had an uncle and an aunt she was proud of. Arthur and Margaret in their turn would have been keen to meet Evelyn. By this time Arthur was increasingly handicapped by arthritis, but his mind was still lively. Despite his noticeable ill-health he had been given the Edward VII Chair of English Literature and was looking forward to his new project. This was a subject which Evelyn could comfortably engage with. What he thought of the Society for Psychical Research might have been another matter.

Although Anna and Hugh were happy with Evelyn, they were becoming uncomfortably aware that all their children would soon be leaving them. Molly wanted to live near Joan in London, and there were only brief unsatisfactory letters from Cuthbert, who was still in Canada. As usual they dealt with the problem by travelling. They planned a trip down to the south of France, coming back in circuit through Italy. 'Abroad with mother and father', says Joan's diary. Evelyn was to join them later when he could get away from work. Despite the initial absence of Evelyn, the trip feels like an advance honeymoon. It was probably one of the longest periods Joan spent with her parents, a bridge into the adult world. The south of France was still quite an adventurous destination, except for the very rich who holidayed in the grand hotels springing up on the waterfronts. They were closely followed by intellectuals and artists like Virginia Woolf (Joan's contemporary) and her sister Vanessa Bell (who became Joan's friend):

> You who cross the channel yearly, probably no longer see the house at Dieppe, no longer feel, as the train moves slowly down the street, one civilisation fall and another rise – from the ruin and chaos of British stucco this incredible pink and blue phoenix four stories high, with its flowerpots, its balconies, its servant girl leaning on the windowsill, indolently looking out.
>
> (Morris, 1993)

Joan and her parents passed rapidly though Paris before heading south by train to Marseilles. They stayed a few days in Cannes, then still a relatively quiet place, and hired a car for a drive to the Cap d'Antibes. From March they went to Monaco and then for a drive around the Corniche. On 18th March, Evelyn arrived. Throughout the trip Anna would have been keeping a hawk eye on Hugh for signs of tiredness, so there would have been plenty of opportunities for Evelyn and Joan to explore the countryside on their own. It was almost certainly the first time Joan had encountered the Mediterranean landscape. 'The ragged tulips were out in the fields, all the fields were little angular shelves cut out of the hill and ruled and ribbed with vines' (Morris, 1993). By April they had travelled to Genoa, and Evelyn went home. After a few days in Milan the Verrall family took the train home. Joan plunged into her own social life, and by the end of April she was back in Belsize Road.

Judging by Joan's diary she and Evelyn were very much an engaged couple spending time with each other's friends and Evelyn's family. They went to Epping Forest twice in May – suggesting that they were fond of it. In June 1905 Joan writes 'dressmaking'. Was it just the usual importance she placed on this, or had she gone back to Mrs Nettleship to do some work? Most of Joan's life seems given over to pleasure and preparations for her life with Evelyn. Although Joan went back to Brighton for visits, she spent more time with Evelyn in London. Christmas was spent at Flaxley with the Rivieres and Joan records that she wore her satin dress. For some reason she left Belsize Road and moved in with Mrs Joy at 24 Inglewood Road in West Hampstead, although she returned to Belsize Road the following year. Evelyn transported her possessions in 'Daisy'. Joan's period of engagement seems to have been a round of pleasure. In January 1906, six months before the wedding, she wrote 'shopping, concerts, teas, and dinners with Evelyn'. This sunny period was in contrast to the physical and emotional difficulties which followed.

Joan's diary is laconic.

> 13th July 1906 'At Home' afternoon
> 14th July 'Married St Peters 11.45'

Fortunately, Anna's diary is more forthcoming. The 'At Home' was a tribute to her capacity for domestic organisation and visual sense. 'Good old Clarke' and two other waiters came in the morning to get the room ready, and an extra parlourmaid had been hired for several days beforehand. Tall jars of lilies stood upstairs and downstairs – perhaps a nod to the aesthetic movement, and the tables were decorated with pink sweetpeas and gypsophilia. The family went out for lunch, but Anna stayed on duty and 'had a chop quietly'. As usual what occupies Anna is what she and the girls were wearing, 'Joan a bright rosy silk and old lace, part of my present. I had a pale grey taffetas silk and old Italian lace'. A son-in-law who cared about his clothes was a gift to Anna. Evelyn looked, and was, delightful. But as always there was the undertow of worry about Hugh, and Anna consoles herself he does not look overtired.

In contrast to the 'At Home', the wedding was mostly family, and Anna itemises them carefully. Mr and Mrs Briton Riviere came with three of Evelyn's brothers. Annette and Marion Verrall – Hugh's sisters came, but only Helen from Cambridge. Anna takes no account of Arthur's decreasing mobility, and probably she found it difficult to think about. Within the confines of a conventional wedding Anna was proud that Joan had chosen an unconventional style:

> She was charmingly dressed in quite unconventional style – she wore a lovely old embroidered muslin frock of her great grandmothers with pale blue ribbons run through slits and a leghorn hat drawn down with narrow ribbons. It was *most* picturesque and uncommon. There were no bridesmaids, flowers, favours, white gloves or fuss of any kind.

This was in contrast to Anna's wedding, and she glories in Joan's freedom from 'fuss'. This belies her image as a Victorian housewife and Joan as a Grande Dame.

Chapter 6

Does housekeeping interest you at all?

Evelyn and Joan had a quiet honeymoon in Burley in the New Forest. When they got back they stayed with the Rivieres at 'Flaxley' while they hunted for somewhere to live. On 13th August they found a flat at 16 York Terrace, in easy reach of Lincoln's Inn where Evelyn continued to build up his practice. Everything seemed to be going well. Then on 17th August Evelyn became frighteningly ill. Joan described Evelyn's illness as 'British Cholera', which would have meant sickness and diarrhoea. Only the poor went to hospital, so Evelyn was nursed at home. For Joan, Evelyn's weakness and debility must have had frightening echoes of her father's symptoms. On 16th September Joan wrote in her diary 'E sat in an armchair', and her words breathe relief. Although Evelyn's illness was real enough, its timing suggests that there may have been a psychological element. Like many men of his generation, apart from his time at Oxford, Evelyn had never lived away from home, and he continued to retreat to Flaxley when things were difficult. On 27th September Joan and Evelyn went for a drive. '[Evelyn] 6 weeks ill'. By October, Evelyn was well enough for them to make a trip to Brighton, their first visit as a married couple.

It may have been during this visit that it was decided that Molly would come to live in London. Officially, Joan would be her chaperone and introduce Molly to London life. At first Molly lived with Joan, but she soon rented a flat of her own, suggesting that Anna and Hugh were supporting her financially. Joan's diaries show that the two young women went to the same dances and social gatherings. At this point in their lives they were on friendly terms. At some point Molly was employed at St Thomas's Hospital as an Almoner, but her comings and goings suggest it was at a later date. With Joan and Molly in London, and Cuthbert in Canada, Anna was free to devote herself to looking after Hugh. He only had three years to live.

Once Molly was in London she and Joan organised the move into York Terrace while Evelyn stayed at Flaxley until everything was ready. Part of being ready was having a servant. Joan's diary suggests that at this point they only had one servant – a maid of all work. Often that meant a teenage girl. She would have to cook, clean, carry water for washing, and in the afternoon put on a black dress and white apron to let in visitors and wait at the table. Some households had a second woman to do 'the rough' (Flanders, 2003). Finding a maid was straightforward. The best-known agencies were Masseys and Mrs Hunts in Mayfair. The decor of these agencies mirrored the mistress/servant divide. Prospective employers were interviewed in a room with dainty chairs, servants were seen in an office with a linoleum floor. If finding a servant was straightforward Joan soon found that keeping them was not. Joan's diary lists a rapid staff turnover: '12th December first maid left. One engaged did not come. 18th January second maid left'. It is not clear exactly what went wrong. Working for a couple in a flat must have been easier than working for a family in a house. The problem was that Joan had immensely high standards, but the mechanics of housework did not interest her. She wanted the flat immaculate, and delicious meals at regular intervals. As an older woman she achieved this, but at this stage she did not have the knack which Anna had of mixing careful supervision and taking an interest in the work. The complaints about maids died down, to reappear later as crises with nursemaids and nannies.

Despite these difficulties, Joan was pleased to have her own home. She organised two 'At Homes', and in addition, friends and relatives came in the afternoons (for some reason 'morning calls' were made in the afternoons.) Joan wrote a list of everyone who came in a three-month period, which comes to a total of thirty-seven people. This is typical of Joan's diaries. Each entry is usually no more than a sentence or a few words. At first I thought it was written a long time after the events, however the handwriting when Joan had her breakdown is visibly disturbed. Sometimes it is possible to make deductions. For example 'Aunt May' (Margaret Verrall) is on the list. She must have come to see Joan's new home as well as providing gossip from Trinity and Newnham. Perhaps she gave Joan some advice about the servant problem. Anna's attempts to talk to Joan about it only ended in a row.

The obvious person missing from the guest list was Helen Verrall. However, the two young women had other plans. They were going to Germany for a month. Their trip included Dresden, where they could idle in cafes drinking coffee and eating ices – as well as more cultural pursuits. They also visited Gotha. Both young women had to face the question of what to do with their lives. Helen had a head start. She had a first-class degree in Classics. The stage was set to follow in Margaret's footsteps, which she did, apart from a detour in Psychology at King's College London. Joan had a long and painful road ahead of her. However, at this point they shared a preoccupation with the fight for votes for women.

In 1906, the *Newnham College Letter* (edited by Helen) reported the foundation of a suffrage society with bullish tactics. The secretary, Ellie Rendall (later Virginia Woolf's doctor) held regular cocoa meetings in her room for the conversion of anti-suffragists and the strengthening of the wobblers. The suffragists took their message beyond the bounds of college.

A suffrage caravan pulled by a horse called Jock took a group of suffragists into Scotland, holding rallies and distributing leaflets on the way. Jock was too aristocratic to sleep in a field and had to be found a stable for the night. Joan, who loved her comforts, must have sympathised. Women were not only demanding the vote. Amber Reeves gave a lecture to shocked Newnhamites on the relativity of morals. Shortly after this she put her theory into practice by eloping and becoming pregnant by H. G. Wells (a married man). His checked suit had been seen flashing round the corridors of Newnham beforehand.

When Joan returned from Germany she put her energy, rather erratically, into the suffrage cause. There were two main strands of the movement. The National Union of Women's Suffrage Societies (NUWSS) was a democratic organisation who hoped to make change using the political process. Their leader, elected democratically, was Millicent Garrett Fawcett, who we last met writing to the Merrifields to encourage them to send Margaret to Newnham. A newer organisation was the Women's Social and Political Union (WSPU), ruled by the undemocratic, charismatic Mrs Pankhurst. Their tactics included civil disobedience – often leading to prison – and later violence. Joan joined the NUWSS. In November 1907 Joan hosted a NUWSS meeting at her flat. Alys Russell was the speaker. She was the American wife of the philosopher Bertrand Russell. They were both devoted to the NUWSS cause, so much so that Russell agreed to stand for parliament as the NUWSS candidate in the 1906 Wimbledon by-election. Rather surprisingly he polled 3,000 votes, although he was relieved not to be elected. Joan does not record what Alys spoke about, although she had spoken about 'free love' at Bryn Mawr College in America. Unlike Amber, Alys did not always put her principles into practice and kept Russell on the rack of continence during their courtship. Perhaps Alys felt that there had been too much free love in her family. Her father had been a charismatic evangelist who seduced some of his flock under the pretext that he represented Christ the bridegroom. Once exposed he fled to America. But the clock was already ticking for Joan. By the time Alys gave her talk, Joan was two months pregnant.

In March 1908 Joan got the nursery ready. The walls were distempered and a linoleum floor was put down, which Joan brightened up with rugs. The baby would take its meals in the nursery, so there was a table and chairs and a high chair. A visit to Brighton at this time resulted in a row with Anna. Not a good prognosis. In May, Joan records that she was sewing, but does not say whether it was pregnancy clothes for herself or something for the baby. Behind these preparations Joan may have been anxious about the baby. She probably knew about the death of her older brother, and there were reasons to be anxious. Mortality rates for infants were still very high. In the event all went well:

> June 7 [1908] Diana born 4:30. Pains
> 1am slightly. Nurse came 7:30

Joan seems to have had a fairly easy time in labour. The difficulty came afterwards. The nurse that Joan refers to would have been the monthly nurse, who usually stayed three months. Joan longed for care for herself. She must have been hoping for this when she took Diana and her nurse to visit Anna and Hugh, 'Joan brought her baby to stay a fortnight. H. very poorly'. In fact, Anna could only think of the impending changes in her life. Hugh had decided to give up his work. A new partnership was set up without him, and he only drew a small income from the practice. Their house would be given up, and they would need to find somewhere cheaper to live. They planned to visit Allasio where Hugh could rest in the open air. Joan must have been shocked and upset. Back at home her mood descended further. On 10th October she recorded 'Bad cold. Gave up feeding baby'. The next day she was in bed, and again on 17th October. On 9th November Joan was ill again, although she brightened up a bit when Diana was christened.

Nowadays we would probably think that Joan was suffering from post-natal depression. Instead of having a helpful figure in her mind, a woman with post-natal depression has a harsh critical figure who tells her she is no good as a mother. The problem for Joan was that there was no one in the external world who could help her out of this state. Anna and Hugh came to London to stay at the Grosvenor Hotel, but Hugh collapsed and seemed near death. When he rallied, Anna took him to Dover where they waited in rented rooms for a ferry which they never took. At Christmas Joan was desperate for parental figures to turn to. With characteristic warmth and love Arthur and Margaret invited the family to spend Christmas with them in Cambridge. While Joan and Evelyn were enjoying one of Margaret's delicious meals, Hugh and Anna were spending Christmas alone in lodgings in Dover. It is striking that Joan's diary does not record anything of her father's collapse or her parents' flight. It was a pattern which echoed her childhood experience of her parent's trips abroad for Hugh's health. This must have made her feel that she had no place in her mother's mind. Many years later Joan told her supervisee Hanna Segal 'I could never stand mania'. It was something she had learned to abhor in her parents and herself. Without understanding this it is hard to understand her response to bereavement or the needs of her baby.

Reading Joan's diary it seems she was terrified of being left alone with Diana for any length of time. When the nurse or nanny was not there Anna, Molly, Margaret or the Rivieres were pressed into service. There was a rapid turnover of nannies and nursemaids, as Joan's difficulties did not prevent her being critical and demanding. This regime was not good for Diana. She was frequently ill with colds and coughs, often at a time when a nanny left. Joan was worried about this, but could not provide her with what she needed. In many ways Joan was recreating for Diana the emotional deprivation she herself had experienced as a baby. The only difference was that Anna was better at keeping servants, so Joan had more consistent alternative care. It could be argued that Joan and Anna were behaving like any other middle-class woman of the time. But women differed in their emotional receptivity and interest in their babies. In Joan's defence, she did not have a confidante. Evelyn's name appears frequently in her diary before Diana's birth and hardly at all afterwards. Joan had married a man who dealt with difficulties by going home to his parents.

As Diana grew older Joan found it easier to look after her, and she experienced Diana as more of a person than a persecutor. A diary entry when Diana was four refers to her starting a drill class. Joan was obviously very proud of her, and it is the first time she refers to Diana by name in her diary. In many of the references Diana is being sent to members of the family to be cared for. Anna is the most frequent, but Molly and the Rivieres also took a share. There is a photograph of Joan and Diana taken when Diana must have been five. They both look exquisitely dressed – perhaps by Joan. Joan holds a very adult-looking book and gives the impression she would like to get back to it. The adult Diana told Athol Hughes that Joan once sent her to a boarding school without first visiting the boarding school herself. Yet that cannot be the whole picture. Joan's diary shows that when Diana was at boarding school at King's Langley she visited Diana three times during one term, perhaps when Diana was ill or unhappy. Joan often refers to Diana as 'ill' and records when she is well enough to go out. This is in sharp contrast to Anna's diary which paints a picture of a lively, affectionate child. Joan's preoccupation with Diana's health may have been partly coloured by her depression, and a depressed mother is a burden to a child. In 1909 Joan's depression began to lift. She started dressmaking again, perhaps for the International Ball which she went to with Evelyn. She went to Wagner's 'Ring' cycle – quite a test of endurance – with the mysterious IEE. This enjoyment came to an abrupt stop on 18th March when she was summoned to Brighton because her father was dying.

Anna's diary of Hugh's death was written at right angles to her usual entries, as if her world was turned upside down. Hugh was as charming in death as he was in life. He had a message for Cuthbert, 'Tell my boy to go straight!' When Molly arrived he even managed a little joke, although he knew he was dying. When Joan arrived

> he received her very sweetly but gravely – I have *always* loved Evelyn – even when there have been difficulties and you know there have been difficulties my child! Joan sobbed 'that's all over' and he said 'yes, yes be kind to your mother'.

Joan was overwhelmed and left the room. The following day, his way eased by a tot of brandy, Hugh died. Sitting next to his bed Anna's mind went to another death, long ago: her first baby: '[It] was the sweetest quietest death I have ever seen except my own wee baby who sighed out his little life on my bosom so many years ago'. Anna took comfort from Hugh's courage and the kindness of the nurse looking after him. Characteristically, she basked in the beauty of the room that Hugh had died in. On 23rd April, Hugh was buried in St Peter's churchyard, with its little gravestone for the baby and bigger one for Hugh. The next day Joan returned to London. That evening she went out with a man called Murray Kendall to a performance of his play. Murray Kendall was an architect whose American parents settled in London. They lived in West Hampstead, which is probably how Joan met him. She also went out with him the next evening – presumably leaving Evelyn behind. Was Joan desperate to be with someone who would be emotionally receptive? Or was this the sort of manic flight she would later come to abhor? It does seem likely that Murray Kendall was one of the 'difficulties' that Hugh referred to. Joan spent hours in his company – walking, talking, visiting galleries. Whatever Evelyn felt about this, it did not affect his commitment to Joan. Joan was hungry for new projects, and in January 1910 they took a whole house at 10 Nottingham Terrace. This is a tall thin house behind what is now Madame Tussauds and overlooking Regent's Park. Joan enjoyed herself choosing rugs, fireplaces and wallpaper. Murray Kendall worked on the panelling for the new house. As before, Evelyn retreated to Flaxley while the hustle and bustle of moving was going on. Joan interviewed for a cook and a house parlour maid. A cook was a step up and very welcome to a woman who was fond of her food. Finally, in April, Diana and her nurse and Joan moved in.

Their first visitor was Helen Verrall. Margaret was probably unwilling to leave Arthur, who was increasingly affected by arthritis. Helen had become a research assistant at the Society for Psychical Research. Joan also did work for them, but on a more casual basis. It was one of the things which drew them together. As before, Joan organised two 'At Homes' but was now too sophisticated or too busy to write a list of the guests. However, her diary entries show she was moving into the fringes of Bloomsbury and haute Bohemia. The bustle of the move covered up the anniversary of Hugh's death. It was easier for Joan to respond to the death of Edward VII. She watched his funeral from the Colonial Office. Joan was restless. She did not enjoy being a mother. She wanted solid activities to occupy her time. In June 1910 Joan was asked to work on a suffrage banner for the NUSWW. This was a significant task. Banners were becoming increasingly important as a way of getting the suffrage message across. The 1908 NUWSS March had eight hundred banners, each one billowing out like a sail with the suffrage message. Afterwards they were displayed in sympathetic shops to keep the suffrage message alive. The Artists Suffrage League was founded in 1907 to help with the famous 'Mud March' of the NUWSS (a march in February was not a good idea). Artists worked without pay to design banners which were then worked with embroidery and appliqué work by women volunteers. This is probably the work Joan was doing, although she may have had some input into the design because of her dressmaking skills. On 18th June 1910 Joan's diary records that she walked in a suffrage procession from Charing Cross Bridge to Hyde Park Corner. Although such marches were increasingly common, to take part in one still required courage and dedication for a woman. The Suffragettes (the WSPU) were becoming increasingly frustrated at the slow progress of the cause. Although more MPs supported a vote for women, actual progress was hampered by complex party-political alliances as well as the hostility of Asquith, the Prime Minister. Perhaps it is not a coincidence that 1910 saw the development of the 'hobble skirt'. A long skirt with a band around the hem, so the wearer could only take tiny steps. Joan also went to a suffrage conference in Brighton. She does not seem to have been involved with any further suffrage activities, although she continued to be involved in a variety of women's causes. She may have been alienated by the NUWSS alliance with the Labour Party.

Joan was passionately devoted to the ballet, something which lasted throughout her life. On 3rd May, 1910, Joan went to see Anna Pavlova with Murray Kendall. On 17th May they went to see the Ballets Russes for its first visit to England. Although the eroticism was toned down for an English audience the experience was still stirring, in particular the costumes, designed by Leon Baskt in vivid clashing colours and integrated with the sets. Joan was not the first person to see the crossover potential for fashion, 'So chic was the Russian ballet that the line between stage and couture salon collapsed' (Davis, 2006). Working with couturier Jeanne Paquin, Baskt designed 'street dresses' linked to the Ballet Russes productions, such as *L'Apres-midi d'un Faune* and *Sheherezade*. Joan was fired with a wish to have her own salon where she could design and make exotic dresses. Evelyn, as always, was willing to support Joan's projects and offered to pay the rental for Joan's future salon. However, Joan had only worked as a junior member of staff at Mrs Nettleship. Her dressmaking skills were sophisticated, but her business knowledge was limited. Within a month she arranged to spend some time at a dressmakers called 'Sheba' to learn the business side of things.

After taking a holiday in August, Joan had another spell at Sheba's in September, but she must have felt she had learned enough, because she left Sheba on 10th September, and within a week had found rooms in Manchester Street, not far from Nottingham Terrace. As a token of her serious intentions, Joan opened a bank account and moved furniture into the Manchester Street rooms. By October or November Joan must have had customers as her diary records fittings in November and December. But at the point of success Joan broke down, 'Collapsed with gastritis', 'Home: home to bed'. Although Joan did a bit of work after she recovered it was the end of her business. Anna's diary describes the situation very concisely: 'Joan was very poorly – and had to give up work and go away. Asked me to go to London and keep house for her'. Within a week of arriving in London, Anna records 'Baby very ill'. What was going on?

Chapter 7

'Nerves'

'Molly and I had the donkey, and took tea up to Buckthorne Hill'. In the period immediately after Hugh's death, Anna was still able to enjoy herself. Her catalogue of visits has a Jane Austen-ish quality. However, there were some unpleasant things to do. She sold the furniture from the big house and moved into Heath Cottage, one of a group of cottages owned by Hugh. As time went on she let out the cottages, bringing in a much-needed source of income. She even managed to let Heath Cottage when she was away on visits. From time to time Anna went to visit Joan and baby Diana in London. Joan also came with Diana and her nurse to visit Anna, 'Had a very happy week with the darling, who is very sweet and attractive now'. Anna's view of Diana was in marked contrast to the sick baby seen through Joan's eyes. Anna spent a peaceful Christmas in 1909 with Molly and two of her sisters. After Christmas Molly went back to London. Left alone, Anna's thoughts took a turn for the worse. She realised that there were now no Verralls left in Brighton. This seems to have brought home her own loss, and the brisk tone of the diary collapsed, 'And so ends the most terrible year of our lives'.

1910 began more cheerfully. There was rare news from Cuthbert: 'I hear my boy thinks he can come home in or about October 1911 when he hopes to be a qualified surveyor'. The Richardson's head clerk, who had visited Canada, described Cuthbert as 'very tall, very quiet, very nice and don't drink'. With this news Anna went to visit the Verralls in Cambridge. Helen and May were abroad, so Anna encountered Arthur on his own. She was shocked by the deterioration in his health. It must have brought back memories of Hugh's illness in a very concrete way. The effect on her was immediate: 'Felt very ill'.

Despite this, Anna carried on. After a round of visits, including her faithful servant, Page, who had recently married, Anna went to 10 Nottingham Terrace to help with Diana while her nurse was away. Joan was also away, as if taking flight from a Diana without her nurse. After a week of this, Anna unsurprisingly grew worse and consulted Dr Hugh Wingfield, who told her she was suffering from 'acute Neurasthenia brought on by many shocks and strain'. He ordered a complete long rest. Neurasthenia was the current term for depression and other ailments. Anna was lucky only to be prescribed bed rest. The standard treatment for neurasthenia was developed by an American neurologist Silas Weir Mitchell in 1873. He prescribed not only bed rest but massive overfeeding. A patient could be expected to gain 50 lbs (Showalter, 1987). No exercise was allowed but a nurse came each day to administer massage and a doctor also visited. With such a draconian system some patients felt they had no choice but to recover. Virginia Woolf, who was prescribed a version of this treatment, wrote poignantly of being left alone in the dark (Lee, 1996). Weir Mitchell's treatment was introduced into England in 1880 by W. S. Playfair, professor of obstetrics at King's College. His experience with women who had lost their babies led him to link neurasthenia with grief. Dr Wingfield seems to have been familiar with his ideas. Anna's initial response to the instruction to rest was to return to Crowborough to get Heath Cottage ready for letting. Then she came back to London to rest at a friend's house. Rest seems to have made Anna worse. She called in a Dr Sainsbury. Consulting a number of doctors was normal practice when there were mental health problems, probably because treatments were so ineffective. Anna devised her own rest cure. She visited friends and rested at their houses. So far Anna only had herself to worry about, but at the beginning of November, Joan collapsed with gastroenteritis and had to spend time in bed. This was the beginning of a terrifying slide into depression.

Initially, Joan rallied and had dress fittings booked at her business on 24th, 25th, and 28th November and 1st December. This suggests she already had a number of customers and the business was going well. However, Anna's diary presents a bleaker picture: 'Joan was very poorly and had to give up her work and go away. Asked me to go to London and keep house for her'. When Anna came to 10 Nottingham Terrace, Joan and IEE went to stay in Heath Cottage. Then Joan went to Arthur and Margaret in Cambridge. She was restless and desperate to be with people she felt close to. It must have been hard work for Margaret to look after Arthur, handicapped by arthritis, and Joan in a state of collapse. Reluctantly, Joan went back to London. She seems to have been barely aware that the problem was in her mind. In London she turned to a Dr Cyriax who offered 'orthopaedic medicine' which was based on a diagnosis of muscular lesions. The treatment depended on very careful history taking which probably had a therapeutic value in itself. Anna took the opportunity to slip away for a few days to Brighton to visit friends. She was still not feeling well, and had another consultation with Dr Sainsbury. Not surprisingly, her doctors felt that she was still not getting enough rest. Finally, at the beginning of March, Anna decided that Joan was much better and went to her friend Ethel to spend a week in bed.

Anna was wrong about Joan. Unable to sleep or eat, Joan was terrified by her state of mind. Instead of consulting a fashionable London doctor, Joan wanted to be looked after by her mother. She saw a woman doctor, Dr Boyle, in

Hove, and Anna grudgingly allowed Joan to stay for two months, and Evelyn came down on visits. By July, Joan had acquired three doctors, Dr Basdene, Dr Boyle and Dr Falkener, who irritated Anna with their comings and goings. The number of doctors reflected Joan's fears that she was not going to get better. Dr Boyle was probably the most effective doctor. She had a speciality in treating women. Census records show that Joan was a patient in her private hospital. Poignantly the records describe her as a 'dressmaker'. Although Anna had nursed Hugh when he was dying, she did not want to nurse Joan. This difficulty was not new, but Anna was also struggling with her own state of mind. Anna felt 'tired and worn out' and in June, while Joan was still staying in Heath Cottage, Anna went to a Mrs Howells for a rest. Anna did not return to Heath Cottage until 15th July. By then Joan and Evelyn had got the message, and Joan went into Mrs Chater's nursing home.

In reality, doctors had little to offer for depression except bromides and sedatives. The real curative factor was almost certainly the nursing. Nursing homes offered rest, seclusion and feeding up. The problem for patients like Joan was the other patients. Virginia Woolf, Joan's contemporary, describes in a letter a visit to her friend Jean Thomas's nursing home:

> I went down to Twickenham (Miss Thomas) last week and had a most interesting time, trying to ignore the oddities of several not altogether like other people women. One of them leapt with fright when one looked at her and shook her fork in one's face.

A little later she presented an even more dramatic picture: 'Miss Thomas came down for a night in an interval between discharging a woman who wished to commit murder, and taking one wants to kill herself'. Virginia's detachment was more apparent than real. This was Virigina's idea of humour. She herself had been a patient in Miss Thomas's nursing home in 1910 and would go again in 1913 after the publication of her first novel *The Voyage Out*. At the time her delusions, refusal to eat and sleeping difficulties were put down to the strain of finishing the novel, and her worry about what her family and critics would say about it.

Freud would have seen it differently. In a paper on 'character types to be met with in analysis' he described a group of patients who were 'wrecked by success'. These patients break down when they achieve a longed-for goal. In Virginia Woolf's case this was the publication of her first novel. In Joan's it was the establishment of her own business. Unlike Virginia Woolf, Joan was later able to turn this breakdown into a professional success when she published a dazzling paper on 'Those Wrecked by Success' in 1936 (Riviere, 1936a). For now, Joan's recovery was slow, but by August 1911 she was well enough to move with a nurse into a cottage in Walberswick with Diana, Diana's nurse and Molly. The dry, sunny Suffolk climate was thought to be helpful for tuberculosis. The regime at the sanatorium was very similar to Weir

Mitchell's but combined with fresh air. Not surprisingly, it was also thought helpful for 'nervous exhaustion'. Walberswick is a beautiful part of the coast and was much favoured by painters including Charles Rennie Mackintosh, though it is unlikely that Joan could appreciate it.

No sooner was Joan a bit better, than she illustrated Freud's theory by coming down with tonsillitis. They moved out of the cottage into rooms. By now Joan, like Diana had a nurse of her own. Joan's longing to be looked after is painfully clear in her scrappy diary where she has inserted 'my' every time she writes 'nurse'. Eventually, Joan was well enough for the whole entourage to move back into 10 Nottingham Terrace. Joan's nurse left and she got Miss Whitlock. In July Diana's nurse left. As always this was a crisis and a new nurse, Ethel, was rapidly hired. By 1912 Joan was leading a more normal life and going out to visit friends, although she made a trip to Brighton to see Dr Boyle, whom she found particularly sympathetic. Despite these improvements Joan's diary is a careful catalogue of minor illness, as if her body was a sick child that needed nursing. Some of these illnesses were probably psychosomatic. She had frequent styes, one of which required lancing. The modern view is that psychosomatic illness is linked to psychological states which are denied expression, but emerge in the body as illness. Dr Alexis Brook, psychiatrist and psychotherapist had suggested that styes are expressions of unresolved mourning (Brook, 1995). We have seen how Joan took flight from the death of her father. When Arthur Verrall died in June 1912, Joan records this in very small handwriting as if minimising the event, but does not seem to have gone to the funeral, although he was very important to her.

As Joan's professional venture had collapsed, her friendships were increasingly important. There were three overlapping circles. Those involved in painting and writing, including members of the Bloomsbury group. There were the people involved in the Society for Psychical Research, and later the Medico-Psychological clinic. Finally, there was a group of people she had known for a long time and felt close to. Molly, Helen, Aunt May, Murray Kendall and the enigmatic IEE. However, when Joan broke down in 1910, IEE came with her to spend time at Heath Cottage. It seems unlikely that Anna would have allowed this if IEE was a man. The relation with IEE had a similar pattern to Joan's relationship to Anna, with rows and reconciliations. Perhaps it was sexual.

It is an indicator of Joan's recovery that she began dressmaking again. Molly had moved into a flat in Upper Baker Street, close to Nottingham Terrace, and Joan did her dressmaking work there. It also allowed her to spend more time with Molly. Despite the later rows over Diana's care, the two sisters were close and went on holiday together. In August 1912 they went to Saint Jacut in Brittany, a fashionable resort. An unusual diary entry records that Diana went to drill class for the first time. So many of Joan's records of Diana comment on her illness that it is refreshing to read signs of progress. It may have been a sign that Joan was feeling better in herself, as well as more positive feelings about Diana, Joan went to coffee parties, literary parties and even held a St Jacut party at her house. Shortly after the party, Joan took Diana to the Bells for tea. It was a rare outing for Diana without a nurse. However, a few months later, when Diana's nanny left, Joan immediately sent Diana to the Rivieres at Flaxley until a new nanny was found. To a certain extent Joan was like many middle-class mothers of the time. Vanessa, despite her bohemian principles, made some desperate and unsatisfactory arrangements for her children to be looked after. But there was something quite extreme in Joan's fear of being left alone with Diana. Perhaps Joan's attitude to Diana was more like Georgina Burne-Jones's description of her first child as 'the small stranger within our gates'.

Somehow Joan met the Sickerts (probably through the Rivieres), E. M. Forster and Lady Ottoline Morrell. Judging by Joan's diaries her relationship with the Sickerts developed and she went on motor outings with them. Sickert's second wife Christine Angus was a professional embroiderer and tapestry maker, so there may have been common ground there. However, Sickert was known for his appreciation of beautiful women – his first marriage collapsed under his many infidelities. Joan was both beautiful and decorative. Although Sickert enjoyed upper-class society his paintings reflected bleak emotional truths. His famous painting *Ennui* is a bleak portrait of a marriage gone stale. Joan's willingness to face the truth may have found an echo in Sickert. Joan was gradually moving into friendships which helped her face the reality of her mental state.

Joan met Clive and Vanessa Bell at a party. Vanessa was the daughter of Sir Leslie Stephen, editor of the *Dictionary of National Biography*. Her sister, Virginia, was about to marry Leonard Woolf. Vanessa was becoming established as an artist, and Clive as an art critic. Like Joan, Vanessa was emerging from a period of depression. During this time she had fallen in love with the painter and art critic Roger Fry, the organiser of the first Post-Impressionist Exhibition. This relationship did not ruffle the Bell's relationship as Clive kept a mistress. The marriage was moving towards a liaison of convenience. Perhaps the same could be said of Joan and Evelyn although it seems unlikely that Evelyn kept a mistress. Members of Bloomsbury had a reputation for talking about everything, although in practice there was some selective frankness. However, Vanessa would have had no hesitation in telling Joan about her sister Virginia's breakdowns. Virginia's family openly regarded her as 'mad'. This straightforward discussion may have made Joan more aware of the psychological nature of her breakdown. When she felt herself sliding downhill in 1915 she recorded it as 'nerves'. Vanessa probably gave Joan the name of Dr Maurice Wright who Leonard Woolf had consulted for a nervous tremor. Leonard also took Virginia to see him. Joan saw Maurice Wright eleven times in February and March 1915. It was not psychoanalysis but it was a more intense experience than her previous encounters with doctors; it was an attempt at treatment rather than a diagnosis. She must have found it helpful because she went to see Wright again the following year.

It was probably through the Bells that Joan met Amber Blanco White. Vanessa and Amber had planned to have their children looked after together. This arrangement broke down when Julian, Vanessa's son, pelted one of Amber's daughters with cow dung. Amber would not have been shocked. Her own background was more bohemian than the Bells. Her family came from New Zealand and both her parents were committed Fabians. Amber's mother Maud edited a collection of accounts of working-class life, *Round About a Pound a Week*. At Cambridge, Amber was a brilliant and charismatic student. We have already encountered her preaching moral relativity. Through the Fabians she got to know H. G. Wells and was the model for the eponymous Ann Veronica. In real life Amber and Wells eloped to France; but unlike the fictional Ann Veronica who marries her university tutor, Wells had no intention of leaving his wife Jane. However, there was a happy ending of sorts. Amber married a fellow Cambridge student, and they brought up Wells's daughter together with their own. In some ways Amber did not live up to her early brilliance but she did become a lecturer in psychology at Morley College and wrote a book called *Why Women Worry* in which she acknowledged her debt to Freud and Klein.

In 1913, probably at Amber's suggestion, Joan and Amber went to a meeting of the Medico-Psychological Clinic at the house of the psychological novelist May Sinclair. This organisation was founded by Dr Jessie Murray. Dr Murray had studied at the School of Medicine for Women at the Royal Free Hospital and at Durham. She had a particular interest in psychology and had been to France to attend Pierre Janet's lectures in Paris. The clinic was intended to treat nervous disabilities by medical and psychological methods. Shortly before Joan and Amber's visit the clinic opened at Dr Murray's home in 14 Endsleigh Street. Among the staff were Julia Turner, Dr Murray's friend and possibly lesbian partner. As time went on they were joined by many students and staff who went on to become early members of the Tavistock Clinic and the British Psychoanalytic Society. These included Dr Sylvia Payne and Ella Freeman Sharpe, who would become colleagues of Joan, and Susan Isaacs, who would become Joan's patient. Initially, the clinic concentrated on women patients, but as the First World War gathered momentum it began admitting soldiers suffering from shell shock. It offered psychoanalytic and psychological treatments and more conventional medical help. As well as treatment, there was also training for therapists which welcomed women as well as men. The clinic spread into several houses in Brunswick Square, where it was possible to offer early forms of occupational therapy such as dancing, gardening and art.

This therapeutic Garden of Eden was not to last. It ran into financial and ideological difficulties. Too many patients were taken on at no cost, and the clinic had expanded beyond its means. A member of staff, Dr James Glover, was invited to the sixth psychoanalytic conference in The Hague. Here he met Dr Karl Abraham who persuaded him to go into analysis with him and have a taste of real psychoanalysis. Glover persuaded his brother Edward to have analysis with Abraham as well, an arrangement which was to have dire consequences later. Glover was impressed by his experience of the real thing, and returned to London determined to reform the, by now, shrunken clinic. Jessie Murray tragically died of cancer and Julia Murray was unable to accept the change of ethos or manage the accumulated debts. Eventually James Glover, like a pied piper, led those willing to follow Freud's ideas to Ernest Jones's newly formed British Psychoanalytical Society in 1919. Joan soon joined the society herself.

The First World War, which provided so many traumatised soldier patients for the Medico-Psychological clinic is very much in the background in Joan's diary, possibly because it coincided with changes and upheavals in her own life. She made no attempt to make a contribution to the war effort, unlike Anna who provided soldiers with baths and entertained them with tea. Later, Anna worked at St Thomas's Hospital. Like many of the upper–middle classes it was hard for Joan to regard Germans as the enemy. She still maintained links with friends in Gotha. Germany was the country of culture and music and psychological novels. The Royal Family were, after all, German. However, Evelyn volunteered for training as an air defence gunner. Murray Kendall went to camp with the Sportsmans Battalion. The war also hastened weddings.

In September, 1914, Molly got married. Joan made Molly's dress. The faithful IEE came to stay for five days immediately after and in October Joan and Evelyn went away together for five days. At times, Evelyn seemed like a guest in his own marriage, but Joan was grateful for his support. In February, 1915, Molly's husband, Jim, was sent to the front. In September, 1915, Helen got married to a fellow SPR member William Salter. Joan made her dress and prepared herself for the wedding by having a Helena Rubinstein face treatment. Joan used the opportunity of being in Cambridge to visit Jane Harrison, ostensibly to discuss her Russian lessons. Harrison and her companion Hope Mirrlees had been having Russian lessons in Paris. At this point the horrors of war were still distant for many people, but Harrison had been shaken by German shelling of the North East. A family servant who she had been close to was killed with a grandchild on each knee. After visiting Jane, Joan had dinner with Aunt Margaret. Despite poor health Margaret was loyal to her French background and belonged to a committee which looked after the needs of Belgian refugees. These meetings with women who were so important to Joan seem to have stiffened her resolve to do something with her life. As well as the Russian lessons she began to go to psychology lectures. Helen was working as a demonstrator in psychology at King's College, so it is likely that Joan went to lectures there. Joan also went back to see Maurice Wright – an indication that all was not well.

At Christmas, Joan and Evelyn went to stay in Cambridge with Aunt Margaret, who was rather lonely now that Helen was married. Joan basked in Margaret's sympathy and quick understanding. In 1916, Margaret wrote to Joan that she was dying. It was an opportunity for Joan to see Margaret and say goodbye to her. There is no evidence that she went. The deathbed farewell to her father had been unbearable. It was left to Jane Harrison to spend the last few weeks with Margaret. Margaret was not afraid to die. On the contrary, she had been looking forward to it for years. Although she was sceptical about some psychic phenomenon her belief in life after death was absolute. Jane found Margaret's beliefs exasperating but did not try to disabuse her. As Jane put it 'death meant to her fuller knowledge, fresh opportunity to live and work'. She also expected to meet Arthur and her two dead babies (Robinson, 2002).

On 5th July, 1916, Joan went to Margaret's funeral. Within a few days she went to see her mother at Redhill and they had, as she puts it, a 'reconciliation'. The loss of Margaret seems to have driven Joan to make peace with her mother. There is no mention in Joan's diary what the argument was about. However, the usual running sore was Joan's treatment of Diana. Joan's determination to send Diana away with people she hardly knew, and to places she had never been, make painful reading. Of course this is how Anna had treated Joan. However, by the time Diana was born, Anna's capacity to enjoy a baby had increased. It must have been painful to Joan to see Anna spending time and playing with Diana in a way she had never done with herself. Joan's supervisee, Hanna Segal, thought that Joan did not like children. It would be more accurate to say that Joan could not cope with children, but deeply admired those who could. It was part of the basis of her friendship with Melanie Klein. In the late 1940s Joan wrote of:

> those gifted intuitive mothers and women who nurse children, who have always taken for granted that a baby does feel and 'think' and 'know' and react and respond emotionally *ie* psychically, to whatever happens to him and is done to him.

It was probably a measure of Joan's guilt about Diana that when she was an adult Joan begged Hanna Segal to take Diana into analysis. Sadly, or wisely, Segal refused.

Chapter 8

Ernest Jones

At the beginning of 1916, Evelyn was taken ill with pleurisy. As usual he retreated to Flaxley to be nursed. He was away for three weeks – long enough to worry Joan. While Evelyn was away, Cuthbert passed through London on his way to fight in France. If Joan met him, her diary does not record it. Joan was disturbed that the two most significant men in her life were under threat. She developed a bad stye. However, she seems to have become more aware of the significance of her own illness, perhaps with the help of Dr Wright. On 12th February 1916 she went to the SPR library and borrowed books by Freud and Ernest Jones. By 21st February she had started analysis with Ernest Jones on a daily basis. It was a terrible mistake.

Joan's choice of analyst was not surprising. Ernest Jones was one of the earliest British adherents of Freud. He was the founder of the London Psychoanalytic Society in 1913. Maurice Wright was a member, and may have recommended Jones to Riviere. Jones thought of himself as Freud's representative in England. He had read Freud and Breuer's 'Studies in Hysteria', and had finally met Freud at the first Psychoanalytic Congress in Salzburg in 1908. Jones made a favourable impression on Freud, who invited him for a meal when Jones travelled to Vienna. At this meal, together with Freud's first English translator Brill, they discussed some of the difficulties of translating Freud's work into English, a job that would occupy Joan for many years. Freud was worried that psychoanalysis would be seen as a Jewish science, so he was very pleased to welcome a gentile into the fold. However, Jones's difficulties with boundaries soon became apparent. Otto Gross, another psychoanalyst, asked Jones if he would analyse his wife. Freud was concerned and wrote to Jung.

> Jones wants to go to Munich to help the Grosses. The little woman seems to be seriously smitten with him ... It looks as if this were going to end badly.
>
> (Quoted in Maddox, 2006)

This was not the first time Jones had taken risks with therapeutic boundaries. After he qualified as a doctor he failed to get the hospital job he expected. He turned his hand to doing medical odds and ends such as coaching students. He was pleased to accept an appointment as a medical examiner of 'mentally defective' children at a school run by the London County Council. On 2nd March 1906, Jones was examining children without the presence of a nurse, which would have been normal practice. Afterwards, one-by-one, four children made accusations that Jones had exposed himself and made sexual overtures. The father of one of the girls laid a complaint with the police. The police surgeon found 'certain marks' on the green baize tablecloth and the complaint went to court. In court the LCC's Dr Kerr took Jones's side and suggested the children had made up the story between them. The fact that they were mentally handicapped finished Jones's defence and the case was dismissed. Brenda Maddox, Jones's biographer, carefully weighs up the evidence and finds Jones guilty. She considers the fact that the children were adolescent means that their statements were more likely to be true. Nowadays we take children's evidence very seriously in sexual abuse cases. However, in the case of Ernest Jones this was not an isolated incident. By the time Joan saw him he had a history of being accused of boundary violations. He seems to have been aware of this as a problem, and told Freud he had successfully conquered certain difficulties in himself.

At the very least one could say that Jones was a very self-destructive person. In 1908 he was working at the West End Hospital for Diseases of the Nervous System. A senior colleague told him of a girl with a paralysed arm. He challenged Jones to prove that this was a case of hysteria with a sexual basis. Jones questioned the girl (without a nurse present) and discovered that she had been playing with an older boy who made sexual advances towards her. She used her arm to fend him off. Jones proved his case, but the damage was done. The girl accused him of talking about sex to her. In this case Jones's story is very likely to be true, but it does not alter the folly of talking about sexual matters without a third person present. As this was the second accusation Jones lost his job, and he had no chance of getting another.

Jones was resilient. He applied for a job in Canada and took his wealthy Jewish mistress, Loe Kann, with him – lying to his parents that she was his wife. Once in Canada, Jones got himself into erotic difficulties again, this time with adult women. One patient accused Jones of having sexual intercourse with her. He paid her five hundred dollars in blackmail money – a very large sum, possibly paid by Loe Kann. This patient was followed by a female protector with a gun. Loe Kann paid for someone to protect Jones. This Feydeau farce did not of course do Jones's reputation any good. Another patient who felt she was entangled with Jones sought an interview with Brill to discuss this. Fortunately her intentions towards Jones were friendly. Brill, Freud's first English translator, probably passed on this information to Freud (Maddox, 2006).

Not everything in Canada went wrong. Jones was eventually given an assistant professor post at Toronto. This honour was due to the intervention of Sir William Meredith, who was pleased with the outcome of his daughter's psychoanalysis. However, Loe was increasingly unhappy and giving herself huge doses of morphine. Matters were not helped by the fact that Jones had started an affair with her maid Lina. Jones poured out his worries about Loe to Freud (omitting mention of the affair). To his amazement Freud offered to analyse Loe. Eventually Loe went to Vienna and Jones decided that he would set up as a psychoanalyst in London. Loe was happier after her analysis with Freud and married a man called Herbert Jones. She continued to correspond with Ernest Jones.

This then was Joan's first psychoanalyst. At her first meeting she saw a small dapper man with regular features and a confident manner. Jones regarded himself as a changed person, thanks to his self analysis. Joan was in a vulnerable state following the death of Margaret, who in many ways had been a mother to her. Unlike Anna, Joan could confide in Margaret and rely on her kindness and good sense. Jones fired off comments that were insightful and Joan was not the first woman to feel she had a special relationship with him. In a letter to him she analysed his appeal: 'you irresponsible puck! Irresistible to women, meeting them on their own ground, the emotions'. Helen and Molly were married. Evelyn was kind but shied away from anything emotionally demanding. Riviere began to believe that she was falling in love with Jones. Freud had anticipated this sort of difficulty, but he believed it was a transference phenomenon, and he advised analysts not to be flattered by this. Jones was a vain man who prided himself on his success with women. However, he also seems to have felt sympathetic to Joan, and some of his behaviour was guided by mistaken good intentions. Jones was a well-read man, and they both shared an admiration for D. H. Lawrence, and were subscribers to his magazine *The Signature*. (Lawrence had had a consultation with Jones, who had written a letter exempting Lawrence from military service.)

Jones himself had been refused by the army on the grounds of his arthritis. The war meant he could not travel abroad to meet his psychoanalytic friends and colleagues. Freud himself had two sons in the army, and was very preoccupied with worries about them. To satisfy his urge to travel, Jones bought a motorbike and side car and drove around the south of England. On his travels he came across a Jacobean farmhouse in the village of Elsted in Sussex. It was at the foot of the South Downs and close to the sea. He named it 'The Plat'. During the summer of 1916 Joan complained that she had nowhere to go. It is not unusual for psychoanalytic patients to be anxious about the long summer break, but Jones treated this literally and offered to lend The Plat to Joan. It was to do great harm to the nature of their psychoanalytic relationship. Initially Joan was pleased to be able to stay in Sussex again. She gave Jones advice about the decor, and invited IEE and Murray Kendall to visit. Riviere was falling in love with Jones, and staying at The Plat supported the idea that he was in love with her. Joan was in the grip of an erotic transference, but Jones's behaviour gave it substance.

What made Jones behave like this? It could be argued that in the early days of psychoanalysis, boundaries were more flexible. Freud had been known to exchange presents with his patients. Anna Freud was said to have knitted a blanket for a patient's baby during his sessions. Jones's only experience as a psychoanalytic patient was three months with Ferenczi. In between sessions the two men went for vigorous walks together. However, to lend your house to a patient for nine days is a much more intimate thing to do. It is an indication of how oblivious Jones was to the storm brewing with Joan that he wrote to Freud on 31st October: '[I] am glad to reassure you finally about any fears you may have concerning my sex life. I am a "reformed character"'. A few months later, Jones wrote to Freud that he had 'parted with Lina', Loe's maid. He had found her a flat and arranged for her to have some work. Lina was desolated. These letters to Freud are written from 69 Portland Court which is the flat he had lived in with Loe. He also saw his patients there, possibly adding to Joan's feeling of an intimate contact with him.

On 19th September, 1916, Joan saw Murray Kendall off to the front. There was now more public awareness of the bloodbath of the war, and Joan must have been afraid of losing Kendall. The Battle of the Somme was a couple of months before, and a film made at the time was showing all over England. Although somewhat edited, it did convey the horrors of war. All this added to her susceptibility to Jones. Jones lent The Plat to Joan again, she was there from 18th December to 22nd January. Once again she invited friends, including Helen. Were Evelyn and Diana there? Was Jones himself? On 18th January, 1918, Jones proposed to a beautiful young musician, Morfydd Owen, who was ten years younger than him. It was a whirlwind romance, and for some reason Jones insisted they marry without her parents being there. Within hours of proposing Jones was telling his patients he was getting married. The reasons for this are not clear; it seems to have been a narcissistic gratification. Needless to say Joan was devastated. She accused Jones of marrying Morfydd as a substitute for herself. Interestingly, Morfydd did share Joan's preoccupation with clothes. Her mother was a milliner and she had a talent for creating beautiful hats which she wore with 'aesthetic' clothes. Joan bombarded Jones with letters in between her sessions. On 31st October, 1918, she wrote:

> the more I think over this the more clear it becomes that underneath the present conflict concerned with myself lies the Oedipus complex. Part of the Oedipus conflict is the illusory belief that one is special to the parent of the opposite sex.

The problem for Riviere was that Jones treated her as if she *was* special. However, at the time of his wedding, Joan had not arrived at this insight. Her response to the wedding was to go into a sulk and send herself to a Nordrach Sanitorium.

The original Nordrach colony was in the Black Forest and offered fresh air treatment to patients with consumption. A relative of the Garrett family, Edmund Garrett, spent time there and improved considerably. He was visited by Dr Elizabeth Garrett Anderson and another woman doctor, Dr Jane Walker. Jane Walker set up a similar programme in a house in East Anglia where the dry climate suited the regime. The demand for places was so high that the East Anglia Sanitorium Company Ltd was set up with Millicent Garrett – the suffragette leader – as chairman, and Jane Walker as one of the directors. Eventually, a beautiful Arts and Crafts building was erected at Nayland in Suffolk. Patients had individual rooms with huge windows letting in the fresh air and sunshine. Healthy, substantial food was served in the communal dining room. It is extremely unlikely that Joan had consumption, although later in life she suffered from bronchitis and emphysema. However, the regime at Nordrach was thought suitable for patients with nervous exhaustion (Crawford, 2002). Wartime restrictions would have made it impossible for Joan to travel to the sanitorium in Germany. I like to think of her basking in her room at Nayland. If Joan felt uprooted by Jones's marriage she certainly visited it upon her family by uprooting them. She abruptly let Nottingham Terrace and the family moved into rooms. Perhaps this was a may of making money for her treatment. Diana and Kwang, the Pekingese dog, were sent to stay with Anna.

By June 1917, Joan was back in London, only to go off to Cambridge with the faithful IEE. Joan did not know where to put herself or what do with herself. In July she had an operation on her nose. The scenario is rather reminiscent of Anna's description of the operation 'without which she will never be well'. In August, Arthur Waley came for two weeks. He and Eva Hubback were friends whose names begin to appear in Joan's diary. Arthur Waley is now best known for his translations of Chinese poetry. Eva Hubbock was the daughter of wealthy Jewish parents who were observant, but assimilated. She studied economics at Newnham, which is probably how Joan got to know her. Eva and Joan had both been involved briefly in the suffrage movement. Hubback became a close colleague of Elinor Rathbone and worked for the National Union of Societies for Equal Citizenship. This was the successor organisation to Millicent Garrett Fawcett's NUWSS. As we shall see, Joan had the casual anti-Semitism of the period, but Eva with her socialist views – which Joan also disliked – was one of the many exceptions to Joan's social rules. She was a good friend to Joan, and even though her husband was killed in 1917, she took Diana away on holiday with her three children.

In 1917 a new horror was unleashed on Britain. In addition to the devastation caused by U-boats and the terror of Zeppelin raids there were now air raids in broad daylight with civilian targets. One of the most horrific took place in June 1917 when a fleet of Gotha Bombers took off from occupied

Belgium. One of the bombs fell on a three-storey school building. It crashed down to the basement where the youngest children were, leaving a sea of smashed bodies and severed limbs. Eighteen children were killed and thirty horribly maimed. After this, waves of bombers carried on coming over. Joan's relationship to the war changed radically. She longed to do something useful and meaningful. Anna was already involved offering tea and baths to soldiers. In October 1917, Anna went to work at St Thomas's Hospital. Evelyn was making use of his training with the anti-aircraft gun. In Joan's diary there is a neat little entry Psa 2.45, but no comment about how she felt about going back to Jones. The year 1918 is a catalogue of Joan's attempts to get involved with worthy causes. She started by putting her own house in order. They moved to a new house in Berners Street, and Joan tried to let Nottingham Terrace. The move seemed part of Joan's drive to change things. Next, Joan decided to find a suitable boarding school for Diana. A Miss Gross came to see her about Coombe Hill School near Kings Langley. Joan then went to visit the school, and a few days later Diana went. Joan visited her twice in the next month. During this time there were three more air raids on London and this may have been one reason for sending Diana away on a more organised basis. The adult Diana told Athol Hughes that Joan sent her to a school without visiting it. It certainly was not the case with this school, although Diana was packed off to a family in Southampton in the holidays. Diana's more consistent time at the school made her feel a bit more part of a family of older and younger girls.

While Diana was at school, Joan saw a Mrs Fowler about becoming a solicitors clerk. The next month she started training to be a secretary using the triangle method. In April she started work with the Divorce Reform Society. These activities seemed to be a wish to identify with her father or Evelyn, but she could not sustain any interest in them. She also began working at the Society for Psychical Research, which she managed to do more consistently, although it was not a new cause in the sense that her other attempts had been. On 18th April, 1918, Joan writes in her diary: 'EJ cannot continue anals. Arranged borrow money'. Does this mean that Jones would not continue if his fees were not paid? The move of house and Diana's new school may have absorbed a lot of money, although she managed to let Nottingham Terrace. In May, Joan was being treated for a vaginal inflammation, in August she had influenza. All probably psychosomatic reactions to Jones's refusal to see her. After alterations to Nottingham Terrace the family moved back in. Joan wanted to move back into her analysis when a bombshell came, 8th September: 'Telegram Mrs Jones dead'. The marriage had lasted only eighteen months.

A cloud of unknowing hangs over Mofydd Jones's death. At the end of August 1918, Morfydd suffered from recurrent bouts of pain and fever. Jones was afraid she had an abcessed appendix and telephoned his friend Trotter, who was now a distinguished surgeon. Trotter seems to have told Jones that she should be operated on immediately. A surgeon from the local hospital came and it is possible that Jones helped to administer the anaesthetic – chloroform. It is not known what was found, although Brenda Maddox suggests, from a comment of Jones to Freud, that Morfydd may have been pregnant. However, Morfydd went into a coma and died several hours later. No autopsy was done, so nothing was established conclusively. Trotter thought Morfydd should have been given ether instead of chloroform. Whatever the truth was, Jones must have felt a double dose of guilt. First, because he was not able to get better medical help. Second, because the relationship between Jones and Morfydd had seriously deteriorated. Morfydd wanted to spend time with her younger friends, and she did not want to run Jones's household. Sometimes she took off for days at a time. Morfydd's death released Jones from the burden of an unhappy marriage. Jones staggered around with his burden of guilt and ambivalence, staying with friends for a few days at a time, unable to work or settle anywhere. Joan herself was torn between rage and sympathy for Jones. On 25th October, 1918, she wrote to Jones: 'I am always painfully wondering how you are in mind and body … Night and day I can only think one thing – god keep you – god help you'. As Jones struggled with grief and guilt, Joan realised something very important about her relationship with analysis. Regardless of Jones's state of mind she fired off a letter on 26th September 1918.

> In the last 2 or 3 months I have come to realise clearly that psychoanalysis is the only thing left me to care about and to which I have to look forward for any interest in life.

Despite the obvious streak of depression, there had been a sea change in Joan's relationship to analysis. Initially she had approached it with desperation as a cure for her depression. Now it was a valued body of knowledge. Within six months she was seeing analytic patients herself. Jones wrote to Freud that she knew more about psychoanalysis than anyone in the British Society – except possibly Flugel.

After Jones came back to work, Riviere spent hours writing long letters to him and occasionally saw him. Despite this she spent October 1918 working mornings on the War Pensions Committee. She also worked in St Thomas's Hospital with Molly. Molly may have become a hospital Almoner and it is more likely Joan had a clerical or social work role. However, her depression was bubbling underneath and after a period of feeling ill and sleepless, Jones agreed to take her back. She barely registered the Armistice on 11th November 1918, and it is impossible to imagine her dancing in the streets. Besides there were horrors as well as rejoicing: horribly mutilated soldiers, and able-bodied soldiers desperate for paid work. There were even strikes. In contrast to the triumphalism of the peace there were families who had lost at least one member – often under horrific conditions. Spiritualism, the uncritical wing of psychical research, blossomed. Conan Doyle was a firm believer, and Oliver Lodge, a distinguished physicist, wrote a very successful book about communications via a medium with his dead soldier son. Those soldiers who had survived could not be all brought home at once. Many were traumatised, wounded or horribly scarred. Molly's husband, Jim, came home and Cuthbert seemed to have survived. However, there were other losses too. Hugh's sister Annette died in a convent. Anna was suddenly taken ill; possibly the loss of Annette reminded her of Hugh's death. Joan spent the night with her and then took her to St Thomas's. Her diary records two weeks travelling to and from Battersea – presumably to visit Anna. This entry suggests Joan was feeling emotionally stronger. She may have gained something out of the wreckage of her analysis with Jones.

Joan and Evelyn now had lodgers to bring in some much needed cash. Diana was settled at school in Kings Langley, and Joan and Evelyn visited her there from time to time. Many women who find it hard to manage a baby find it easier once they have a child. Joan was not one of these women. In the holidays a succession of unsatisfactory 'day governesses' came and went. At some point in early 1919 Jones began to refer Joan psychoanalytic patients. The first one was 'Gray' who started on 17th March, coming at 12.20pm daily. On 12th May 'Lomax' started, and on 30th May a Miss Grunbaum came. Modern psychoanalysts usually have an initial training such as psychology or psychotherapy which gives them experience of working with patients. Joan had plunged in the deep end. It is possible that Jones gave her some support or supervision. Her diary notes 'Jones in evening about patients'. But Joan was, as James Strachey would say, not afraid. Her diary entries are more alive and not simply a record of social engagements. Joan bought a corduroy sofa for her patients to lie on. Some of Joan's liveliness crept into her marriage. She and Evelyn went on holiday together to Newport.

By October 1919, Joan had four patients who were probably coming five times a week, which would mean twenty hours work a week. Jones had formed a London Psychoanalytic Society in 1913. However, the entry criteria were vague and some of its members had embraced Jungian ideas. As a way of getting rid of these members Jones dissolved the society and inaugurated the British Psychoanalytic Society in 1919. The new society had rigorous entry requirements. New members had to be proposed by someone who knew them and nominated by the council before a ballot was held among the members. New members attended for a year as Associates and had to read a paper. As Jones was chairman it is likely that Joan had an easy ride. According to Jones other members regarded Riviere as his favourite. The new society wanted to become part of the international society. Ever-inventive Jones founded the *International Journal of Psychoanalysis* in 1920. For such a journal to meet the needs of members there had to be a mechanism to provide translations. Joan was to play a key role in this, and by March 1919 she was already translating one of Freud's papers. Jones travelled to Switzerland in an attempt to make contact with Freud after the war. Joan gave him a pen to take to Freud. Probably a useful present but, as we shall see, a highly symbolic one.

After the catastrophe of the dressmaking business, Joan had at last found a profession. In May 1919 she went to her first meeting of the British Psychoanalytic Society and also to a meeting of the British Psychological Society (Medical Section). Although Jones had tried to persuade members to train as doctors first, it was accepted that the most important qualification was a personal analysis. This made it easier for many women from the Brunswick Square Clinic to enter the society. Many of Joan's fellow psychoanalysts were women and like Joan they would play an important part in the development of British psychoanalysis. The climate was more accepting of psychoanalysis. Psychoanalytic methods had been found effective for shell shock. In 1919, legislation had been passed opening up the professions to women. At a simple level Joan was having a new experience. She was contributing money to the family.

Jones's first attempt to meet Freud after the war failed. The Austrian treaty with Britain was not yet signed. Wartime hardships still prevailed in Vienna. Food was scarce and there was no fuel for heating. Freud had to analyse patients wearing a hat and overcoat. This had not frozen Freud's creativity and he managed to write important papers during the war. While Riviere planned for her first long analytic break from her patients, Jones was planning to use his break to make another attempt to see Freud. Joan agreed to look after Jones's dog, a rather extraordinary thing for an analyst to ask of a patient. It may be that Jones saw Joan as more of a colleague now that she had patients of her own. For Jones that trip was momentous. After persuading the Austrian Ambassador in Berne to grant a visa to visit Vienna, Freud and Jones were reunited after nearly six years. Freud was greyer and very much thinner, and Jones had the pleasure of treating Freud and his family at the Hotel Cobenzl to the first proper meal they had had for years. They were joined by Ferenczi, Jones's old analyst. Ferenczi was currently Acting President of the International Psychoanalytic Association. Freud decided to shift the centre of analytic gravity westwards, so he persuaded Ferenczi to pass the Acting President role to Jones. This was not the only change in status for Jones.

Before he left England, Jones was looking for a secretary who was fluent in German and English to help him with the *International Journal.* Hans Sachs recommended the younger sister of his mistress. Kitty Jokl had a doctorate in Economics from the University of Zurich. It is not clear if Sachs mentioned that she was young and pretty, but Jones was eager to have her and had arranged the necessary permit for her to come to England. After a delay, while Kitty nursed her mother through an illness, Jones and Kitty met in Zurich. Jones wooed Kitty at high speed. A basket of flowers, a walk in the woods and a promise to take her to Lugano – as his wife. Despite the rushed courtship this marriage was lasting and happy. Jones and Kitty married in

Zurich Town Hall on 9th October 1919, and after his visit to Freud, Jones and Kitty arrived back in London.

Joan's diary for this period presents an orderly picture. Her patients came back after the holiday. On 1st October a new patient, Miss Hands, started. Electric light was installed at 10 Nottingham Terrace. On 27th October she resumed analysis with Jones and 'the dog returned'. Behind this orderly facade Joan was enraged. Jones must have told her about his marriage before he got back to England. On 12th October 1919 Joan wrote:

> Dear friend ... I have 5 patients I do not know how I am going on – for I am horribly ill. I am frightened of illness and exposure of every kind ... god bless you and give you happiness my dearly beloved one – weddings and funerals and weddings how many more times will you kill me Bluebeard and shall I always love you?

Ostensibly this letter is Joan's response to Jones's marriage. However, I think it takes us back to Joan's collapse just as her dressmaking business got going. However, Jones must have done something right because Joan's life and analytic work did not collapse. She visited Diana at school when Diana had chickenpox, she had a weekend break in Market Harborough and most importantly she went to a meeting at the British Psychoanalytic Society, and arranged a week off from her patients at Christmas.

How do we understand Joan's collapse or threatened collapse on the point of success? Freud was about to throw light on this and Joan would write a major paper on the topic.

A bizarre addendum to the story of Ernest Jones comes from an account given by Diana Riviere to Athol Hughes. She was visited by Vincent Brome, the biographer of Ernest Jones, who told her that he was going to prove that Riviere had an affair with Ernest Jones. He wanted to break the news to Diana before he published it. Diana seems to have greeted this news with sangfroid, and he left hastily leaving his coat and umbrella. There does not seem to be any assertion of the affair in the biography, although one does get a sense of how powerful Joan's feelings were. Unlike Freud, Jones was not able to use the transference as a therapeutic tool.

Figure 1 Joan Riviere and her father *c.*1885

Figure 2 Joan Riviere *c.*1895

Figure 3 Joan and Diana Riviere *c.*1910s

Figure 4 Molly Verrall *c.*1910s

Figure 5 Joan Riviere *c.*1920s

Figure 6 Evelyn Riviere *c.*1930s

Figure 7 Joan Riviere *c.*1930s

Chapter 9

Freud

> 22/1/22
>
> Dear Professor,
>
> I thought it would interest you if I told you a few words about your new patient Mrs Riviere ... She plays a considerable part in the society here. It is a case of typical hysteria almost the only symptom being sexual anaesthesia ... I underestimated the uncontrollability of her emotional reactions, and in the first year lent her my country cottage. This led to a declaration of love (she has been the mistress of a number of men). From that time on she devoted herself to torturing me without any intermission.
>
> (Paskauskas, 1993)

In fact, Jones was not entirely sincere. In the letter he implies that he persuaded Joan to go to Freud. But when Joan announced she planned to do this, the previous summer, he was alarmed about what she would reveal, 'I fear her motives are not of the best'. However, he suggested she wrote to Freud. Freud was delighted to hear from her. He had read her translation in the first issue of the *International Journal of Psychoanalysis*: 'It goes without saying that if you want to enter into analysis, you will take precedence over all the others as my translator and as an outstanding member of the London group'.

Freud would also have seen Joan's clinical vignettes in the same issue of the *Journal* which show an intense devotion to psychoanalytic understanding. Friendly, business-like letters passed between Joan and Freud until finally Freud had a vacancy at the end of February 1922. Joan was very different from the shy seventeen-year-old girl who set off to spend a year in Gotha. She had a husband, a child and a profession. But she felt vulnerable. Her analysis had gone wrong. How would she get on with Freud? Her anxiety was so great that when she lay on Freud's couch she was totally unable to speak. A more conventional analyst would have allowed the silence to develop, but Freud was not a conventional analyst:

> My first analytic hour with him he opened – contrary to rule and inadvisably – saying 'Well I know something about you already; you had a father and a mother!' meaning of course 'Quick I can't wait for you and your inhibitions, I want something to start with'.

This picture of Freud shows something of Joan and Freud. Not only Freud's warmth and impatience, but Joan's awareness of the correct way an analyst should behave. Joan's psychoanalytic correctness is hardly surprising, of course, after her experience of Jones.

Gradually, Joan developed a routine. She was up and ready when her coffee was brought to her room in her pension. There is a hint in a letter from Freud that her landlady may have been a Frau Frisch. Many middle-class Viennese let out rooms. Most had bought government bonds which were now virtually valueless. It was possible to get breakfast and a substantial dinner in the pension for a very small sum. Joan was constantly surprised at the amount she was able to buy for small amounts of English money. Freud managed to keep his family by charging substantial fees. After the privations of the First World War many families were living in desperate poverty again. Alix Strachey, Freud's former patient, was in Berlin having a second analysis with Abraham. She wrote to her husband James how she assuaged her loneliness with food. One day at her pension she had a huge steak and potatoes followed by bread and cheese, washed down with vast quantities of tea. Joan's passion was for ices. Writing later in the year to Anna and Molly from an analytic conference in Berlin Joan described: 'an ice, the like of which could only be found again in heaven' (Hughes, A., 1992).

Abram Kardiner, an American Psychiatrist whose analysis finished just before Joan's started, described being greeted at the beginning by Freud, Martha Freud, Anna (Freud's daughter) and Paula the maid (Kardiner, 1977). It is unlikely this line up appeared for Joan as she had already met Freud at the congress in The Hague in 1920. Jones's letter had not alienated Freud from Riviere and it is likely he already had a plan to use her muscular and poetic style of English and her excellent German. In fact, Freud had hoped to conduct Joan's analysis in German, but Joan did not think she could freely associate in German. Freud spoke excellent English, but he had a bad experience with James Strachey whose mumbled English was a torment to his attention. Freud eventually decided it was a symptom in itself. Joan's voice was also in its way her first symptom with Freud. On her first day she climbed the steps at 19 Berggasse. The door on the left was for Freud's family and the door on the right was for patients. Once inside there was a waiting room with red plush furniture, and a table with a photograph album. Freud appeared to collect her. He was diminished by the privations of the previous war, but still a formidable figure:

> His most striking feature, however, was the forward thrust of his head and critical exploring gaze of his keenly piercing eyes. Finally, this rather awe-inspiring appearance was lightened by the glow of an enchanting humour.

It was this humour, 'you had a father and a mother', which settled Joan into her analysis. Freud's consulting room was furnished like a religious sanctum. There was the couch, where the patient reclined on oriental rugs, with a blanket for the cold. At the foot of the couch was a porcelain stove giving off a warm glow. Freud's desk was covered with the antique figures he collected and resembled an altar for the worship of psychoanalysis.

Freud was a very strange altar for a snobbish, casually anti-Semitic woman to worship at. He was the son of a wool merchant and his second (or possibly third) wife. Hard times led Jakob Freud to move his family from Freiburg to Vienna. Freud was the eldest of eight children, but the most brilliant and academically successful. There is a well-known photograph of him with his still-beautiful mother who is splendidly dressed in a crinoline. One can see where his self-confidence came from. This grandiose picture is very different from Freud's picture of his father. He remembered a story his father told him of an anti-Semitic attack. Jakob was wearing a new fur hat when a Christian knocked it off into the mud. Freud hoped to hear that his father retaliated but he meekly picked it up. Perhaps because of this Freud firmly clung to his Jewish identity, even though he was an atheist. He belonged to his Jewish Men's Lodge – the B'nai Brith – and played Tarok with a group of elderly Jewish friends on Saturday evenings. Anti-Semitism in Vienna was not simply a matter of social prejudice. In 1895 an actively anti-Semitic government was elected under the leadership of Karl Lueger. The whole fabric of Jewish assimilation was destroyed. Freud's response was robust. In a speech to the B'nai Brith in 1926 he said 'because I was a Jew I found myself free of many prejudices which restrict others in the use of their intellect: as a Jew I was prepared to be in opposition' (Beller, 1995). It is unlikely that Joan knew of this speech, but many years after Freud died she described what she felt was the unique quality of his genius:

> He established an instantaneous direct relation to his perception which automatically excluded cut and dried assumptions or arrieres pensees. Second thoughts and suspended judgement came much later.
>
> (Riviere, 1939)

Ironically, it was anti-Semitism that set him off on his unique career. He was training a neurologist with an interest in cerebral palsy and aphasia. But the institutional anti-Semitism of the university prevented him from advancing up the hierarchy. By now he had a reason to earn more money. He was in love with Martha Bernays. To make more money Freud started to take private neurotic and hysterical patients. These patients were difficult to treat, so Freud went to Paris to observe the work of Charcot, who used hypnosis to treat hysterical patients.

Back in Vienna, Freud soon gave up the practice of hypnosis, partly because he found he was not very good at it. He and an older colleague Josef Breuer simply allowed their patients to talk about whatever came into their minds – free associations. Gradually Freud evolved the idea of forbidden thoughts which are rendered unconscious by a force of repression. This was the subject of Freud's paper in the *Proceedings of the Society for Psychical Research* (Freud, 1912), and the first place Joan had encountered Freud's ideas. She had come full circle. Meanwhile, Freud was feeling very pleased with his new patient:

> Mrs Riviere does not appear to me half so black as you had painted her. We agree quite nicely so far. Maybe the difficulties will come later. In my experience you have not to scratch too deeply the skin of a so-called masculine woman to bring her femininity to the light. I am very glad you had no sexual relations with her as your hints made me suspect.
>
> (Paskauskas, 1993)

Jones was quick to reassure Freud that she was not his type, although he admired her intelligence as he would a man. Once Freud discovered that things between Riviere and Jones were not as bad as he feared, he got to work at once, not simply to get Joan to do some translations, but to make her the principal translations editor for the *International Journal.* His faith in her abilities is striking, as he had only seen one short piece which she translated, and translations of his introductory lectures. I think he must have been impressed by her way of expressing herself. Freud had an ear as well as an eye for literary style. Jones was relieved and alarmed by Freud's plan. On 1st April 1922 Jones wrote to Freud: 'I received a handsome offer from Mrs R to take over translations from the journal. There is no-one who could do it as well and there is no work I would more gladly be relieved of'. This is followed by protestations about the difficulty of relieving John Rickman of the job – although Rickman's work was marked by grammatical and spelling mistakes. Freud was very aware of Jones's reluctance to give up control of anything and was quick to settle the deal. On 6th April he wrote that he was 'glad to inform Mrs Riviere that you had accepted her offer and would write to tell her so' (Paskauskas, 1993).

Jones was forced to give up. Freud was right that Joan would be a 'powerful helpmeet'. Between 1922 and 1937 Joan laboured over the *Journal* translations, editing other people's work as well as carrying out her own translations. It is not clear if Freud told Joan that he had also asked James and Alix Strachey to translate other parts of his work. The Stracheys were not only rival translators, but also analytic siblings. They must have known of each other's presence at the time. James knew Joan from meeting her at Margaret and Arthur Verrall's house. There is evidence that analytic siblings got to know each other quite well. James Strachey, John Rickman and Abram Kardiner got together to compare notes about Freud's technique. According to Kardiner, Strachey and Rickman found Freud very silent; as Kardiner found him quite talkative he felt he had a 'better' version of Freud (Kardiner, 1977). Reading contemporary accounts by Freud's patients it seems that each created a version in their own image. Kardiner was interested in dreams and admired Freud's capacity to interpret them. James Strachey likened Freud's verbal fireworks to his favourite tutor at Cambridge, Arthur Verrall. More convincingly he wrote to his wife Alix of the awful feeling of resistance sitting on his stomach which disturbed him for the rest of the day. There was one analysand who did not share her views of Freud with this sibling group, and that was Anna, Freud's daughter. As the youngest child in the family she felt acutely jealous of her analytic siblings – particularly Joan Riviere. She wanted Freud to herself and as an older woman she ruthlessly cut out her mother. At this time it was thought that the best person to analyse a child was the parent, but it could be argued that Anna's analysis with her father distorted her life. According to Kardiner Freud lamented Anna's lack of interest in getting married, 'Look at her father', replied Kardiner (1977).

As Joan's analysis progressed letters flew back and forth between Jones and Freud discussing Freud's developing understanding. He wrote:

> she is a real power and can be put to work by a slight expenditure of kindness and 'recognitions' ... My diplomacy is to be as kind to her ... in order to make her open up her mind.

Jones was outraged by this kindness, 'People wonder how I endure her behaviour'. This intense correspondence could be seen as a breach of confidentiality. It has to be understood in context. Today it is routine practice for analytic patients to be discussed with a supervisor or peer supervision group. This was not available to Freud for his difficult patient. Freud was used to thinking about patients by writing about them and his thoughts about Joan's difficulties became part of one of his most famous papers, *The Ego and the Id* – which Joan would later translate into English.

Jones's complaints about Riviere finally roused Freud into reminding him why Riviere had come to him: 'finally you took the stand that you had sent her to me for finishing and correcting the analysis she had with you ... Now this situation given you must be prepared to my taking her side'. At this point Freud becomes Jones's supervisor, 'When Mrs R brought up her unpleasant reactions you seem to have treated her as a bad character in life but you never got behind her surface to master her wickedness'. Here Freud points out that Joan had been just as unpleasant to him as to Jones. The next part of Freud's letter shows his greatness as a thinker – his capacity to turn his experiences with patients into a theory which illuminates and explains them:

> One important point soon emerged. She cannot tolerate praise, triumph or success. Not any better than failure, blame or repudiation. Whenever she has got a recognition, a favour or a present she is sure to become aggressive and unpleasant ... it is an infallible sign of a deep sense of guilt, of a conflict between Ego and Ideal.

What is interesting is that Freud also suggests that an early severe ideal (superego) developed in Joan. Here Freud's findings have echoes of the early harsh superego discovered by Melanie Klein. Freud never made common cause with Klein, but Joan brought Freud and Klein together in her magnificent paper on the negative therapeutic reaction.

Freud tells Jones: 'she projects her self-criticism to other people, turns her pangs of conscience into sadistic behaviour, tries to render other people unhappy because she feels so herself'. He combined a trenchant understanding of his patient with a wish for her to develop. The rest of his letter makes the case for Joan to have the title 'translating editor': 'she is an uncommon combination of male intelligence with female love for detailed work'. Freud shows a care and concern for Joan beyond that of his other former patients. There is a touching account of Freud's grandson, Heinz, somehow getting into his consulting room. Freud introduced him to Joan, who he remembered later as 'the tall auntie'. When Joan clashed with Freud's daughter Anna this fondness preserved their relationship. Jones's letters also display an increasing fondness for Riviere, 'She and I have spent one long evening talking over matters and in my opinion the result was very satisfactory'. Joan was happy with her analysis but felt it was not finished. She decided that after the summer break she would return to Vienna to spend a bit longer with Freud. She combined this with taking part in the 1922 Psychoanalytic Conference in Berlin. Freud allocated an eleven o'clock slot for Joan, but in a moment of irritation told Jones she would need special regard indefinitely. In this he was wrong.

Joan spent the summer with her family, then on the 23rd September 1922 she travelled by boat and train to Berlin. By a fortunate chance a letter to Molly and Anna has survived in which she gives a detailed account of her time at the conference (Hughes, A., 1992). The letter shows the intensely contradictory nature of Joan's character. On the way there she was feeling 'blue' and lonely and puts on a carapace of snobbery and anti-Semitism.

> I got my sleeper all right on the train, but another woman was shoved on top – I always seem to have the same type in sleepers, common little actresses in fur coats, very much made up and covered in scent.

She also comments on the woman's husband, 'a Maida Vale Jew'. This crude anti-Semitism comes as a shock, particularly because of Joan's admiration for Freud. I think Joan fell back on such statements partly because the couple wanted her to move out of her bunk so that they could share it. Her mood changed when she felt welcomed by Jewish colleagues at the conference. Arriving in Berlin, in the dark, Joan was dismayed to discover she had been booked in a dingy pension. Venturing out for a meal before the conference a kindly commissionaire directed her to the Hotel Hassler. Despite the presence of many Jews, Joan reports that the food is marvellous. Cossetted and mollified Joan changes into her black dress with white sleeves and feels able to face the conference. Once at the reception and greeted by friends, she is flattered to be discreetly pursued by Dr Sachs, who later arranges to sit next to her at the conference dinner. They soon discovered that they shared an interest in the arts. Later, Joan visited Dr Sachs's apartment. She tells her mother and Molly there was another woman there, but I wonder, Dr Sachs has a reputation as a womaniser. Like all psychoanalytic conferences the atmosphere was charged with the unexpressed feelings of analytic patients for their analysts. Status is partly decided by who your analyst is. Adrian Stephen was not an object of interest to Joan because he was Virginia Woolf's brother. She respects him because he was analysed by Dr Glover, who was analysed by Dr Abraham, 'who is in the first rank'. This was the first time an analytic conference had been held in Germany since the war. However, there were no traces of anti-German feeling. Many of those present had spent time in Germany or Austria being analysed, and felt loyalty to Freud.

The following morning, Joan spent an anxious few hours arranging her journey back to Vienna to restart her analysis with Freud. Some of this anxiety was probably related to the fact that she was due to have lunch with Freud and Anna at the house of Max Eitingon, an immensely wealthy Jewish psychoanalyst. Joan was aware the invitation was an honour, but it is not easy to have lunch with one's analyst, to see them eat and talk to other people. Eitingon was kind and attentive to Joan. Joan carefully explains his status to Anna and Molly, 'Dr Abraham is the scientific leader of psychoanalysis in Berlin and Dr Eitingon is the social and material leader'. In keeping with this, Eitingon's wife was stunning in her own right: 'a well-known Russian actress – a very piquant and notable person with piled up masses of black hair, and exquisite clothes – very Parisian in effect'. Joan also admires Lou Andreas Salomé, 'the only woman Nietzsche ever loved … a wonderful intellect'. Not surprisingly

Joan does not say a word about Freud or Anna to her mother and sister, instead she loses herself in admiration of the decor, 'wonderful paintings, panelling, chinese wallpaper ... beautiful bookshelves, pictures, rugs, objets d'art and marvellous *food*'. What is characteristic of Joan in this letter is that where she admires she does not hold back. In contrast to this, when Alix Strachey visited the house, she admired the bookshelves but only conceded that two or three pictures were worth admiring. Bloomsbury snobbery.

When Joan speaks of Eitingon as the material leader in Berlin she means that with his own money he built and furnished a psychoanalytic clinic and training institute (Danto, 2005). Freud expressed a wish that psychoanalysis should be available to all, regardless of their means. The clinic was staffed by psychoanalytic trainees and this was part of their training. However, experienced analysts were also expected to give time to it. This was in contrast to the British Psychoanalytic Society (and many psychotherapy trainings) where only trainees staff the low-fee schemes. The Berlin Policlinic and the Vienna Ambulatorium, which opened in May 1922, while Joan was there, were part of a wider socialist enterprise to provide housing, healthcare, sex education and other services to all sections of the population. In 'Red Vienna' these services were provided by taxing the rich. Joan was not a socialist; in fact, she referred to socialism as 'that religion of younger siblings'. Nevertheless she seems to have taken her turn with a low-fee patient. Unlike the Policlinic, the Vienna Ambulatorium was housed in a shabby house shared with the ambulance service and heart clinic. Joan took a professional, even business-like approach to patients. She shocked her supervisee, Hanna Segal, by referring to some of her patients as 'pot-boilers', presumably people she saw only for the money. However, as was so often the case with Joan, she had another side. She kept up a correspondence with one patient for many years and signed the letters 'your friend, Joan Riviere'.

Altogether, Joan spent six months with Freud plus a further six weeks a few years later. By the standards of today's analyses, which usually go on for years, it was very little time, yet its effects were long-lasting. According to Jones, the members of the British Society found Joan much easier to get on with when she returned from Vienna. At the Berlin Congress Jones took Riviere to visit Abraham at his house in the suburbs. The visit was a disappointment as another guest dominated the proceedings, but they shared a taxi there and back in a comfortable way. Joan and Freud stayed in touch by letter. A good deal of this correspondence concerned translation issues, but Freud remained concerned about Joan as his patient. On one occasion Freud expressed regret that he had not kept Joan for a further six months:

> I might have succeeded in letting you see the connection between neurosis and national or social prejudice and we may both have derived some benefit from this study perhaps after several stormy hours.

It was a gentle rebuke for Joan's anti-Semitism. In this letter of 1923, Freud concludes 'the times are bad and full of dark warnings'. Perhaps he already felt the rise of the horrific anti-Semitism which would eventually sweep Freud and his family to London. Four of Freud's sisters died in concentration camps.

Even on the one occasion when Freud was angry with Joan his letters to her are tender and fatherly. He also confided in her about family illnesses and losses. Later, in 1923, Freud told Joan about the growth on his jaw which initially he thought was non-malignant, but which he nonetheless experienced as the 'first tolling of the bell'. Joan wrote Freud a letter which touched him deeply: 'Your expression of sympathy moved me so much that I could hardly prevent myself addressing this letter to your first name'. Freud described the improvements brought about by the operation and the fears that still hung over his family, 'I am being so frank in this communication because I intend it only for you, officially a more harmless version will be put out'. 1923 was a very difficult year for Freud. In July he wrote from Badgastein where he had retired to try and gather some strength. This was not due to the growth on his jaw, but to the death through miliary tuberculosis of his favourite grandson Heinz, aged four and a half. This was the little boy who had run into the consulting room when Joan was on the couch. 'with his death he has taken from us some portion of our joy in life'. Joan replied immediately to Freud's sad letter. What she said pleased Freud and he also replied promptly, 'What you say about the dear little child is so apt that we can only marvel that we did not notice it earlier ... It is difficult to get over his loss'. It is interesting to find Joan perceptive about a child. Her attitude to children was markedly more sympathetic after her analysis with Freud.

Much of Freud's correspondence is about translations and the Psychoanalytic Press, which was financed by a wealthy brewer, Anton von Freund. However, in November 1923, Freud tells Joan of yet another operation on his jaw. This time a larger part of his jaw was removed and he had to have a prosthesis to enable him to speak and eat. This was to become the bane of his life until he died. Freud's predicament brought out a very important aspect of Joan's character which we will see again: the capacity to give prompt and practical expression to her concern. Within days Freud received a copy of *The Tomb of Tut Ankh Amen* by the Earl of Caernarvon and Howard Carter. This was absolutely designed to appeal to Freud's interest in antiquities and he was delighted to discover that there would be further volumes, 'How great, then, was my joy and surprise to hear that it is your kind sympathy, of which I was convinced anyway without this beautiful gift'.

In 1924 it was Freud's turn to be anxious about Joan's health. She told him that she was due to have an operation for fibroids. He begged her to make sure she had a second opinion before she had the operation, 'There is nothing left for me to do but plead on my own behalf as well as that of my daughter that you send us news as soon as possible'. Freud did not leave it at that. He sent Joan flowers and wrote to Jones for news of Joan's health. Joan decided to come and see Freud for some sessions later in 1924. This may have been because of the psychological aftermath of her operation, which was possibly a hysterectomy. Letters pass backwards and forwards between Joan and Freud, often about translations; for example, he compliments her on her translation of the *History of Psychoanalysis*. Over the years the relationship between Freud and Joan weathered battles about child analysis, and Freud's cavalier way of disposing of his translation rights.

On 5th May 1936 (Freud's birthday), Joan read a paper as part of an exchange series between London and Vienna. Her paper was on 'early psychological development' (Riviere, 1936b). This seems to have passed without overt conflict, although Joan took a hard-line Kleinian position. The next day Joan went to visit Freud. She could not fail to recognise the deterioration of the situation in Vienna. When the Imagist poet Hilda Doolittle went to see Freud in 1934 there were swastikas chalked around Freud's house and gold foil swastikas floating in the air. Cracker mottos said 'Hitler gives jobs', 'Hitler gives bread'. Behind this glitter there was violence. Although Freud did not want to leave, the last straw came when Anna and Martin were arrested by the Gestapo. Joan wrote to Freud as soon as he arrived in England on 15th June 1938. He replied: 'Many thanks for your friendly words of welcome. I am glad to have come to England'.

In the years before and after Freud's death, Joan was sometimes asked to write about him. These writings are quite revealing, sometimes about Freud and sometimes about Joan. In 1937 Joan was asked to write a review of Freud's 'autobiography', which was first published in 1925. It was for a series about medical men in the *Journal of Medical Psychology*. Paula Heimann and Hanna Segal both thought that Joan had difficulties expressing herself in writing; this review contradicts that. She picks out key aspects of the autobiography and by clever turns of phrase renders them fresh and unfamiliar, making Freud's achievement more vivid. Those who flinched at her comments about the 'Maida Vale Jew' might find this interesting:

> his curiosity and concern about human affairs would not brook the restrictions of human prejudices ... his capacity for scientific detachment and an open mind ... was *excited* in him as a boy by finding at the University, that no matter what his attainments, as a Jew he was expected to regard himself as inferior; this, he tells us, he resolutely refused to do. [My emphasis]

Freud not only ran into prejudice about his religion, but also the nature of his hysterical patients and how he was treating them. The Laboratory of Cerebral Anatomy where he had lectured with great success was closed to him. Freud eventually withdrew from academic life, '*Left alone at the age of thirty with the nervous patients in his private practice*, he discovered the uselessness of fashionable remedies' [my italics]. Here Joan communicates vividly the lonely path that Freud chose to tread. Joan admires his 'fearlessness, patience, and indomitable persistence'.

Joan did not idealise Freud. She did not hesitate to criticise the work of Anna Freud, or Freud's ideas of female sexuality. Robust disagreement was possible between them. There was, however, one occasion when Joan talked of Freud with bitterness. In 1953, when Joan was seventy, the American psychoanalyst Kurt Eissler embarked on a project to record the memories of all the people who had known Freud. This eventually amounted to about sixty people. The interviews were tape recorded and transcribed in minute detail by Eissler's secretary, Pearl Melniker. The tapes and transcripts were deposited in the Library of Congress in Washington, but closed until 2020. However, they could be viewed. Astonishingly, when I rang to ask about the tapes, I was told they had been lost. The Swiss psychoanalyst Nina Bakman has viewed the transcript.

What is surprising about the interview is that Joan completely downplays what Freud did for her. She says he only analysed her penis envy. The various strands of correspondence between Freud, Riviere and Jones make it clear that Freud did a great deal more than that. Eissler asks Joan to put something in writing, but she never does. Was she envious or ungrateful? I think the large scale of Eissler's project made it clear that *she did not come first*. Freud understood this. On 10th September, 1922, he wrote to Joan: 'You should not regret that I came to know you through analysis. I hope you will now be better able to bear a word of appreciation in private'.

Chapter 10

A devilish amount of trouble

'Always one of the most interesting things to me about Freud was his writing; I met him first in his writings before I knew him'. Joan's first encounter with Freud's writing was his paper on the unconscious in the *Proceedings of the Society for Psychical Research.* Ironically, she did not have to translate it as he had written it in English himself. In 1916, when Joan borrowed some of Freud's books – probably *The Interpretation of Dreams* and *The Psychopathology of Everyday Life* – from the SPR library, they were translations by A. A. Brill. Ernest Jones was aware of the need for good translations to promote the work of Freud. He conceived of a series of uniform volumes, beautifully translated and under his control. He was reckoning without the initiatives of Freud himself.

When Joan went to Freud for analysis in 1922, he immediately treated her as his translator-in-chief: 'As my translator you will take priority [over other patients]'. At that time Joan had translated a paper by Freud for the *International Journal*, but she also translated Freud's *Introductory Lectures on Psychoanalysis* which were published by Allen and Unwin in 1923. Her translations are magnificent. The words leap off the page. Joan succeeded in retaining an aspect of Freud's work she admired: his capacity to speak directly to the reader. She was also familiar with the novels and poetry which were so important to Freud. This edition of the Introductory Lectures is one of the few opportunities to read her translations in an unmodified form. The elegance of her prose style can be seen in her later translation of the title of Freud's booklet *Das Unbehagen in der Kultur* as *Civilisation and its Discontents*.

Joan did not only have the advantage of fluent German and a compatible prose style: she was also Freud's patient and was familiar with his latest psychoanalytic ideas. When Freud completed *The Ego and the Id*, which changed his model of the mind from the topographical model of conscious and unconscious to the structural model of id, ego and superego, he wrote to her three times to ask her to translate it. He wanted to be assured that Joan herself would do the work, and not delegate it. Freud was aware that Joan would recognise herself in a type of patient whom he describes for the first time:

> There are certain people who behave in a quite peculiar fashion during the work of analysis. When one speaks hopefully to them or expresses satisfaction with the progress of the treatment, they show signs of discontent and their condition invariably gets worse … They exhibit what is known as a negative therapeutic reaction.

Freud's letters to Ernest Jones make it clear that Joan showed negative reactions during her analysis. While translating this paper, Joan absorbed its ideas so thoroughly that she was later able to use them in a ground-breaking paper on 'Those Wrecked by Success' (Riviere, 1936a).

Although Freud's letters to Joan make it clear that she was his favourite translator, she was not the only one. As Freud became more famous he had many English and American patients. For the first four months of Joan's analysis Joan had two analytic siblings, James and Alix Strachey. They had left England immediately after their marriage so that James could have an analysis with Freud. Ostensibly this was to follow an intellectual interest, but James had been severely depressed while a student at Cambridge. Afterwards when he was working for *The Spectator* his brother Lytton was worried he might commit suicide. Ostensibly the depression was because of unrequited love for Rupert Brooke but it was unlikely that this was the whole story. He transferred his sexual interests to Noel Olivier and Alix Sargant-Florence, where they settled. James did very little work at Cambridge, which was probably a symptom of his mental state. One lecturer he did enjoy was Arthur Verrall (Joan's uncle) and he compared Freud's interpretations to Arthur Verrall's verbal fireworks. Although James regarded Joan as coming from the same social box as himself, in reality his family experiences and personality were very different. This was to have an impact on his style and aims as a translator, and would bring him into a potential conflict with Joan.

James was the youngest of twelve children of Sir Richard and Lady Strachey. The Stracheys both considered themselves Anglo-Indians, and Sir Richard spent long periods in India working chiefly as an engineer, although he had many other scientific interests. Lady Strachey, who had a talent for drama, said their lives had been 'spent in the arduous and noble service of rescuing the natives of India from intolerable oppression' (Caine, 2005). Within the family, James's closest ally was his brother Lytton. James followed Lytton to Cambridge, occupied his old rooms, and was also elected to the Apostles as a time when the society had a distinctly homosexual ethos. His apparent limpness and passivity was misleading as he was a serious student of music and later wrote programme notes for Glyndebourne. Apart from music, James had a keen interest in psychopathology and his wish to become a psychoanalyst was the solution to the problem of what to do with his life. This approach was in contrast to Joan who entered psychoanalysis as a cure for her depression. Her professional interests came later, but were no less serious than James's.

Once James and Alix arrived in Vienna, Alix showed signs of needing analysis too. After Alix had an attack of 'palpitations' at the Staatsoper she and James persuaded Freud to take her on. Freud was interested in the technical problems of working with a couple, but Alix was convinced that she was the less important patient. As usual this was expressed through her body and she ended up in a sanitorium looked after by Freud's doctor. James felt that he got to know Joan better while all three were in Vienna. It is possible he found her company particularly welcome while Alix was ill. They were two very cultured people who shared interests in the ballet and literature. James was a member of the original Bloomsbury group – Lytton, Vanessa and Clive Bell, Leonard and Virginia Woolf, Maynard Keynes. Joan had met Vanessa and Clive Bell as well as other 'outer' Bloomsburys Ottoline Morrell and E. M. Forster. The Bloomsbury group was to become very significant in the spread of psychoanalysis. This was particularly so with publication, but Virginia Woolf's brother and his wife were also psychoanalysts.

Alix and James finished their analysis with Freud in June 1922. He recommended that both be made full members of the British Society as they were 'first rank' people. Jones resisted full membership status as members had to be associates for a year. Interestingly, Freud warned Jones not to underestimate Alix. This was very prescient as Alix was responsible for a huge upheaval in Joan's life and that of the British Society. Like Joan, James and Alix were now Freud's personally sanctioned translators. Only a few weeks after they began their analysis Freud asked them to translate *A Child is Being Beaten*. It was not as innovative as *The Ego and the Id* but it was important to Freud as it was based on the analysis of his daughter Anna, who also became a psychoanalyst in 1922. At that time it was acceptable for analysts to psychoanalyse their own children, but this only seemed to be applied to young children. The consequences were not good for Anna or analysis. Freud based some of his ideas of female sexuality on Anna. He seemed unaware that they were particular to her. Later when Joan was developing her own ideas of female sexuality she did not hesitate to contradict Freud in print. As James Strachey put it, 'she was not afraid'.

Once Joan and the Stracheys were back in England, Ernest Jones organised all three into a 'glossary committee' to decide how to translate Freud's technical terms into English. They met at Jones's consulting room in Harley Street. Anna and Freud were also involved at a distance. Part of the problem, as far as Jones was concerned, was that Freud did not use technical terms. When Freud wrote *Ich*, *Es*, and *Überich* a literal translation would be *Me*, *It*, and *Above-Me*. Jones felt that people would accept Freud's ideas more readily if they were expressed in technical-sounding words. Jones particularly wanted to be accepted by the medical establishment. In England psychoanalytic ideas were in favour because they had been effective in treating shell shock. In 1918 Jones was invited to speak at the Royal Society of Medicine on 'War Shock and Freud's theory of Neurosis'. In America things had developed differently.

Psychoanalysis had been taken over by the medical establishment and anyone who was not a doctor was not allowed to practice it. Freud was suspicious of the American attitude. After all, his daughter was a lay analyst.

The glossary committee was split. Ernest Jones and James wanted a scientific language. Although James only managed three weeks medical training his father, Sir Richard, was a dedicated scientist and was at one time President of the Royal Geographical Society. Alix was out of the picture for a while in Berlin having a second analysis with Abraham. This left Joan to advocate an approach that represented Freud's language more closely as well as the rhythms of his sentences. With Jones's approval, James invented a scientific language based on his partially remembered Latin and Greek. This did not always facilitate understanding. In fact James himself described a scene fit for P. G. Wodehouse at the Howard League for Penal Reform on 'corporal punishment': 'In the middle of it the clear ringing tones of an upper class lady's voice was heard – old Lady Dyke-Acland "will you spell them please S-A-D-I"' (Meisel and Kendrick, 1986). Some of the technical-sounding translations worked quite well: *Id*, *Ego*, and *Superego* for *Ich*, *Es*, and *Überich*. Joan herself used *Id* and *Ego* in her translation of Freud's introductory lectures. James cheerfully owned up to one which obscured more than it clarified: shaulust – the pleasure in looking – was translated as scoptophilia, which sounds like a rather unpleasant disease. James pointed out that 'scopt' is a Greek root which means 'to make fun of'. Here Joan's lack of a classical education put her at a disadvantage, for the term slipped into the four volumes of the *Collected Papers* which she was now editing. The translators for these included John Rickman, who probably did not notice. In James's obituary of Joan he pays tribute to her qualities as a translator: a thorough knowledge of the German language, a highly accomplished literary style and a penetrating intellect. In an earlier letter to Alix in 1925 his attitude is more ambivalent. Speaking of Joan's translations of *On Narcissism: An Introduction* and *Instincts and their Vicissitudes* he says:

> I must say the translations are extraordinarily well done. They're very clever and the sense seems always to be correct. The woman must have taken a devilish amount of trouble with them. However I'm glad to look through them, as there are occasional points that are susceptible of stylistic improvement (Ahem).

Despite James's admiration for Joan's translating skills, his envy found expression in two Freudian slips:

> Well that's a good one! I absolutely cut a tea-party engagement with Mrs Riviere yesterday. It went smack out of my head. – But the point is its the second time I've done exactly the same thing in the last three months. At all events one knows that apologies are of no avail.

Finally, on the third attempt, James arrived at Joan's for tea. He seemed surprised that she was 'slightly stiff'. The purpose of these tea parties was to discuss translation problems. It was the beginning of a conflict between James and Ernest Jones's quasi-scientific style and Riviere's translations which are closer to Freud in meaning and rhythm. This conflict still rumbles on today, and each side has its advocates.

The early editions of Freud's collected papers were by different translators, edited by Joan. The role of the editor was important not only to detect errors but to ensure that there is enough unity in the translations so that the reader is not confused. Jones held on to the idea of a 'Standard Edition' of Freud's work. The Glossary Committee was a step in the direction of standardised translations. James was a very willing recruit to this model. Despite his self-effacing manner he had some of his parents imperial ambitions. James approached his fellow Bloomsbury member Leonard Woolf. Leonard and Virginia Woolf owned the Hogarth Press. This had been originally seen as therapy for Virginia, who carried out the soothing work of typesetting. However, they also published work by their friends. Freud's collected works was a much bigger venture. Fortunately Leonard had read *The Interpretation of Dreams* as a preparation for reviewing *The Psychopathology of Everyday Life* for the *New Weekly*. Leonard's view of Freud's writing style was much closer to Joan's view: 'he writes with great subtlety of mind, a broad and sweeping imagination more characteristic of the poet than the scientist or medical practitioner' (Glendinning, 2006). The contrast between James and Joan's style of translating Freud is illustrated by some examples chosen by Nina Bakman:

> Freud writes *ein Wortstreit*; Riviere, *a war of words*; Strachey, *a verbal dispute*.
>
> Joan intensifies Freud's image, James flattens it.
>
> FREUD: 'An diesem Ich hängt das Bewußtsein'
> RIVIERE: 'It is to this ego that consciousness is attached.'
> STRACHEY: 'This ego includes consciousness.'
>
> Riviere keeps a similar verb and sentence construction. Strachey changes the sentence construction and loses the original meaning of the sentence.
>
> (Bakman, 2013)

James's dry scientific style was intended to woo an American medical audience. However, Joan preserves the aesthetic dimensions of Freud's writing – which of course appealed to her. Joan's style also derived from her dressmaking skills, endlessly careful and precise. She even entered into a correspondence with J. W. Fowler, author the *Dictionary of Modern English*, to decide small points of grammar. It is sometimes assumed that working on the Standard

Edition was too difficult a task for Joan. It would certainly have brought her into constant conflict with Ernest Jones and James. Instead, with Freud's help, she negotiated a very different translating role.

In April 1922, Ernest Jones wrote to Freud telling him that Joan had offered to take over the translations of for the *International Journal of Psychoanalysis*. Jones's response to this was a masterpiece of ambivalence. First of all he acknowledged that no one could do it better. Then he thought he would prefer to work with Rickman (despite his difficulties with spelling and grammar). Then he worried that the Americans would not like another lay analyst. Finally he decided that it was up to Freud. Freud told Jones that he would tell Riviere that her offer was accepted and Jones would be writing to her. To hammer things home Freud told Jones that he owed Riviere some compensations for 'aggravating her analysis'.

As Joan's analysis progressed, Freud's fondness and admiration for her abilities grew. They spent time talking about the forthcoming collection of Freud's papers which was coming out. Joan told Freud that she thought that there were too many different people working on it, and it would be difficult to get uniformity. Freud's response was to suggest some papers were withdrawn from other people and given to Joan to translate and edit. Jones did as he was told, with a good deal of huffing and puffing. Fed up by his prevarication Freud fired off a decisive postcard:

> Mrs R proposed to me some alterations in the arrangement of the Sammlung [volume] which appeared to me quite good ... I am becoming ever more pleased with her. Will you not transfer to her the whole responsibility for this job, establish her as a Redacteur en Chef [editor in chief].
>
> (Paskauskas, 1993)

There was still some whining from Jones, who could not bear to give up any bit of power, 'She is put at the head of a translating staff, but the important question of capacity to work with other people is not yet proved'. In the end, Freud was proved correct and Joan worked as translations editor from 1922 to 1937. Her contributors showed no signs of mutiny. Freud was so pleased with her work that he signed over royalties from his books to pay Joan and some of his other translators, including the Stracheys and Rickman. Working in collaboration brought Joan and Ernest Jones closer together. Jones wrote to Freud after Riviere returned from her analysis in July 1922: 'She and I have spent one long evening talking over matters, and in my opinion the result was very satisfactory'. I have a copy of the collected papers, published in 1940 which shows that Jones and Riviere had arrived at a compromise. On the first page it says 'Edited by Ernest Jones', on the second page 'Authorised translations under the supervision of Joan Riviere'.

The transfer of the *International Journal* and the publishing of Freud's works in England marked a move in the centre of gravity of psychoanalysis from Vienna and Berlin to England, although this was mainly caused by financial difficulties. It was fortunate in the developing political climate. The rise of Hitler and the National Socialists eventually led to the burning of Freud's books. Freud himself was forced to flee to England with his family. (Curiously, a modified version of psychoanalysis was practised at the Göring Clinic.)

Joan remained as translations editor of the *International Journal* until 1937. Although James Strachey portrays this as a tedious task, Joan did not complain. It gave her a chance to work with friends such as Paula Heimann and Eva Hubback. Joan's only complaint was that during her analysis with Freud she would arrive filled up with things she wanted to say, whereas Freud had a knotty translation problem he wanted to discuss with her.

There is now a substantial literature about Freud's translators, much of it centred on the Standard Edition. There is general agreement that it is clear, but that this clarity comes at a cost. For example, James may use one word where Freud uses several to enable the reader to come at the topic in different ways. James says he adopted the style of a nineteenth-century man of science – probably his father. Joan would have Freud's voice in mind. Riccardo Steiner points out that James produced the Standard Edition by retranslating other translators, such as Joan. Sadly this obliterates her work unless one can find an old edition. Ironically, both James and Alix made mistakes in their translations. It is hard to imagine Joan with her minutely careful work doing this. A recent study of Klein's first book, *The Psychoanalysis of Children* by Sue Sherwin-White (2017) reveals that Alix translates 'Weidergutmachung' (which means 'reparation') as 'restitution', which is a different word, 'Wiederherstellung'. This gave a negative cast to Klein's work which it did not have in reality.

Obviously factual accuracy is important, but so is style. Many readers prefer Scott Moncrieff's translations of Proust, although modern ones are more accurate. It is important to remember that the city of Frankfurt awarded Freud the Goethe Prize. Their description of his work is a summary of what a good translation might look like:

> With the strict method of Natural Science, at the same time boldly interpreting the similes coined by imaginative writers ... psychoanalysis [has] enriched medical science.
>
> (Gay, 1988)

Here is the initial paragraph to Freud's introductory lectures. Firstly translated by Joan, and then re-translated by James. Readers can judge for themselves:

> I do not know what knowledge any of you may already have of psychoanalysis, either from reading or hearsay. But having regard to the title of lectures – Introductory Lectures on Psychoanalysis – I am bound to

> proceed as if you know nothing of the subject and needed instruction even in its first elements. (Riviere)
>
> Ladies and gentlemen – I cannot tell how much knowledge of psychoanalysis each of you has already acquired from what you have read or from hearsay. But the wording of my prospectus – 'Elementary introduction to psychoanalysis – obliges me to treat you as if you knew nothing and stood in need of some preliminary information. (J. Strachey)

Although James's version of *The Standard Edition* was a territorial coup, Joan's influence on psychoanalytic translation was considerable but more hidden. The *International Journal* lived up to its name. Many papers must have come from Germany and Austria. Joan's role as translations editor meant she influenced the form in which they appeared before the English-speaking public. Paula Heimann (1963) describes going to Joan's house to work on translations. After a number of hours of hard work, a delicious meal was laid on the table and Evelyn came to join them. This sounds a bit pretentious, but an exchange of letters between Joan and James Strachey after she gave up editing shows a laid-back, humorous approach:

> 30th April 1949
>
> Mr Strachey
>
> Herewith the proofs. I think the interminable one is a very nasty horrid translation and I don't like my name being attached to it. (Are we *sure* I did it … I could only [read] it by listening to a Mozart Mass on the wireless at the same time.)

In a later postcard Joan tells James that all she now takes into consideration is the *sound*.

Chapter 11

I would be inclined to bet heavily on her

Hanna Segal, Joan's supervisee and Melanie Klein's patient thought that Joan was 'swept off her feet' by Klein. Many people have commented on Klein's tendency to arouse strong positive or negative feelings wherever she went. For the next thirty years Joan loved Klein, and even when she was angry with her, she forgave her. This warmth and softness was a side of Joan that few people saw – except perhaps Evelyn (and I hope Diana). At first sight they were on an ill-assorted couple. Joan was tall and elegant, Klein considerably shorter with a penchant for embroidered blouses and floral hats. Klein could have been a target for Joan's snobbery and anti-Semitism, but Klein's intense little patients with their violent feelings won her admiration. Even the cynical Alix Strachey was entranced by Klein's work, 'I would be inclined to bet heavily on her' (Meisel and Kendrick, 1986). Joan was not only prepared to help Klein, but she was willing to arouse the anger of Freud and Anna on Klein's behalf.

Klein was only a year older than Joan, but her life with its hardships and tragic losses was very different. Klein's father, Moritz Reizes, grew up in a strictly orthodox family, however he broke away to train as a doctor and marry the beautiful Libussa Deutsch. Klein was the youngest of their four children. Emmanuel, the eldest, was brilliant and gifted, but tubercular. He gave up studying medicine and drifted round Europe trying to write. He died at 25, possibly of self-neglect. Klein, recently married, took responsibility for burying him. Emmanuel was not her first loss. Her sister Sidonie died aged nine of scrofula. Before she died she taught Klein how to read, and Klein was very grateful, 'I was wildly keen on knowledge'. By now the family had moved to Vienna, but Moritz faced the same anti-Semitic prejudice as Freud. Libussa opened a shop selling exotic animals to help make ends meet. Unfortunately male customers were more interested in Libussa than the reptiles (Grosskurth, 1986).

Klein had hoped to go to university to read medicine, but at 17 she fell in love with Arthur Klein, a friend of Emmanuel. Characteristically, she was attracted by his intelligence. They had three children, Melitta, Hans and Erich. For the first years of their married life they moved around various small towns in Slovakia and Silesia for Arthur's work as an engineer. Klein, like Joan, probably suffered from post-natal depression. However, in 1910, Arthur got work in Budapest. Here Klein, with her thirst for knowledge, found Freud's popularising book on dreams. She approached Sandor Ferenczi, the president of the Budapest Psychoanalytic Society. (As she said herself, she was not shy.) Ferenczi had not yet adopted the 'active' technique of forced associations which would alienate him from Freud. He was perceptive and sensitive and soon observed that Klein had potential for working with children. Ferenczi encouraged her to develop this. In 1919, Klein graduated in the Budapest Society by presenting a paper on 'The development of a child'. Strictly speaking this was psychoanalytically informed observation. The child was her son, Erich, aged 4 ½, whose slow development worried her. Klein tried to keep an analytic hour, but Erich was more interested in his toys than talking. Klein's brilliant insight was that his play was a form of communication. From now on, this technique would allow her to work with very young children and to map previously unknown aspects of child development. Klein's boldness and rigour put her at odds with Hermine Hug Hellmuth who worked in the Vienna Society, and also used play. Hug Hellmuth believed that children under six could not be psychoanalysed and also believed that the analyst should foster a positive transference. Joan and Klein were not afraid of sadism and rage in the consulting room. Joan knew very well what it was like to feel rage with her analyst, and the relief that Freud could tolerate this.

Klein's early work in Budapest came to an abrupt end in 1919. A complicated series of communist governments led to a 'white terror' and ferocious anti-Semitism. Klein and her family had to leave. Arthur went to Sweden, and Klein stayed with his parents before moving to Berlin. The Berlin Society was chaired by Karl Abraham. He was one of Freud's inner circle, but he had his own ideas. Unlike Freud he put more emphasis on the significance of the mother. He was known for his rigorous approach, and his presence attracted other analysts as well as Klein. Klein met him at the Congress in The Hague in 1920. He encouraged her to come to Berlin, but he refused to take her into analysis, as he did not believe in analysing colleagues. Despite this initial setback the Berlin Society was crucial for Klein's development. Berlin was the heart of the Weimar Republic, and socialist projects sprang up to improve the lives of the poor. At the 1918 Congress in Budapest, Freud gave a stirring speech which advocated free psychoanalytic clinics where poor people could receive help for their minds just as they received medical care for their bodies. Within two years Freud's dream was realised in Berlin (Danto, 2005).

Joan's Berlin was a city of luxury hotels and fine art. In contrast to this, many people lived in grinding poverty. The Weimar Republic tried to provide for poor people with worker's housing and free health clinics. The Berlin Psychoanalytic Clinic (Poliklinik) was in keeping with this trend. When Joan came for the 1922 Psychoanalytic Congress as a patient of Freud she was invited, with Freud and Anna, for lunch at the house of Max Eitingon.

Eitingon was not highly regarded as a psychoanalyst, but his huge wealth and organising powers made him one of the leaders of the Berlin group. He financed the new Poliklinik and employed Freud's son Ernst (who had trained with Adolf Loos) to design everything down to the chairs and analytic couches. It was a message to people that their mental sufferings were being taken seriously. A modest advertisement was placed in a newspaper that the clinic was open. The analysts were astonished by the flood of patients. Some children even referred themselves. A waiting list soon built up. Thanks to Eitingon, treatments were recorded in a systematic way, which allowed the effectiveness of the work to be evaluated. Klein complained about her time in Berlin because of the hostility of some of her colleagues, but the setting of the clinic enabled her to treat children and young people from a variety of backgrounds, many of them extremely poor or delinquent. She also treated the children of some colleagues. Karen Horney sent her two daughters to Klein, although possibly more as a gesture of support than a deep belief in Klein's methods. Klein discovered that one patient a colleague had left her to look after was psychotic. Courageous as ever, she interpreted his fear that she would send him back to the asylum. Her colleague found the patient had improved when he returned.

For Klein this was simply part of her principle of interpreting the transference. But Freud did not believe psychotic patients formed a transference. Later when Klein developed her theory of manic depressive illness even some of her English colleagues were outraged. Many years ago I was working with a thirteen-year-old boy who had psychotic ideas. I was not sure how to make contact with him. My supervisor, a delightful elderly lady who had trained with 'Miss Freud', told me I should find a Kleinian supervisor. Even today psychoanalysts and psychotherapists who would not call themselves Kleinians still seek out Kleinian supervisors for difficult patients.

The Berlin Poliklinik was not only a place for treatment, it also offered a training for psychoanalysts. Anyone doing training had to have a personal analysis. There were also seminars given by members on a variety of topics. After Klein gave a presentation in 1924, the normally phlegmatic Abraham declared 'the future of psychoanalysis lies with the play technique'. After this, Klein was able to persuade him to take her into analysis. Not only did Klein benefit personally from the analysis but she got to know an analytic sibling who would change her life, and to a certain extent Joan's. We last met Alix Strachey when she and her husband James were in analysis with Freud. Joan's analysis with Freud also overlapped with theirs. Alix was not satisfied with her analysis, partly because she had to share Freud with James. Freud, who thought highly of Alix, suggested she go to Abraham.

Abraham was the analyst's analyst. Some people thought he was better than Freud. James would have liked to join Alix but Alix was determined to have Abraham for herself. The advantage of this arrangement was that they wrote to each other almost every day. It is sometimes possible to glimpse Joan in James's letters, usually seen through a thin fog of malice:

> after dinner I have to go to Mrs R's [Joan] to a committee to discuss the question of an index for the four volumes of [Freud's] collected papers. Bryan has started making a wildly inefficient one, and for a moment I thought of offering my services instead.
>
> The meeting [at the British Society] was much livelier than usual, I must say the English are a minderwertig [inferior] set, especially the ladies. Miss Searl struck me as a mere jelly of sentimentality and prejudice. Mrs Isaacs is conceited beyond words ... Mrs R's *morale* is all right, but her mind is decidedly enfeebled.

James is describing major players in the forthcoming conflict between Anna Freud and Melanie Klein (Meisel and Kendrick, 1986).

Initially, Alix took a similar snobbish view of her German colleagues. She spent a lot of time in the Romanisches Cafe drinking coffee and writing letters to James. As Freud's ex-patient and Abraham's current one, Alix was invited to Max Eitingon's house – an oasis of good taste. This was an honour, as Max's wife Mirra was not keen on his colleagues. Meanwhile, Alix was getting to know her analytic sibling Melanie Klein. At first they were united by a shared love of dancing: 'I've promised to go to a Maskenbal with Frau Klein tonight. It's darned expensive, she dances like an elephant'. After the dance Alix viewed Klein more kindly: 'She's really a very good sort and makes no secret of her hopes and fears and pleasures which are the simplest sort. Only she's got a damn sharp eye for neurotics'. Within a few days Alix had snapped out of her languid Bloomsbury snobbery and became a serious advocate of the work of Melanie Klein:

> I meant to tell you how exciting last night's sitzung [seminar] had been. For Die Klein propounded her views and experiences on kinderanalyse, and at last the opposition showed its hoary head ... The *words* used were of course psychoanalytical: danger of weakening the Ich Ideal [ego ideal] etc. But the *sense* was purely anti-psychoanalysis. We mustn't tell the children the terrible truth about their repressed tendencies.

Alix immediately grasped that far from running riot in their sessions, children were crushed by a harsh early superego. The conflict with Freud was immediately obvious. Freud thought the superego arose as an outcome of the Oedipus complex at the age of five or so, Klein's little patients were two to four years old.

Klein was chipping away at one of the cornerstones of Freud's work – the Oedipus complex. Klein believed in describing the reality of her work, apparently unaware that she was entering the lion's den. The psychoanalysts in the

Berlin Society were the shape of things to come. The women, Karen Horney, Josine Müller and Ada Schott who had all spent time with young children were basically supportive. Josine Müller suggested that some children project their harsh ego onto their parents who then appear more frightening than they are in reality. However, the male analysts, Alexander and Rado, were violently opposed to Klein's work. Alexander declared that small children would not understand Klein's interpretations; and if they did they would faint with horror. (Perhaps those were his feelings.) In a vain attempt to disprove this speculation Klein described a small boy who resolutely ignored her. Desperate to make contact with him, she decided to make an interpretation: 'You know why you break all your toys and can't play with them, it's because you want to break your brother's widdler because you are jealous of him'. Far from fainting with horror the boy became friendly and confiding. Children did not have a problem understanding Klein – she spoke their language.

Klein not only spoke children's language but she was prepared to be an actor in their private dramas. Trude, age 3 ¾, suffered night terrors and wet herself when left alone. She repeatedly played a game where she and Klein were both asleep. Then she would creep out of the corner she called her bedroom and steal up on Klein making all sorts of threats, 'She would stab me in the throat … or give me to the policeman … she lifted the sofa cover and said she was making *po kaki kuki*'. Translated this meant she was looking in Klein's buttocks for babies which she equated with faeces. A modern reader who probably spends quite a lot of time with their children might find this sort of material familiar. However, in an age when babies and small children spent most of their time with nursemaids, Klein's material was electrifying. At the time there was a tendency to confuse the woman with her patients. James wrote to Alix 'what an awful woman she must be, I pity the poor kiddies who fall into her hands'. Despite James's horror he asked Alix if she could produce an abstract of Klein's presentation at the Berlin meeting. Unfortunately, Klein, oblivious to the difficulties she faced, had arranged to go to the Vienna Society to present her work in front of Freud and Anna.

Klein's autobiography makes no mention of the Vienna meeting. Understandably she chose to draw a veil over the experience. She seems to have hoped that the weight of her evidence would convince Freud to revise his theory. This was something Freud was good at doing, provided the evidence came from himself. The Viennese Society were also still reeling from the murder of Hermine Hug Hellmuth by her nephew. She had probably analysed him. Alix anticipated that the biggest opposition to Klein would come from Anna Freud. Anna viewed herself as the keeper of her father's flame. However, her opposition to Klein was not only theoretical. As Alix put it 'she thinks Klein is a low woman'. It is certainly difficult to imagine Anna allowing a child to search in her buttocks for babies. In fact, she developed a form of child analysis which involved a great deal of control over the child. She promoted a positive transference, going to great lengths to maintain this.

While Klein was being snubbed in Vienna, Alix was struggling with her abstract of Klein's Berlin paper, 'I have made a few notes on the meeting in which Klein's paper was discussed and I think I can produce a (very inadequate) short account of it, about 5–6 pages long'. Fortunately a frantic letter from Alix reached Klein in Vienna. It would have been balm to Klein's wounds. She replied at once, although it was Christmas Eve.

> Dear Mrs Strachey,
>
> I am replying at once to your letter which I received today. Above all I thank you for having taken the trouble to comment about my lecture and certainly – as I gather from the formulations of the questions – in a most knowing way.

Klein gave further case histories which emphasised how she established an analytic contact directly with a child through its play. When people expressed shock at Klein they were really expressing shock at how children's minds work. Unfortunately, faeces were a common preoccupation. However resistant children were to Klein they seemed to intuit that Klein would understand them. Klein described a four-year-old girl brought to analysis by an escort. She ignored Klein until Klein interpreted to her some of her play. (1) She rummaged through the handbag of the escort, then closed it, she said, so that nothing should fall out. (2) She did the same thing with a purse with money in it. (3) She drew a glass jar in which there were marbles, drew a lid in order to close the glass jar so that the marbles would not fall out. Klein gave a *transference* interpretation that these were faeces which she did not want Klein to produce and also not other children, 'A changed relationship between us was established'. This immediate transference link was completely at odds with Anna Freud's approach.

In January 1925, James read Alix's abstract to the British Society. It was the beginning of Klein's courtship dance with a new group of potential followers. James's letter to Alix makes it clear that the topic of child analysis was already a live one in London. The evening started with short papers by Riviere, Glover and Jones, and a paper by Nina Searl on 'A question of technique in child analysis in relation to the Oedipus complex'. Joan seems to have made some crushing comments about this. However, Klein's work was almost universally acclaimed, despite some mutterings that she did it by suggestion. As Alix experienced in the Berlin Society, Klein's work stirred up everyone's feelings and afterwards James stayed up until two in the morning at Rickman's house discussing child analysis and other topics.

Unlike the Viennese and Berlin Societies, in London there was already an active interest in the psychoanalysis of small children. The reasons for this were complex, but an important factor was that there was a high proportion of women analysts, such as Joan, in senior positions in the society.

Many of them, such as Nina Searl and Ella Sharpe, came from the Brunswick Square clinic with its emphasis on the *application* of psychoanalysis. Nina Searl had papers on child analysis published in the *International Journal of Psychoanalysis* from 1920 to 1936. Despite its title, the *Journal* was under the control of Ernest Jones (with Joan Riviere as translations editor). It would have an important role in the battle to come. The interest in children in the British Society cannot be put down solely to the presence of women analysts. Many of them did not have children, and Joan, although she had a child, found children difficult to tolerate. The men were also interested. Ernest Jones claimed to have worked with a nine-year-old boy. Even James Strachey began to look for evidence of Klein's theories among the children of his acquaintance. A Mrs Hussey had a one-year-old baby girl who repeatedly thrust the thumb of one hand into the fist of another, before looking around at her audience 'with a leer of delight'. James looked for evidence whether boys have an awareness of a vagina. In this climate a discussion of faeces was quite acceptable.

News of the success of the abstract soon got back to Melanie Klein: 'at last night's sitzung Melanie swam up and was *most* gracious … *how* had I kept it so clear etc. etc. … She says she has designs on England and is going to talk to me about it tonight'. Alix heaves a sigh. 'Melanie is rather tiresome as a person – a sort of ex-beauty and charmer'. As was so often the case by the next morning Alix's views of Klein had changed, 'I met Melanie last night and really was immensely impressed by what she told me. She really is the only person who's ever regularly analysed children'. In no time at all Alix and Klein had devised a programme of six lectures covering early analysis, latency analysis and adolescence. After a while the practicalities asserted themselves. Was Klein's English good enough? Was there a demand? Alix was sure there would be, but would Jones support it? How much would Klein be paid? Alix became so involved with Klein's forthcoming seminars that she decided to teach her English. Klein read Freud's paper 'Little Hans' in English and Alix then questioned her on it. Alix soon discovered that although Klein understood English quite well, she found speaking it more difficult.

The arrangements for Klein's seminars gradually increased in complexity. Alix decided Klein should go to a specialist English teacher. Then Klein's German lecture notes needed to be translated into English and typed. James thought that Joan was too busy with Freud's collected works. It seems likely that Joan would have wanted to do some of the translation for Klein, had she known about it. James's rivalry with Joan may have influenced his idea that she was too busy. James's self-effacing manner covered up an intense wish for control. Eventually James and Alix did most of the translation for Klein. Ella Sharpe, one of the psychoanalysts who came from the Brunswick Square clinic to the British Society offered a room in her house for the seminars. However, as more and more people expressed a wish to come, a larger room was needed. Adrian and Karin Stephen offered a bigger room in their house at 50 Gordon Square, although Karin demanded money for a charwoman to clean the rooms after each lecture – all of this was deducted from Klein's fee. Adrian was the younger brother of Virginia Woolf and Karin had been a brilliant philosophy student at Cambridge. Klein would literally and metaphorically be at the heart of Bloomsbury. Adrian and Karin had both been persuaded to do medical training before becoming psychoanalysts. Unlike James Strachey, who had only lasted a few weeks, they had stuck it out until qualification. The issue of medical training was still an acute one. Jones was struggling to have psychoanalysis recognised by the medical establishment. This drive was probably fuelled by his earlier disgrace as a doctor before he went to Canada. Many senior psychoanalysts such as Joan, James and Alix were not doctors. This was a potential rift within the Society which was dealt with by British compromise. This was the shape of things to come.

The wish to make psychoanalysis scientific remained a live issue. We saw it in James Strachey's quasi-scientific translations versus Joan's more accurate and aesthetically pleasing ones. In America, only doctors could practice psychoanalysis. An exception was made for Anna Freud. As well as the Freud name she developed scientific frameworks for evaluating her work with children. Despite these 'scientific' issues Anna Freud and Klein aroused different feelings. Anna Freud was often idealised, and Klein was often attacked for psychoanalysing her own children. Yet Anna Freud analysed all four children of her life partner Dorothy Burlingham. All remained very troubled, and one of them, Mabbie, Anna's favourite, killed herself. This fact is rarely mentioned, yet Klein's daughter's adolescent spat with her mother is often held against Klein. However, in the summer of 1925, the English psychoanalysts took Klein to their hearts.

In her autobiography Klein described her three weeks in England as one of the happiest periods in her life. She stayed in a small hotel in Bloomsbury, and delivered two seminars a week in her heavily accented English. She found it hard to understand the questions, but felt she managed to satisfy her audience. People were kind, hospitable and interested. No one laughed at her yellow hat with its floral decoration. A photograph of Klein and Joan at the Innsbruck Conference in 1928 suggest that Joan had taken Klein's clothes in hand. Instead of a large hat and embroidered blouse, Klein is elegantly dressed in a silk dress and discreet hat. Did Joan make any clothes for Klein? She would certainly have told her about her apprenticeship with Mrs Nettleship, and the two women could have gone for tea in Marylebone High Street, just round the corner from Mrs Nettleship's shop. Klein was not snobbish. She was interested in everything, and her warmth melted Joan's stiffness of manner. The few letters we have from Joan to Klein are very different to those she wrote to other people.

Klein returned sadly to Berlin. Abraham, who had been very ill, eventually died on Christmas Day 1925, probably of lung cancer. Alix Strachey went back to London and James Eitingon took over from Abraham as chair of the International Psychoanalytic Association and Simmel became chair of the Berlin Seminars. He was well disposed towards Klein, but not strongly enough to defend her from Alexander and Rado. Rado's animus to Klein was lasting and he later tried to block attempts to defend her from the attacks of Anna Freud. Lonely and despairing, Klein wrote about her predicament to Joan and Alix. Both of them spoke to Jones, reminding him what a success Klein had been the previous summer. They were pushing at an open door. Jones had also met Klein at the International Congress in Salzburg in 1924. Klein had presented her first paper on the technique of child analysis. 'An approach' Klein wrote 'which was entirely new, completely controversial, and strongly doubted by many analysts' (including Anna Freud). Although Jones wanted to curry favour with the medical establishment, at heart he was a rebel, and like many in the British Society he was convinced by Klein's clinical data. The British Society had always been the younger sibling of the Berlin and Viennese Societies. Vienna had Freud and Berlin had their splendid Poliklinik. With a clinician of Klein's brilliance England could become a centre of child analysis.

In addition to these professional and political factors Jones's interest in child analysis was very personal. He was no longer a lone philanderer. He was a happily married man with two children: Gwenith, aged 5, and Mervyn, aged 3. Unfortunately Kitty, Jones's wife, was finding the children very hard to manage. Jones decided to bet on Klein. He wrote to ask her to come to England for a year to analyse Kitty and the children. With three English patients guaranteed, Klein packed her bags and set off for England. She was to live there for the rest of her life.

Chapter 12

Child wars

Up until 1925 the British, particularly Jones and Riviere, could claim to be devoted to Freud. Jones saw himself as Freud's bulldog, defending his work against all comers. When he found Jungian tendencies in the London Society he closed it down and founded the British Society in 1919. Joan was one of its first members. Its purity suited her perfectionist character. In 1924 James Strachey negotiated a contract with Leonard and Virginia Woolf's Hogarth Press to publish Freud's complete works in a unified English translation. Yet, within a year of this, Jones would be writing to Freud to praise a woman who had not been to university, who was not a doctor, and who questioned Freud's dating of the superego and the Oedipus complex. Not only this, Melanie Klein would later introduce a new concept of developmental stages. Why was she not expelled like Jung or Rank? Why did Freud make almost no public criticism of Klein, except a footnote agreeing with her? As we shall see, Anna Freud more than made up for Freud's reticence.

The opening shot in the battle was fired by Ernest Jones. Aware of Anna Freud's hostility to Melanie Klein he wrote to Freud on 17th July 1925.

> Melanie Klein has just given a course of six lectures in English before our society in Frühanalyse. She made an extraordinarily deep impression on all of us and won the highest praise both by her personality and her work.
> (Paskauskas, 1993)

Freud sounded a note of warning on 22nd July: 'Melanie Klein's works have been received with much scepticism and opposition here in Vienna', Jones was not to be deterred. He regarded the Viennese opposition as 'indicating nothing but resistance against accepting her conclusions concerning infantile life'. At this stage Freud's response was laconic, Klein was safely tucked away in Berlin surrounded by hostile colleagues. Abraham showed no signs of recovering from his illness, and on Christmas Day 1925 he died. Klein lost her strongest supporter. Rado reigned supreme in the Berlin Society, and refused to publish any of Klein's works in the *Zeitschrift*, the European equivalent of the *International Journal.*

Jones's motivation in inviting Klein to England was twofold. He was aware of her difficulties in Berlin – probably via Riviere. However, he also had a very sincere wish for her to psychoanalyse his wife and children. His marriage was a very happy one, but Kitty's difficulties with the children distressed him. Mervyn Jones's analysis started on 15th September 1926, Gwenith started on 27th September and Kitty began on 4th October. No one today would think about psychoanalysing a mother and children together. At the time the full power of the transference was underestimated. Complications arose immediately as Kitty felt rivalrous with this woman who was going to manage her children better than she did. Klein asked Jones to avoid mentioning her positively in front of Kitty.

In the few years since Joan and Klein met they had become close friends. According to Diana Riviere, Joan's daughter, Klein was accompanying Joan and Evelyn on holiday from around 1925. A letter from Joan to Klein, dated 27th April 1926, makes it clear that Joan was aware of Klein's plans to come to England very early on.

> My dear Frau Klein
>
> I am delighted to think it is settled about your coming. I heard this week of a case of a dreadfully naughty little girl of 2½ which I might be able to get for you … I have just finished Das ich in Das Es … I now have the festschrift to do …' [At this point Joan's affection bursts out] '… I *am* so glad you are better and more "arbeits lustig" [ready for work?]. It will be delightful to have you here and I do hope you will find all you hope for.
>
> Yours ever
> Joan Riviere.

Klein kept this letter and several others from Joan for the rest of her life. In these early days Joan set herself up as Klein's bulldog in much the same way as Jones and Freud. She was aware of Klein's need for patients if she was to survive in England, and the political necessity of keeping on the right side of Ernest Jones. Riviere suggested Klein ask Jones to write a preface, presumably to her first book, *The Psychoanalysis of Children*. In a more immediate way Joan encouraged Klein to write to Jones to get his support for her to move to England on a more permanent basis. Klein's ostensible reason for coming to England was to have her son Erich living with her, and away from the influence of his father. However, her positive experience of the seminars she gave in 1925 made her feel that England was a place she could develop her work. Her letter to Jones is a magnificent mixture of truth and diplomacy.

> Mrs Riviere went into my worries with great warmth and thus it happened that in the course of our conversation the idea of settling down permanently in London emerged. However I stated at once that this could be

> considered only after I had found out what you would think of such a possibility.
>
> (Grosskurth, 1985)

Klein goes on to say that she knows that Riviere has spoken to Jones on her behalf. Having disposed of the delicate preliminaries, Klein followed herself to make her ambitions clear. She wanted 'a viable analytic basis' not only for her work, but also for working for the establishment and expansion of child analysis (this last bit was probably at Riviere's suggestion – she was aware of Jones's ambitions). Klein's glowing picture of London as a centre for child analysis was deeply attractive to Jones. For many years he had been chafing at being second to Berlin and Vienna. After Abraham's death it was Eitingon, rather than Jones, who Freud chose to be president of the International Psychoanalytic Association. However, it was not only ambition which led Jones to back Klein. There were already British psychoanalysts working with children. Susan Isaacs had become the headmistress of the first school run on psychoanalytic lines in 1924. All this accounted for the intense interest in Klein's seminars in 1925. As Nina Searl put it, Klein had given her a technique she could rely on.

Juliet Mitchell has suggested that the British empirical tradition puts its faith in what works (Mitchell, 1986). When Ernest Jones wanted to convince Freud of the value of Melanie Klein's ideas he wrote in May 1927:

> Dear Professor
>
> Though the gratitude I owe you for many years is too great to be adequately expressed ... I am writing today to express some more of it ... it concerns my children. Since September [1926] they have with the exception of some weeks of holidays and illness been analysed ... The changes already brought about are already so striking and so important as to fill me with thankfulness towards the one who made them possible, namely yourself.

Although Jones does not mention Klein, he was aware that Freud would guess who was analysing his children. With a mixture of flattery and empirical evidence Jones was trying to convince Freud of the value of Klein's work. Meanwhile Klein was slowly settling into English life. After a number of moves she eventually had a house big enough to see her patients and have Erich come to live with her. Following Joan's advice Klein sent Erich to the Hall Prep School in St John's Wood, while he was learning English. After a year he transferred to St Paul's School in Hammersmith, a highly academic school. This was probably at the suggestion of Evelyn Riviere, who had been a pupil there. Klein must have been very satisfied with the school because Hanna Segal, her patient and star pupil, sent all three of her sons to St Paul's. Erich did not lose contact with Arthur Klein, and there are a number of affectionate letters from Arthur to Erich in the Klein Archive.

One of the less attractive aspects of Klein and Joan was their tendency to dispose of their children to suit their own needs. As a child analyst, Klein was very aware of Erich's difficulties and once she moved to England there were people who could analyse him. Klein successfully prevailed on Donald Winnicott to analyse Erich, although she bombarded him with supervisory letters. Joan was less fortunate, as we saw: her supervisee Hanna Segal refused to psychoanalyse Diana Riviere. Diana told Athol Hughes that she felt closer to Evelyn and her Aunt Molly, Joan's sister. Whatever Diana's difficulties were, she did go to Oxford and worked as a journalist. There is also some indication from Joan's letters that she and Diana spent more time together as Diana got older.

When I spoke to Hanna Segal, Klein's patient and Joan's supervisee, shortly before she died, she told me that Joan wanted Klein to take her into analysis. I am not sure if this is true, as Riviere's experience with Jones had made her careful about boundaries. However, even if this is not literally true, Klein and Joan were very close. Klein's last paper was called 'On the sense of loneliness'. In this paper Klein says:

> However gratifying it is in later life to express thoughts and feelings to a congenial person, there remains an unsatisfied longing for an *understanding without words* – ultimately the earliest relation to the mother.
>
> (Klein, 1963)

I think this wordless understanding was the creative spark between the two women. I do not think it is a coincidence that Joan wrote her three most original papers in the eight years after Klein came to England. 'Womanliness as a Masquerade' (1929) describes a type of defensive femininity. 'Jealousy as a mechanism of defence' (1932) introduces the significance of envy twenty years before Klein's controversial paper on the subject. 'A contribution to the understanding of the negative therapeutic reaction' (1936a) was Joan's response to Freud's analysis of her in *The Ego and the Id*. In this paper Joan uses Klein's newly minted concept of the depressive position to understand why some patients resist recovery. Joan's brilliance as an explicator of Klein has obscured the originality of her ideas. In this paper Joan introduces the concept of a defensive organisation which is extensively used by Kleinians today.

As well as these intellectual links, Joan and Klein looked after each other in a maternal way. When Klein collected her early papers into a book (translated by Alix Strachey), she wrote in the preface 'I also owe a deep debt of gratitude to my friend Mrs Joan Riviere, who has given such active support to my work and has always been ready to help me in every way'. One of the ways in which Joan helped Klein was to arrange an inexpensive holiday for Klein in the house of a friend of her Verrall aunts. The tone of Joan's letter has a warmth and affection that few people saw.

> My dear Melanie, I went to see my aunt (Miss Verrall) … I saw Miss Belcher and she showed me the room you will have. It looked *very* nice, the whole place was so pretty and bright and the garden … you can have your meals where you *like* – in bed in the garden or anywhere … It really is exactly the place you want. I am sure it will do you good.
>
> With love yours J Riviere.

This affectionate and unbuttoned tone gives a picture of a side of Joan that few people would see. The friendship between Joan and Klein lasted until well after the Second World War. Even in 1952 Joan was still writing:

> Dear Melanie,
>
> I think the tone and style of your paper is excellent … For myself I am proud to be reckoned as a friend in scientific matters as well as personally. Love from
>
> Joan R.

There follows a *cri de coeur*. Joan is having servant problems as usual: 'Do you think Mrs Pearce's sister would come here to wait dinner and help after 9th. My Mrs Smith can't come'. During Klein's first few years in England her relationships with most of her colleagues were friendly and collegiate. The wish she had expressed to Jones to establish child analysis on a firm footing in England looked as if it would be fulfilled. However, a dark cloud was looming over the horizon. It took the shape of Anna Freud.

In 1927, Anna Freud published her first book *The Psychoanalytic Treatment of Children*. This describes an approach which was entirely different to Klein. Woven into it is an intense personal hostility to Klein herself. Behind this lay some of the unresolved dynamics of the Freud family. Anna Freud was born in 1896. She was the youngest of six children. By the time she was born, Martha Freud was worn out by babies, and when Anna was 10 months old Martha had her first holiday from the children. Anna was looked after by a devoted nurse, Josefine, who cared for the younger three children. Anna was confident she was Josefine's favourite. Unfortunately, Anna was also aware that her beautiful and fragile older sister Sofie was her parents favourite. However, the Freuds also worried about Anna. She lived in daydreams and resisted growing up. There may also have been a problem with anorexic tendencies. It was decided that Anna should go on a health-giving tour of Italy with her aunt Minna, Martha's sister. When they arrived at a pensione in Merano, Minna was suddenly called back to 19 Berggasse. The reason for this was that

Sofie had just got engaged to Max Halberstadt in Hamburg. Martha hurried to help the young couple set up house and Minna was needed to look after Freud and the rest of the family. Why did Minna not take Anna back with her? There is some evidence that Martha and Sigmund found Anna rather tiresome and intrusive. They decided that Anna should stay in Italy until after Sofie's wedding. After a lonely five months Freud came to collect Anna. As a reward he took her for a short tour of Northern Italy, including Venice. Anna was marked by this experience of exclusion. She was determined to annexe her father for herself (Young-Bruehl, 1988). When Joan met Freud in Berlin, it was Anna who accompanied him, not Martha. One a more personal level a few years later Freud went to the Tegel Sanatorium. Anna managed to elbow aside her mother and accompany her father. It was not only Anna who was possessive. When Anna began to think of being a psychoanalyst Freud could not bring himself to send her to one of his colleagues, but analysed her himself over two quite long periods. This gave substance to her fantasy of sole possession of her father. Interestingly, when she and Joan were analytic siblings, Anna was very jealous of Joan. This may have been Joan's beauty – reminiscent of Sofie – but also because Freud must have expressed his fondness for Joan. When the conflict between Klein and Anna came to a head it did not stop the warm relationship between Joan and Freud. Freud's letters to Joan often include a message from Anna, possibly given through gritted teeth.

Anna initially trained and worked as a teacher. From 1919 she started attending the Vienna Society as a visitor. In 1922 she graduated with a paper on beating fantasies, which was entirely based on her own analysis with Freud. At this stage she had no patients of her own. Both Freud and Anna seem to have been oblivious to this bizarre piece of nepotism, which also revealed Anna's intense identification with her father. Freud's cancer must have made it difficult for Anna to express negative transference feelings towards him. This in turn influenced the technique Anna developed with children. Anna learned her technique from Hermine Hug Hellmuth. Hug Hellmuth thought that children under latency age could not be analysed. She worked in the child's home and insinuated herself into the child's confidence by a variety of techniques which often involved deception. Anna adopted these ideas without really acknowledging their source, or questioning their efficacy. Hug Hellmuth's murder by her nephew, who she brought up and probably analysed, must surely have called her techniques into question. Anna's approach to child analysis went even further than that of Hug Hellmuth. She deliberately cultivated a split transference by binding a child to her by a variety of means including writing letters for them, knitting clothes for their dolls, owning up to their misdemeanours to their parents. She believed the child analyst had to work with a positive transference. If the children misbehaved at home she would give educational instructions to the parents – who she believed were responsible for the child's difficulties. This approach is a variant of Anna's analysis with her father where the negative transference was located elsewhere – often in letters to Max Eitingon. A wealthy American woman, Dorothy Tiffany Burlingham, came to Vienna in search of an analysis for her son Bob, who had suffered from asthma. Anna took on Bob and his sister Mabbie and later their two younger siblings. Dorothy herself was in analysis with Theodor Reik. Dorothy's husband suffered from manic depression and the two were separated. Anna eventually accepted that she wanted Dorothy for herself, and she used Freud to lay claim to her. She persuaded Dorothy to leave Theodor Reik and go into analysis with Freud. She also moved the whole Burlingham family into 19 Berggasse. Dorothy and Anna were to live together for the rest of their lives. Having laid claim to Dorothy in a way that she could not do with Martha Freud, Anna's hostile transference to a maternal figure lighted on Melanie Klein. In 1927, Anna Freud published a collection of lectures she had given in Berlin and Budapest, *The Psychoanalytical Treatment of Children*.

The purpose of this book is not just to put forward Anna Freud's technique of child analysis, but also to show that Melanie Klein's technique is wrong. This is not simply a disagreement between two workers, but in Anna's case a highly personal animosity revealed not only in the content, but the tone of the writing. Here Anna Freud is talking about the absence of a sense of illness in the child:

> in many cases the child is not the sufferer, for it often does not perceive the trouble in itself at all ... And so the situation lacks everything which seems indispensable in the case of the adult ... This does not impress every analyst of children as a serious obstacle. You will be aware from Mrs Melanie Klein's writings how she comes to terms with these circumstances.

and so on. Not surprisingly, Klein and some of her colleagues including Joan wanted to respond to this contempt by a paper in the *Zeitschrift*. Rado, the editor, had great pleasure in telling them that only a positive review of the book would be acceptable.

Ernest Jones was not deterred by this. He set up a symposium at the British Society at which all of the interested members gave papers which responded to Anna Freud's book. As well as being President of the British Society Jones was Editor of the *International Journal of Psychoanalysis*. He published papers by Melanie Klein, Joan, Nina Searl, Ella Sharpe and Edward Glover. These papers were not simply a critique of Anna Freud's views, they put forward Klein's views with great clarity, and present an inspiring picture of the possibilities of child analysis. Klein's own paper is the most substantial. Joan translated it from the German and its clarity and irony suggest that she also edited it. Klein makes it clear that child analysis is exactly like adult analysis. An analytic situation can only be established by analytic means:

> Now I think it is surprising and illogical that Anna Freud who does not use the necessary measures to establish an analytic situation but substitutes others at variance with these, yet continually tries to prove … that it is *not possible* to establish an analytic situation with children.

Klein goes further. She suggests that when Anna Freud brings into consciousness a boy's worry he might go mad, she does not attack this anxiety at its unconscious roots which would allay the anxiety. Piece by piece Klein demolishes Anna Freud's ideas, and puts forward her own, which are rigorously analytical but sympathetic to the child's difficulties.

Joan's defence of Klein is brief but precise, showing her mother's capacity for hitting a target. She writes from the point of view of an adult analyst, which incidentally gives us some sense of how she herself works. First, she questions Anna Freud's fundamental assertion that children and adults behave differently in the analytic situation: 'this difference though apparent is merely apparent'. Next, she tackles Anna Freud's assertion that the child does not know it is ill. Joan points out that even if an adult takes themselves to be analysed they often show a great reluctance in practice, and a lack of awareness of their problems: 'I should imagine that to be spared these rationalisations and to have the patient's continued attendance ensured by the parents would be advantageous features in the analysis of children'. Here, Joan shows an awareness of the reality of child analysis when she concedes that the parents can be a help as well as a problem! It seems likely that Joan discussed her contribution with Klein. One of the key issues in Anna's argument is that children do not develop a transference neurosis because the 'original edition' in the parent is still dominant. Here, Joan hits on Anna Freud's key weakness: she is being too literal. The transference is based on the child's unconscious fantasies and is not a mirror of the relationship to the *real* parents. Continuing this line of thought, Joan points out that the 'lower classes' do not offer much in the way of 'moral training', yet their children have a cruel conscience which tortures them with guilt and drives them to provoke punishment. Joan has been criticised for talking about the 'lower classes' this way, yet the real issue is whether she is making an accurate observation. One could say that nowadays most classes are reluctant to provide consistent discipline. The issue of the savage superego is one that Joan returns to in her paper on the negative therapeutic reaction.

The publication of the Symposium provoked a war of words between Jones and Freud. Jones fired the first shot:

> It is a pain to me that I cannot agree with *some* of the tendencies in Anna's book, and I cannot help thinking that they must be due to some imperfectly analysed resistances, in fact I think it is possible to prove this in detail.

Jones was probably right, but Freud's complex involvement with Anna did not allow him to consider this:

> In London you are organising a regular campaign against Anna's child analysis, accusing her of not being analysed deeply enough. Is anyone actually analysed enough? I can assure you that Anna has been analysed longer and more thoroughly than you yourself.

Freud is deceiving himself here. We have seen how Anna turned to Eitingon to express her negative feelings, and how her identification with Freud enabled her to present his work with her as her own. It is not surprising that Klein observes that it is difficult for Anna to interpret the Oedipus complex when it appears. It is interesting that Klein, the real villain of the piece, is a no-go area for both Jones and Freud; probably for both of them she was an ambivalently regarded maternal figure. Instead Freud gradually worked himself into a state of rage with Riviere:

> In this symposium an otherwise sensible person such as Riviere lets herself be carried away by theoretical assumptions which run counter to everything we know.

Jones sturdily defended Riviere:

> Mrs Riviere's views [are] expressed in her characteristically uncompromising and vehement fashion, all that matters in the present connection is that she was not *hirgerissen* [carried away].

But Freud cannot let go of his anger with Joan, perhaps because he is aware that her strong personality can withstand him:

> More disconcerting to me than these tempests in a teapot are the theoretical statements of Riviere, especially because I have always had such a high opinion of her understanding ... I am writing to Mrs Riviere herself about this.
>
> (Paskauskas, 1993)

In fact, Joan and Freud had already exchanged views on child analysis. She wrote to Freud from Kitzbühel telling him firmly that she could not agree with ideas in Anna's book. Freud replied quite benignly:

> It is curious that Anna's views on child analysis have met with so much contradiction in London and so much unanimous applause in Berlin. I think one can safely leave the resolution to future experience. Child analysis is still very young.

In a second letter written later Freud is more angry, provoked by Jones's remark about Anna:

> I hope you will not contest my right to irritation … and do not attribute my conduct to my having been insufficiently analysed … I have always had a high opinion of your understanding of analysis and your intelligence.

Freud acknowledges that Joan does not bear Anna any ill will. He then returns to his grievance with Jones, and his anger with Klein for suggesting that Anna does not analyse the Oedipus complex. He asserts that the young child has a weak ego and superego – in contradiction to Klein's views. In this muddled letter, Freud obscures the possibility that some very able people – including Joan – think Klein is right. Despite this, his letter ends 'I greet you warmly'.

In a memoir of Freud, written after his death, Riviere makes a cryptic observation: 'the power to see new facts and to check his observations diminished considerably in him after his operation in 1924'. I think that Joan is referring to Freud's unwillingness to examine Anna's clinical material carefully, and his refusal to accept Klein's new ideas. However, he made no attempts to excommunicate Klein – that threat came later and not from Freud. By 1935 Freud's attitude to Klein had softened and he wrote to Jones:

> It is true I am of the opinion that your society has followed Frau Klein on a wrong path, but the sphere from which she has drawn her observations is foreign to me, so that I have no right to any fixed conviction.

Experience led Anna to give up her elaborate preparatory period and work with younger children. In 1914 Jones wrote to Freud about Anna who had been on a visit to England, 'She has a beautiful character and will surely be a remarkable woman later on, provided that her sexual repression does not injure her. She is of course tremendously bound to you'. That bond would lead Freud up the wrong path in his thinking on female sexuality. Once again Joan would be together with Klein on the front line.

Chapter 13

Female sexuality and femininity

On 6th February 1925, James Strachey wrote to his wife Alix, who was still in Berlin having her analysis with Abraham:

> On Wednesday there was a meeting of the Pyschoanalytic Society ... devoted exclusively to the question raised by Bryan upon whether some kind of excitation of the clitoris was after all essential before a female could have an orgasm ... and the extraordinary thing was that no-one seemed to know what an orgasm was. Mrs Riviere asserted flatly that there was a vaginal orgasm and a clitoris orgasm, that they were qualitatively different, and that you could have one or the other or both. But the gentlemen of the party seemed not to agree with this.
>
> (Meisel and Kendrick, 1986)

The gentlemen do not seem to have given Joan any credit for inside information. Perhaps the gentlemen did not like the idea of a woman having two sources of orgasm. Not only were the gentlemen an obstacle, but later in the year Joan found her experience of her own body in conflict with Freud. In 1925 Freud wrote 'Some psychological consequences of the anatomical distinction between the sexes'. This was read on his behalf by Anna Freud at the Bad Homburg conference the same year. This is the first of three papers which take an increasingly derogatory view of women. These views were challenged by women analysts such as Karen Horney and Helene Deutsch. But the most forceful and comprehensive challenge came from Riviere and Klein (Klein, 1928). According to Freud, one of the central factors in girls' development is penis envy. She discovers that her brother or playmate has a penis of 'large proportions [and] at once recognises it as the superior counterpart of their own small and inconspicuous organ'. When the girl realises that she is like other women in this respect 'she begins to share the contempt felt by men for a sex which is the lesser in so important a respect'. Penis envy is a factor in turning the girl away from her mother who has failed to provide her with a penis.

According to Freud, the clitoris is the equivalent of the penis, and the development of femininity depends on the suppression of clitoral sexuality. This takes place at puberty. If the girl is lucky she replaces the wish for a penis with the wish for a child – ideally a male child. She turns to her father for this and her mother becomes a rival. When the girl has to give up her father she may replace him with an identification with him. Freud's analysis of Anna ended as he was writing the 1925 paper. Gradually his views on female sexuality came to resemble Anna's personal psychosexual constellation, which Anna enacted in a highly concrete way. Anna had masturbation fantasies which were accompanied by vivid masochistic fantasies of a knight and a boy – no sign of a woman. Freud himself wrote a paper called 'A child is being beaten'. Anna cannibalised it to produce her own paper on beating fantasies as a membership paper for the Viennese Society. Her identification with her father was complete, and her mother was viewed in a denigrated way. Joan was to write a paper which throws light on this constellation and how it impacted on Anna's relation with her life partner Dorothy Burlingham. Even before the publication of Freud's paper women psychoanalysts were adding an injection of common sense (and personal experience). Karen Horney wrote:

> an assertion that one half of the human race is discontented with the sex assigned to it, and can only overcome this in favourable circumstances – is decidedly unsatisfying not only to feminine narcissism but also to biological science.

Horney suggests that the experience of satisfaction from sucking at the mother's breast is the prototype of adult female sexuality – giving back a key role to the mother. Possibly in response to dissatisfactions with the 1925 paper, Freud wrote another one in 1931 on 'Female Sexuality'. This covered much of the same ground, but at least with a mention of female analysts. This paper was translated by Joan for the *International Journal of Psychoanalysis*. It is difficult to know why Joan translated this, as she must have disagreed with much of it. Perhaps Freud asked her, and her fondness for him was undiminished. But also this paper contains a rare mention by Freud of Melanie Klein (Freud, 1931).

Freud acknowledges that Klein locates the Oedipus complex 'as early as the commencement of the second year of life'. Initially he rejects this: 'This dating of it would necessarily imply a modification of our view of all the rest of the child's development'. Freud adds that it is incompatible with his finding of the long duration of a girl's pre-Oedipal attachment to the mother. However, Freud seems to feel that Klein's ideas deserve consideration, and he accepts the influence of accidental experience, biological factors and seduction, which might lead to the presence of an early Oedipus complex. I think behind Freud's willingness to concede lies a hidden respect for Klein, as if Freud recognised her innovatory genius. Unlike other dissidents such as Jung and Rank, Freud never wished to exclude Klein from the fold, even during the dispute between Klein and Anna about child analysis.

At the Innsbruck Conference in 1927, Klein shocked the analytic world again with her findings about female sexuality and the timing of the Oedipus complex, dating it far earlier than Freud (Klein, 1928). It is started by the experience of weaning and toilet training and leads to a turning to the father. Klein agrees with Helene Deutsch that there is a displacement of libido from the mouth to the genital, but also believes that the *vagina itself has sensations*. The mother is felt to contain good things including the father's penis. All this increases the turning to the father. The girl has rivalrous, hostile feelings towards the mother which lead to guilt and anxiety. Klein accepts that the girl experiences penis envy, but dates it later than Freud. If the girl has loving feelings towards her mother she will be freer of guilt and be able to enjoy the experience of having children, and her love for her mother will be transferred to her husband. Freud attributes women's preoccupation with their appearance as a reaction to their envy of the penis. Klein suggests this originates in the girl's reaction to her mother. Girls wish to rob and destroy mother's insides and babies. This produces feelings of guilt and a fear that mother will take revenge on her for these attacks. Klein says 'at the bottom of the impulse to deck and beautify themselves, there is always the motive of *restoring* damaged comeliness and this has its origin in anxiety and a sense of guilt'. Unlike Freud, Klein sees penis envy and the turning to the father as a relatively late development, a response to the deprivation of the breast. Even in this early paper Klein touches on the girl's envy of mother's capacity to produce babies (Klein, 1928). Klein does not develop the concept of envy until 1957, but as we shall see this is something Joan picked up and developed by 1932.

A photograph of Joan and Klein at the 1927 Congress shows that they have both decked and beautified themselves. As soon as Klein finished a conference paper she turned her mind to the conference hat – perhaps not quite as spectacular as the yellow one with flowers that she wore for her debut at the British Society. Both Joan and Klein had difficult mothers, but they did not simply share a fondness for clothes, they each put something right for the other. Joan was Klein's bulldog. She used her penetrating intelligence and muscular prose to advocate Klein's ideas. Although Klein was only a year older than Joan she was a maternal figure. In defending her, Joan was symbolically making reparation to her own mother. This was rewarded with an outpouring of creativity. Despite her attachment to Klein, Joan did not give up her loyalty to Freud and she confided in him when she started to write. In September 1928, Freud wrote 'I welcome your promise soon to write something for publication. Anything you write about yourself personally is sure of my interest'.

'Womanliness as a masquerade' was published in the *International Journal of Psychoanalysis* in 1929. It is about the difficulties of a woman who is working in a man's world. It could not have been written at a more apposite moment in the social context. After years of foot-dragging the Representation of the People Act become law in England in 1928. This finally allowed all women over twenty-one to have the vote. Nicknamed the 'flapper vote' it referred to the increasing androgyny of women's appearance: short hair, flat chests and a type of dress called a 'garçonne'. A photograph of Joan taken in 1928 shows her with short curled hair and a suit with a matching shirt – perhaps made by herself.

The paper describes a woman who is mainly heterosexual but displays features of the other sex. Unusually for a psychoanalytic paper, Joan locates her patient in her social milieu, where many women 'fulfil the duties of their professions at least as well as the average man'. The patient's work involves writing and public speaking, and her anxieties about this bring her into analysis. Despite giving papers in a clear and dispassionate way she feels compelled to seek sexual attentions from men afterwards. She also feels acutely anxious about the quality of her presentations. Analysis showed that Oedipal rivalry with the mother was acute and had never been resolved. Her rivalry with her father was also very great. Her father was a literary man who later went into politics, and her adolescence had been characterised by contempt and revolt against him. She experienced her successful performances as a speaker as proof she had her father's penis, having castrated him. The patient described a dream which shows how her femininity functioned as a defence: 'She was alone in the house; then a negro came in and found her washing clothes with her sleeves rolled up. She resisted him with the secret aim of attracting him sexually'. Joan's interpretation was that she has killed her parents – 'home alone' – and she is washing off the guilt and the evidence of the murder. In the dream she is disguised as a castrated woman, the opposite of the competent lecturer. This masquerade of femininity is intended to placate the man who would otherwise attack her.

However, it is not only the father who is feared this way. Following Klein, Joan suggests that hatred of the mother develops during the oral biting stage of development. There is a wish to penetrate and devour the contents of mother's body including the father's penis. In order to escape retribution from the mother the girl puts the penis she has stolen at the service of the mother. She becomes the father and takes his place. However, she expects 'recognitions' for what she has to offer. Like all psychoanalytic theory it gains conviction if it can explain patterns of behaviour. Is Joan writing about herself? She certainly had difficulty speaking, and Ernest Jones wrote about it to Freud. Like the patient in the paper she had a kind and gentle husband. However, the most convincing clue lies in a eulogy of the work of Ernest Jones. At the beginning of the paper she writes:

> Every direction in which psychoanalytic research has pointed seems in its turn to have attracted the interest of Ernest Jones, and now that of recent

> years investigation has slowly spread to the development of the sexual life of women, we find as a matter of course one by him among the most important contributions to the subject. As always he throws great light on his material with his peculiar gift, both clarifying the knowledge we had already and also adding to it fresh observations of his own.
>
> (Riviere, 1929)

This rather over-the-top praise comes right at the beginning of the paper as if she is placating Ernest Jones for her temerity in writing her first full-length clinical paper. Her reference to Klein is more business-like, I think because Joan had already put herself at Klein's service as her most brilliant expositor. Joan points out that the weak point of this sort of femininity is its megalomaniac character. When the patient's megalomania was disrupted by analysis 'she fell into an abyss of anxiety, rage, and abject depression; before the analysis into illness'. This is so like Joan's behaviour during her first analysis with Ernest Jones that it may be a hidden reproach for his not understanding her better.

Joan's paper remains as relevant today as when it was written. There are still women in powerful positions who feel the need to dress in an ultra-feminine way. One of the most striking examples of defensive femininity among Joan's contemporaries is Anna Freud. Her life-partner, Dorothy Burlingham, arrived in Vienna as a poor, divorced, little rich girl with four children in tow. Anna began by psychoanalysing the two older children, Bob and Mabbie. She then arranged for Dorothy to have a psychoanalysis with Freud, a striking example of putting the penis at the service of another woman. Eventually the two women lived together and Anna analysed all four children while hiring and firing tutors and nursemaids. There is a photograph of Anna and Dorothy wearing identical ultra-feminine peasant dresses as if to deny the element of masculinity in their relationship. This defensive relationship worked for Anna and Dorothy, provided Dorothy did not take an interest in men. By 1928, when her first major paper was published, Joan was a senior member of the British Psychoanalytic Society. The Society itself was evolving. It now had its own institute and clinic. From now on there was a formal training, and Joan was a member of the training committee. Thanks largely to the efforts of Ernest Jones, the British Medical Association had declared psychoanalysis a serious branch of science. (One wonders what they would say today.) The presence of Klein put the Society at the cutting edge of child analysis. Joan and Klein met frequently and talked about everything from psychoanalytic technique to the problems with servants. Klein was much better at keeping hers.

Joan's second major paper, 'Jealousy as a mechanism of defence' was published in the *International Journal of Psychoanalysis* in 1932. It shows her increasing confidence in what she has to say. Instead of a long eulogy to Jones she states at once that she has observed a type of jealousy which is not referred to in psychoanalytic literature, and she believes it may have a wider validity. The paper is written almost like a detective story as we follow her investigation into the phenomenon, and we get some glimpses of her analytic technique. At first the jealousy seemed straightforward. The patient imagined that Joan had in her writing table letters from her husband or other men she desired. Joan quotes Freud's observation that jealousy can be projected as a defence against the subject's own infidelity. Although the patient had some minor flirtations they did not seem an explanation. Joan then observed that the patient indulged in periods of guilty breast-beating immediately after a session that was helpful. After some months Joan observed that the jealousy coincided with a particular sort of phantasy. This was a triangular situation where the patient would take possession of a person or object. An essential part of the constellation was a third person from whom the object was taken, and who suffered a robbery and spoilation. This phantasy permeated all aspects of the patient's life. For example, she imagined that Joan's husband would die but the patient would still have *her* husband. All pleasures the patient had were to be acquired at someone else's expense. In the transference her prevailing attitude to Joan was *envy* (my emphasis) made tolerable by contempt.

Joan describes a masturbation fantasy of the patient which provides an insight in condensed form of the patient's attitudes: 'A young girl is in a doctor's consulting room being undressed and then examined by him; there is another woman in the background'. This scenario can be understood in different ways. In one scenario the patient is enslaving the doctor and robbing the other woman of him. Another version is that the stripping doctor is a version of herself, stripping the woman of all she has. The woman represents the mother with breasts, milk, and the father and his penis. However, this is not a Freudian Oedipal position with love for one person and jealousy of the other. Joan likens it to the early sadistic oral position described by Klein in her Innsbruck paper. Klein's paper mentions envy, but Joan develops the concept further and describes its impact on adult female sexuality. Joan suggests that the earliest triangular situation for the infant is the mother's two breasts. People who are dominated by jealousy and infidelity are beneath this driven by oral envy, and the objects of their emotions are part objects and not real people.

Here we can see that Joan is not simply an expositor of Klein's ideas, but has used them as a starting point for original ideas of her own. The paper ends with a condensed account of *Othello* and its underlying dynamics. Joan suggests that Iago, the personification of envy, is Othello's alter ego. This is demonstrated in the first scene where Othello strips Desdemona's father of his daughter. This is the first time that Joan brought her two passions, literature and psychoanalysis, together. It is a theme she would return to later when she had withdrawn somewhat from the psychoanalytic world.

I had always assumed that the woman in 'Womanliness as a masquerade' was a disguised version of Joan herself. Freud wrote to Ernest Jones about

Riviere: 'In my experience you have not to scratch too deeply the skin of a so-called masculine woman to bring her femininity to the light'. This, of course, is the opposite of Joan's patient who hides her masculinity behind her feminine exterior. By chance, in Joan's archive, I came across evidence of Joan's contact with another woman whose details also fit aspects of her patient. There is a postcard with a drawing of a man in seventeenth-century costume carrying a very large rifle whose symbolic nature would not be lost on Joan. The card had been sent by Joan from Madrid to a Mrs P. S. Florence:

> You should have come – this is much the best country. Also it is very hot. How nice it was to see you in Paris. Tomorrow we shall be in Seville. We have already reached the sun. You can think of us eating oranges and basking on the banks of the Guadalquivir.
>
> *I love you.* [sic]
> Joan

The recipient of the letter was Lella Secor, the wife of Philip Sargant Florence, the older brother of Alix Strachey – which must be how it came to be in Joan's archive. Lella Secor was American, like the woman in the case material. She was vibrant and beautiful, and had raised herself from her family's poverty by her skills as a journalist. When Joan met her she was vigorously campaigning for birth control, and temporarily living apart her husband in Paris. The dream of the negro could possibly be hers. Despite the postcard it does not seem likely to me that Joan was in love with Lella Secor. I think she may have been swept off her feet as she was with Klein.

Being a psychoanalyst is not a guarantee of sexual 'correctness'. There is Joan's mysterious relationship with IEE, with its fallings out and reconciliations and holidays together. However, Joan's only explicit interest in sex between women is a one-line entry in her diary in 1916. She has just finished reading *The Rainbow* by D. H. Lawrence. She was lucky to get a copy, as it had just been banned for its explicit depiction of a lesbian affair between a teacher and her pupil. Did this have any resonance with Joan's experience of Wycombe Abbey? This is the only mention of a book in the diary, although Joan was prodigiously well-read.

Joan's brilliance and beauty seemed to arouse the envy of historians of psychoanalysis, and she is commonly presented as a rigid grand dame. In real life, her friends were often artistic, unconventional and sometimes rather raffish. We get a glimpse of this when she allows herself to be whisked off by Hans Sachs at a psychoanalytic conference. She maintained her friendship with the brilliant and eccentric Jane Harrison all her life. Her diary records a visit to Enid Bagnold, author of *National Velvet* and many novels. For a while Bagnold was the mistress of the notorious womaniser Frank Harris. When the First World War broke out Joan and Molly were on St Jacut, an early version of a 'party island'.

In 1933, Freud produced a new series of 'Introductory Lectures on Psychoanalysis', which were aimed at the lay public, as well as psychoanalysts (Riviere, 1934). The *International Journal of Psychoanalysis* carried a long review, written by Joan. This must be a reflection of her seniority, as well as her reputed loyalty to Freud. From the beginning Joan struggled to reconcile her admiration of Freud with her disagreements with him. She starts with: 'A new book by Freud means much to every analyst'. Within a paragraph she is criticising Freud for putting too much emphasis on *external* causative factors. Although she is not explicitly discussing female sexuality, she is likely to have had in mind the glimpse of a boy's penis which is supposed to be so decisive for the girl (the 'female castration complex').

Joan takes heart from Freud's views about the occult: 'One is displaying no great trust in science if one cannot rely on it to accept and deal with any occult hypothesis that may turn out to be correct'. As Joan was still attached to the Society for Psychical Research this would have pleased her, but she clearly wished that Freud would take this attitude to women. Joan devotes most of the rest of the review to challenging Freud, and giving her own perspective on women.

> His view has always been that the little girl turns to her father, and thus changes her love-object upon the discovery that she is inferior to the boy in having no penis ... From this cause too she renounces her unsatisfying male organ (clitoris) and eventually acquires a vagina instead ... The girl turns against her mother for not giving her a penis.
>
> (Riviere, 1934)

Joan emphasises that this point of view is not a psychoanalytic one. It depends on external factors rather than instinctual development. She also resorts to common sense:

> The boy's genital sensations are the exciting cause of his genital interest. That this might be equally true of girls (in the sense of vaginal sensations) is strenuously denied in the Freudian view.

Joan also points out the unlikelihood of the girl's sexual function being dormant until she discovers she has not a penis. It is hard to believe that none of the women in the Viennese Society had experienced vaginal sensations. As Joan put it: 'this is not a credible view of women'. Although Joan had support from other women analysts and Ernest Jones, her forthright disagreement with Freud over female sexuality was the shape of things to come.

There were other more sinister harbingers of the future. In 1932, Oswald Mosely founded the British Union of Fascists, and in 1936 a gang of 150 members smashed the windows and looted Jewish shops in the East End. They threw a man and a woman through a plate glass window chanting 'down with the Yids'. In the same year Ernest Jones asked Joan to take Klein's new ideas to Vienna.

Chapter 14

The road to war

Psychoanalysis is a demanding profession. Joan spent six or seven hours a day, five or six days a week seeing patients. Work often carried on into the evening as Joan was on various committees, including the Board of the Institute. In the early days these meetings were at members' houses, but by 1926 they had their own building at 96 Gloucester Place. Behind this highly professional structure things ran less smoothly. One might imagine that an organisation consisting of psychoanalysed people would be free of conflicts. In reality the opposite was the case. There were probably a number of reasons for this. First, as we saw with Joan and Freud, most analyses were very short. Joan spent barely six months with Freud plus a few brief top-ups. A year would have been considered a long time. In contrast, someone training today might spend ten years in analysis. This is partly because there is increased awareness of how difficult it is to make changes in people. However, conflicts are endemic in psychoanalytic societies, probably linked to the intense relationships members have with their analysts and analytic siblings. The arrival of Klein in England, bringing radical new ideas, initially stimulated the British analysts, however, as time went on there was greater scepticism about her ideas. Many of the British analysts had their own analysis in Vienna or Berlin, where the ethos was strictly Freudian. Despite her analysis with Freud, Joan remained loyal to Klein's developing ideas. Her most original papers were written after Klein came to England.

Joan's mixture of shyness and harshness could make it difficult for her to have close friendships, and she was often cruel to those she did not admire. There was no risk of this with Klein. Joan's letters to Klein are almost girlishly affectionate. Klein's analytic sibling Alix Strachey admired her work, but mocked her fondness for simple pleasures. Joan was free from this Bloomsbury snobbery, and was happy to go shopping with Klein for one of her famous hats. The friendship between Klein and Joan seems to have developed very rapidly. Klein was going on holiday with the Rivieres by 1925. Joan's daughter, Diana, remembers her as a 'dreamy' person. She was probably thinking about her work, which was the most important thing to her, possibly apart from her children. As the dust from the divorce settled,

Klein made trips to visit Hans. There is a photograph of them both with Hans's arm round Klein's shoulder.

Professionally, things went well for Klein. As well as Jones's wife and children, she was soon made a training analyst, which meant she saw candidates doing the analytic training. In fact, Klein and Joan between them had the most talented psychoanalysts of their generation in treatment with them. Joan's patients, Winnicott and Bowlby, are well known even to non-analysts. In 1929 Klein was one of the organisers of the International Psychoanalytic Congress at Oxford. Diana was now a student there, and Joan was pleased to see her. Klein's daughter Melitta, who was training as an analyst in Berlin also came. Perhaps Joan felt displaced by her, as she packed her off with Diana for a tour of the colleges. Melitta was not happy. On her return she complained 'it was interesting, but not scientific'. Despite the inauspicious start she decided to come and live with Klein while she finished writing her thesis. Klein turned the patient's waiting room into a bedroom for her. Melitta, like Klein, had married when she was very young. Her husband, Walter Schmideberg, was fourteen years older and also a psychoanalyst. While in the army he had met Max Eitingon, who had introduced him to Freud, with whom he remained on friendly terms. Phyllis Grosskurth, Klein's deeply ambivalent biographer, has suggested that Klein was envious of Melitta's medical qualifications and upper class husband. There is no evidence for this. Arthur Klein opposed the marriage because of Schmideberg's drug and alcohol problems.

While Melitta was writing about the history of homeopathy in Hungary, Klein also had her own writing project. She was assembling her early child cases into a book which would be called *The Psychoanalysis of Children*. As Klein's English was not completely fluent, Alix Strachey translated it for her. In the preface Klein also credits Melitta with helping her. However, her warmest thanks go to Joan. In 1932 Walter Schmideberg arrived just in time for the book's publication. He took all those who had supported it for dinner at the Mayfair Hotel. This group included Joan and Evelyn, Alix and James Strachey, and Edward Glover and his wife Gladys. Edward Glover, who was going to become Klein's most implacable enemy, designed a birth certificate for the book.

Initially the Schmidebergs and Klein got on well. They even bought a Sunbeam car together, optimistically naming it 'Sunny', and toured around England. Things changed when Melitta left her analyst Ella Sharpe for Edward Glover, who was ostensibly Klein's supporter. Soon Melitta and Walter decided to buy back Klein's share of the car. This was followed by a letter from Melitta in effect telling Klein to stay out of her hair: 'I do not think that the relationship with a mother, however good, should be the centre of her life for an adult woman'. This was apparently very reasonable. Unfortunately, Melitta was to replace a good relationship with her mother with a very bad one, which became the centre of her life. Edward Glover had a big part to play in this. Instead of helping Melitta separate from her mother he reinforced an angry preoccupation, and joined in the attack. Melitta began attacking her mother's work through the medium of her writing. Initially these papers expressed disagreement in a low key way. One of her papers even won a clinical essay prize in 1933 (Schmideberg, 1934). Of course, all analysts have disagreements about theories or clinical work, but the spirit of these disagreements should be professional. The true spirit of Melitta's criticisms of her mother emerged after Klein suffered a tragic loss, which marked the rest of her life.

Hans, Klein's middle child, was living with his father. He was a keen and experienced walker and climber. In 1934 he went for a walk in the mountains and the path crumbled beneath him. He fell to his death. Klein was too devastated to go to the funeral, although Arthur went. A Czech woman contacted Klein to say that when her divorce came through she and Hans were going to marry. Despite these facts Melitta declared it was a suicide, and blamed Klein. Melitta's theory cannot be ignored. Hans suffered from low moods. A modern view of suicide proposed by Dr Rob Hale suggests there is a wish to live and a wish to die which can be present in different proportions. Melitta later cemented her view by writing a paper on suicide in which she suggests it is due to a breakdown of idealisations (Schmideberg, 1936). There is no evidence for this for Klein and Hans, but quite a lot of evidence that Melitta's idealisation of her mother had broken down. She committed professional suicide by her increasingly vicious public attacks on her mother. Other analysts would think twice before referring patients to her.

Meanwhile, Klein struggled to deal with her grief. She did not go to the Institute for two months. She found that she could only bear to see close friends, and then only one at a time. In a paper written in 1940 – the first year of the war, she describes a 'patient', Mrs A, whose son has died, trying to re-establish contact with her neighbourhood by going out with a close friend. (I like to think it was Joan, but it may have been Paula Heimann.) The sunlight seemed unreal so she took refuge in a cafe, but even this did not feel safe, and she had to retreat to her own home. Klein's mourning was a stimulus to her creativity. Within a year of Hans's death Klein had established a model of early development which was based on the evolution of the infant's relationship to its mother. Instead of Freud's oral, anal and genital stages, Klein describes a pattern of shifting relationships. The complete model was developed over several years and two papers; the first described the later stage, the second described the earlier one. Initially, the baby experiences the mother as two different people. A 'good' gratifying mother, and a 'bad' frustrating one. The chief anxiety is the survival of the self. Klein calls this the *paranoid schizoid position*. As the infant develops cognitively it becomes aware that the 'good' mother is the same as the 'bad' mother. An awareness that it has directed hate and aggression towards a loved person fills the infant with sadness, and Klein calls this stage of concern for another person the *depressive position*. If depressive anxieties are intolerable there can be a resort to manic states, which deny damage and increase omnipotence. This new model had many implications, one of these being that it explained the cycle of mania and depression in manic-depressive illness. In her paper, Klein describes the treatment of a man who is depressed in a rather particular way: 'his depression had been spread out ... over his whole life, but he had not suffered from actual depressed states' (Klein, 1935). Was she thinking of Hans, whose letters to her indicate a chronic unhappiness? Astonishingly Klein, like Melitta, puts forward a way of thinking about suicide. In doing so she draws, comfortingly perhaps, on the thinking of her old analyst Abraham:

> A suicide is directed against the introjected object. But, while in committing suicide the ego intends to murder its bad objects, in my view at the same time it always aims at saving its loved objects, internal or external.
>
> (Klein, 1935)

Klein's theories are often seen as bleak, but this is a more comforting view of suicide than Melitta's breakdown of idealisations. Although Klein's new ideas had been stimulated by her grief and mourning, they were based on the clinical evidence of her work with children and adults. It seems very likely that she discussed her thoughts with Joan, as Joan used Klein's ideas so promptly in her own work.

It is a measure of Joan's familiarity with the work of Freud and Klein that she was to bring their ideas together in a paper which describes 'Those Wrecked by Success'. The paper was modestly titled 'A contribution to the analysis of the negative therapeutic reaction' and was published in the *International Journal of Psychoanalysis* in 1936. It is probably the best known of her papers, and based on her experience as a patient and as a psychoanalyst. It is about those who feel worse when they get better. Freud identified this problem very early in Joan's analysis and discussed it in a letter to Ernest Jones. Freud says 'she cannot tolerate praise, triumph or success ... Whenever she has got a recognition, a favour or a present, she is sure to become unpleasant and lose respect for the analyst'. Freud suggests this is a sign of a deep sense of guilt. Freud discusses this therapeutic problem in more detail in 'The Ego and the Id' – a paper he was particularly keen for Joan to translate. His high opinion of her was a present that she was now able to tolerate. In her paper Joan says that it is a mistake to think that the refusal to get better is simply hostility to the analyst. She picks up Freud's comment about guilt and explores it using Klein's concept of the depressive position. She suggests that the patient is keeping the internal situation static by means of omnipotent, manic defences. What the patient is afraid of, if there is change, is the depressive position.

Riviere's description of the depressive position shows how her powerful writing can communicate unbearable mental states:

> The content of the depressive position (as Melanie Klein has shown) is the situation in which all one's loved ones *within* are dead and destroyed ... nothing is left *within* but utter desolation. Love brings sorrow, and sorrow brings guilt ... there is no escape.
>
> (Riviere, 1936)

There is one consolation for reaching this situation. As the manic stranglehold relaxes the capacity for love increases. The clinical picture is of a patient who seems to refuse to get well because they feel that their internal objects have to be put right *first*. Any improvement in themselves is felt to be a betrayal of their internal objects. Joan makes it clear she is drawing on her own experiences as a psychoanalyst, but we know from Freud's letters that she is also talking about herself. Klein's concept of the depressive position, which appeared the previous year, was the final piece of the jigsaw unavailable to Freud at the time.

Joan's and Klein's papers were both published in the *International Journal of Psychoanalysis*, the house journal of the British Society, but these ideas had already been discussed at scientific meetings (and the Lucerne Congress). Not everyone accepted Klein's new ideas, but the climate of the British Society was becoming noticeably different to that of Berlin and Vienna. In this situation Ernest Jones was pulled two ways. He was convinced by Klein's new theories, but he was loyal to Freud. As an act of scientific fairness he suggested that someone from the Viennese Society should come to London and present their latest views, and someone from London should go to Vienna. It was a strange time to be working out a disagreement between Vienna and London. The members of the Viennese Society, who were mostly Jews, were already under attack from the Nazis. The chalked swastikas that H. D. (the American poet, Hilda Doolittle) observed in Vienna were replaced by casual sadistic attacks on Jews. Perhaps Joan felt safe as an English non-Jew.

Four exchange lectures were given between 1935 and 1936. The first one was by Jones himself, on female sexuality, a subject on which he differed strongly from Freud. In keeping with the Kleinian view, Jones also drew attention to the importance of the early relationship with the mother, a topic which Freud considered impenetrable. It would have been fascinating to be a fly on the wall. Robert Wälder gave the two return lectures, although his superior manner did not make him popular. Joan gave the third lecture. It was an astute move by Jones to choose her to represent a Kleinian view. Not only was she a clear and eloquent speaker, but Freud would forgive her. As Joan's train rattled across Europe she may have reflected on her earlier journeys to see Freud. Then she was going to learn Freud's ideas, now she was hoping to convince Freud and the Viennese about Klein's. The Viennese could freeze out Klein when she came, but Joan was a more formidable opponent. Her argument fills twelve large pages of tiny print. Basically, she was following the development of the baby in minute detail, weaving in the ideas of Freud and Klein. However, it is not simply a repetition of Klein and Freud. As we saw in the previous chapter, she describes mechanisms which were not described by Klein until 1940, or by Bion, Klein's patient, until 1962.

Joan reminds her audience that Freud believes that the deepest source of anxiety is the loss of the mother. She describes in minute detail the complex interplay of feelings between baby and mother before any language has developed. From the beginning of life the baby wants to take in good things and get rid of bad ones. This is based on the experience of eating and excreting. Joan links this to Klein's concepts of projection and introjection, these are methods which enable the ego to take in good experiences and rid itself of bad ones:

> but the ego's need to dissociate itself from the unpleasure is so great that it requires an object upon which it can expel it, and which it can identify with a bad suffering 'me'.
>
> (Riviere, 1936a)

This casually thrown-out idea anticipates the work of Klein's patient Wilfred Bion by well over twenty years. Bion suggests that the baby projects difficult emotions, particularly the fear of dying, into the mother, who processes it in her mind so the infant can now take back an unbearable feeling made tolerable. I think in order to make this suggestion Joan was probably already engaged in this way with her patients.

Although Joan, like Klein, lays great emphasis on positive and negative phantasies, she also takes seriously the impact of the environment. Here I think she gives us a hint of her own early experiences:

> If ... lack of love and helpful understanding is experienced, the child feels its own capacity for good feelings, satisfying to its parents and itself greatly reduced.

Towards the end of the paper Joan makes a direct plea for the importance of Melanie Klein's work:

> It is the wealth of phantasy-like dealings with wishes and aims to do good to the object for its own sake ... found by Melanie Klein and her followers in tiny children that provides the best evidence for our views ... This brings in the huge topic of the attempts at reparation, and their great importance for ego-development.
>
> (Riviere, 1936b)

Here, she emphasises that Klein's work is not only about aggressive impulses and phantasies but love and concern. It would have been wonderful to be a fly on the wall. To give a lecture like this on Freud's birthday in Vienna must have required some courage. It would have been interesting to know what Joan and Freud discussed the next day.

One of the most startling clinical examples in Joan's paper is her description of aggressive phantasies:

> Not only excretory but all other physical functions are pressed into the need for aggressive (sadistic) discharge ... Limbs shall trample, kick and hit; lips fingers and hands shall suck twist and pinch; teeth shall bite, gnaw mangle and cut ... these phantasies transfer the danger from the self into the object.

If this seems extreme, the Germans and Austrians were about to enact this towards the Jews and other vulnerable people. A similar point is made by the German Kleinian analyst Ruth Cycon in 1995:

> Melanie Klein's discovery of gruesome, destructive, psychotic phantasies of dismembering, rupturing, robbing and emptying, burning (through urine), gassing (through gastrointestinal gassing) and the total annihilation of the objects.

Here we have the infantile origins of the concentration camps and the gas chambers. Astonishingly, Joan and Klein's emphasis on reparation is now manifest in Germany through its willingness to accept refugees. Naturally, of course, this is being attacked by some segments of the population.

In a period of international tensions and imminent war, the need for the British Society to reach out to the public was greater than ever. In 1932 a public lectures sub-committee was convened. The lectures were well attended, with sixty or seventy people coming to hear about psychoanalytic topics. With this encouragement it was decided in 1937 to produce six small books in a series called 'Psychoanalytic Epitomes'. Joan and Klein collaborated on one called *Love, Hate and Reparation.* John Rickman edited another less optimistically titled *Civilisation, War and Death*, which was extracts from Freud's work. Joan and Klein's book was based on lectures they both gave in 1936. Joan's lecture was on 'hate, greed and aggression'. Klein's was on 'Love, guilt and reparation'. It is not clear how Joan and Klein chose their topics, perhaps Joan felt more affinity with the negative emotions. When they were talking about aggressive, cruel and selfish emotions she suggests that we can see 'the savage satisfaction, or at least the glee, felt by someone making a cutting retort can often be seen in his eyes'. This certainly applied to Joan. In a seminar for psychoanalytic trainees she said to a clumsy student 'I hear there are good jobs to be had selling vacuum cleaners'. Joan examines the roots of feelings such as jealousy, hate and envy in infancy and looks at ways in which as children and later as adults we defend ourselves against them. This lecture has in places the quality of the seven deadly sins. However, it is interesting how frequently she returns to different aspects of envy. Compared to Joan's other papers, this one lacks sparkle. It is clearly written, but it does not seem to have engaged her interest the way a case history or a work of literature does.

Klein's chapter on love, guilt and reparation is more relaxed in style than Joan's. She devotes one section to friendship between women, and it is hard not to imagine that she was thinking of herself and Joan.

> Let us take as an instance of friendship between two women who are not too dependent on each other. Protectiveness and helpfulness may still be needed at times by the one, at other times by the other. This capacity to give and take emotionally is one essential for true friendship.
>
> (Klein and Riviere, 1937)

At this point in time, Klein was needing Joan's support as Melitta was mounting an increasingly hurtful campaign against her mother. One of the main forms it took was a series of papers, published in the *International Journal* which were highly critical of principles which were important to Klein.

In 1935, Melitta wrote a paper on the treatment of asocial children. The paper presents her as an expert in this topic – which coincided with Glover's interest in delinquency. There is no mention of Klein's work, but she quotes Abraham's theories of libidinal development, as if to remind Klein that, unlike her mother, she had not strayed from Abraham's path. It cannot be a coincidence that this paper of Melitta's was published in the same year as Klein's 'A contribution to the psychogenesis of Manic-Depressive States'. In this paper, and her 1940 one, Klein breaks free of Freud's oral, anal and genital schema and introduced two major positions: paranoid schizoid and depressive positions. It is sometimes said that Melitta was hostile to her mother because Klein psychoanalysed her as a child. However, modern research by Claudia Frank, a German psychoanalyst, has shown that it was only Erich who Klein analysed (Frank, 2009). Melitta's hatred of her mother seems to have been based on envy of her creativity. It seems to have been more like Joan's patient who wanted to achieve at another's expense. In 1937, Melitta read a paper to the British Society called 'After the analysis'. In it she accuses 'imaginary' psychoanalysts of promoting patients' idealisation of them and their work. She also attacks the idea that no analysis is complete without the patient going through a phase of depression. Klein had a policy of not responding to Melitta, but Joan was furious. She let off steam in a letter to James Strachey: 'Melitta says we are all bad analysts'. James is a curious person to have turned to, as he found it impossible to share the intensity of her feelings. Perhaps she hoped he would give a dispassionate view.

Interestingly, around this time, Joan took on a patient who was very envious and has since become highly idealised. His name was Donald Winnicott.

Chapter 15

A front-rank analyst

Considering that Joan never worked with children, it is striking that three of her most famous patients were famous for just that: Susan Isaacs, John Bowlby and Donald Winnicott. Of course, she was well known as a Kleinian analyst, and was steeped in the work of Freud and Klein. However, there were aspects of Joan's personality which were very childlike. The intensity of her feelings, her verbal cruelty and her impulsive expressions of affection. After her analysis with Joan, Susan Isaacs dedicated a book to her: 'To Joan Riviere, who has taught me to understand my own childhood'. During the exchange lectures between Vienna and London, arranged by Ernest Jones, Joan chose to give a paper on 'the genesis of psychical conflict in earliest infancy'. Her rich but precise prose describes how a baby gradually internalises good aspects of the mother, 'The absorbing stare with which a six-month-old baby looks at one plainly demonstrates how he is taking you in'. Here we see that she has not only 'taken in' Klein's ideas, but speaks from her own experience of babies.

Susan Isaacs started her analysis with Joan at a very difficult point in her life. After a distinguished academic career at Manchester University and Cambridge, with qualifications in teaching and psychology, she was chosen by the eccentric and brilliant Geoffrey Pyke to become the headteacher of the Malting House School. This was no ordinary school. Children were expected to learn by conducting experiments. There was no formal discipline, although the children's behaviour was sometimes interpreted. Not surprisingly, there was a good deal of violence between the children, and the situation seems to have been more like *The Lord of the Flies* than an enlightening experience. Despite this, a number of Cambridge dons entrusted their children to this scheme, including Alix Strachey's brother Philip, husband of Lella Secor. Not only were there sexual enactments between the children, but between the adults too. Geoffrey Pyke and Susan had a brief affair, and one of the female teachers, Evelyn Lawrence, had an affair with Susan's husband Nathan. In fact, he married her after Susan's tragically early death. The school came to a premature end owing to Pyke's financial troubles (Graham, 2009).

Susan took refuge in Joan's beautifully decorated consulting room, and her clear but sympathetic mind. The set-up at the Malting House School seems to have been a reflection of the most disturbing aspects of Susan's childhood. She was the second youngest of eleven children. Her father became a journalist and her mother was a highly organised housewife. The home was harmonious until Mrs Fairhurst, Susan's mother, became ill with a degenerative disease which eventually killed her. As she got weaker the house and children descended into chaos. It seems to me that the Malting House School was an unconscious recreation of this unhappy period of Susan's childhood, complete with the enactment of Oedipal phantasies. Isaacs began the Institute's training in child psychoanalysis, and her child cases were supervised by Melanie Klein. She was to repay her debt of gratitude to Joan and Klein by making a decisive intervention in the battle for Klein's legitimacy as an analyst, which was slowly gathering momentum in the 1930s.

In the published letters of James and Alix Strachey we hear quite a bit about James's troublesome patient Dr Winnicott. His most annoying habit was forgetting or delaying paying his bills. James seems to have suffered this in silence, perhaps he did not know that Winnicott had not paid Jones's consultation fee either. This difficulty with money had no basis in Winnicott's financial reality. He was a doctor holding several hospital appointments. His family came from Plymouth and his father was a successful merchant. After ten years of analysis with James, Winnicott was able to marry, although James's letters indicate that he was impotent. Winnicott also began to take a serious interest in the children at Paddington Green Children's Hospital, where he worked as a paediatrician. His membership paper, which he wrote in 1935, was entitled 'the manic defence', and makes clear his growing interest in the work of Melanie Klein. Winnicott's biographer, Robert Rodman, suggests that Winnicott was dissatisfied with his analysis with James Strachey (Rodman, 2003), although, as we will see, he seems to have found it difficult to value anyone who might have something to offer him. He approached Melanie Klein. However, Klein had other plans for him. She was still concerned about Erich, although aware now that she was not the one to help him. She felt that Winnicott was sufficiently Kleinian, and that he should psychoanalyse Erich.

Winnicott reluctantly agreed to this. Klein consoled Winnicott by suggesting he go to Joan Riviere. It is unlikely that Winnicott simply experienced Joan as a consolation prize. She had become a brilliant expositor of Klein's ideas and had the reputation of being a rigorous analyst. She immediately got to grips with Winnicott's financial shenanigans. Winnicott managed to convince her that he could only afford a fee of one guinea per session. She subsequently found out that his financial situation was far better than he had painted it. Her letter to him is a model of its kind. It shows Joan's kindness, her confidence in herself, her analytic rigour, as well as sympathy for her patient.

> Dear Dr. Winnicott
>
> I know that you are not very satisfied with the analysis you have had so far with me. I think this may not only arise from the usual phantasy and transference sources, but may be partly due to the actual circumstances in this special instance.

Joan attributes this to the absence of a preliminary interview. In this situation:

> the patient gives the analyst at any rate one view of himself and his reasons for wanting analysis; and this gives the analyst on his side an opportunity to put certain points of view before the patient.

As well as the absence of a preliminary interview, Joan also suspects that Winnicott may have been pushed into this arrangement by Melanie Klein. Joan stresses the need for analyst and patient to co-operate: 'Among the analyst's motives, his need to make a livelihood plays a part'. Joan goes on to say that her normal fee of two guineas is low for a 'front rank' analyst. 'I am second to no-one here in ability', Joan makes it clear that she is now aware Winnicott can afford her full fee. Joan could have been indignant at Winnicott deliberately misleading her, however, she is sympathetic as to how Winnicott will feel receiving her letter.

> So far I don't think we have gained by ignoring real difficulties. But whatever you feel, please don't feel that I am not wishing to help you as much as I can.

Winnicott's biographer, Robert Rodman, puts Winnicott's fee paying problems down to 'stinginess'. I think Joan was clear that Winnicott's problem was envy, a topic we have seen her investigate. In a subsequent letter she makes this clear: 'It is because it has become clear that you undervalue my work that I think it is right to ask if you can pay my full fee'. This exchange of letters does not seem to have done the analytic relationship between Joan and Winnicott any harm. However, as time went on there would be disruptions in the analysis due to the effects of war and Joan's recurrent chest infections. These were probably exacerbated by her smoking (using an elegant cigarette holder). When Winnicott was ill, Joan wrote solicitously 'I do so hope you aren't being uncomfortable or in any pain'.

Winnicott's experience as a paediatrician naturally made him aware of the importance of the nature of the mother's care. However, as time went on he began to use this factor as a stick to beat Joan, Klein and other analysts. As we saw, Joan made allowances for Winnicott because she felt she had failed to provide the right setting at the start of his analysis. Klein was, in fact, perfectly aware of the significance of the environment and particularly the mother's care. In her 1946 paper 'Notes on some schizoid mechanisms' she makes this clear.

> External experiences are, of course, of great importance … For instance, in the case of a patient who showed depressive and schizoid features, the analysis brought up with great vividness his early experiences in babyhood, to such an extent that in some sessions physical sensations in the throat or digestive organs occurred. The patient had been weaned suddenly at four months of age because his mother fell ill. In addition he did not see his mother for four weeks. When she returned she found the child greatly changed.

This is by no means the only reference that Klein makes to environmental factors. In fact her work makes it clear *why* the environment is so important. Joan put the psychoanalytic approach very clearly when she wrote for the Symposium on Child Analysis in 1927: 'Child analysis is concerned simply and solely with the imaginings of the childish mind'. John Bowlby, Joan's other troublesome patient, wrote in the margin of his copy 'Environment = Zero'.

John Bowlby was born in 1907. Like most middle-class children of his day he was brought up by nannies and nursemaids, and only saw his mother for a few hours a day. His childhood was not without trauma. His favourite nursemaid left and his father died when he was young. After a short period in the navy he went to Cambridge to study Natural Sciences and was awarded a first-class degree. As we have already observed, psychoanalysis seems to have exerted a magnetic pull on Cambridge graduates.

Bowlby went on to medical school, but even at the beginning of his training he knew he wanted to study psychiatry, and ultimately become a psychoanalyst. When he was only twenty-two, Bowlby registered at the Institute of Psychoanalysis, although he had to wait to be accepted onto the training proper. By 1930 he was in analysis with Joan. However, it seems from the beginning there were difficulties. He felt that there were things he could not tell Joan in case they affected his future. Perhaps one of the things was his difficulties with women. He was about to become engaged to Lady Prudence Pelham – with the approval of his mother – when he started an affair with her sister. This pattern was repeated in his analysis, when for some time he flirted with the idea of another analyst. He started a PhD at University College London on 'An examination of guilt and anxiety'. He seems to have had some supervision with Susan Isaacs, who – as a satisfied customer – would have encouraged him to stick with Joan.

In 1933, Bowlby spent eighteen months at the Maudsley Hospital under the supervision of Aubrey Lewis. This cannot have helped his ambivalence towards Joan, as Lewis was very hostile to psychoanalysis. Perhaps Bowlby, who found Lewis congenial, may have shared his views. Not surprisingly, Bowlby could not wait to finish his analysis. However, his request to the training committee to qualify in 1936 was turned down. Edward Glover, the chair, wrote to him: 'the committee cannot fail to be struck by the type of anxiety concerning urgent and premature qualification'. He and Joan had to struggle on for another eighteen months. Joan was unhappy about his lack of progress. He in turn, never gave any indication that she had the slightest impact on his life. Unfortunately, Joan was working before the clinical use of the analyst's countertransference was recognised, although Joan herself had already identified the role of the patient's projections. Most analysts, including Klein, believed that a difficult countertransference was the analyst's problem. While this view is still current, now it is also recognised that through projection patients can transmit unwanted states of mind into their analyst. Bowlby's mother did not seem to regard her children as very important, and Bowlby seems to have passed on this feeling to Joan. He made Joan feel that she was not important to him. This must have had some resonance for Joan, whose mother put her husband before her children. Bowlby finally qualified in 1937. Despite the difficulties of Bowlby's analysis, Athol Hughes, editor of Joan's collected papers, thought that Joan and Bowlby developed a friendly relationship once the analysis was finished. They sometimes met for a meal before an evening meeting.

On 2nd March, 1937, Freud wrote a clear-eyed letter to Ernest Jones,: 'Our political situation seems to have become more and more gloomy. The invasion of the Nazis can probably not be checked; the consequences are disastrous for psychoanalysis as well'. However, even Freud was not prepared for the horrors unleashed by the Anschluss on 13th March 1938. The Viennese embraced German anti-Semitism, and made it their own. Horrific attacks were made on both young and old. Many people committed suicide rather than submit to Nazi sadism. Freud was not exempt. The Gestapo invaded his house and were met with Martha Freud's implacable courtesy. Freud's international links made escape tantalisingly possible, but he dithered. Ernest Jones put his great powers of organisation at Freud's service. He took a plane to Vienna (an unusual thing to do) and persuaded Freud that he must leave. Freud accepted. However, he insisted his whole family had to come, including Martha's parents and Max Schur, his doctor. He even included Paula, their maid. Jones then had the task of getting residence permits for everyone. He drew on the goodwill of his friends Sir Samuel Hoare, the Home Secretary, and Earl De La Warr, Lord Privy Seal. Just as these arrangements were drawing to a climax, the Gestapo twisted the knife. Anna and Martin Freud were arrested. They had prepared for this eventuality by asking Max Schur to give them enough veronal to kill themselves if they were tortured. Fortunately they were released, and Freud committed himself to leaving. The Gestapo put their bureaucracy at the service of their sadism. They insisted that the Freuds have an exit visa. Freud could not afford this. However, Princess Marie Bonaparte, a former patient and friend, paid instead. As the Freuds travelled across Europe by train, they were able to rest in Paris at Marie Bonaparte's house. Freud had been forced to leave his elderly sisters behind. Marie Bonaparte tried to obtain their release, but they died in concentration camps.

In a very short space of time the Freuds were settled at 20 Maresfield Gardens in Hampstead, which was to be Freud's final home. His consulting room was minutely reconstructed with his couch and the huge number of antique figurines which he had collected. Despite his age and deteriorating cancer he saw three patients a day. Freud found that his arrival in England had made him a celebrity. Even *The Lancet* waxed lyrical: 'Now in his old age, there are few psychologists of any school who do not admit their debt to him'. Freud was well enough to visit his dog who was in quarantine in Ladbroke Grove.

However, a few days after moving in to Maresfield Gardens, another cancerous spot appeared. This required major surgery. Freud's surgeon, Pichler, travelled from Vienna to perform it. Although Freud recovered from the surgery he had only another year to live. However, he continued to receive guests and colleagues, including his publishers Leonard and Virginia Woolf. There is no record that Joan visited, although she must surely have wanted to. She did tell the American analyst Kurt Eissler that she saw Freud in a group of people. Was she afraid to encounter Anna Freud after the bitter disputes about child analysis? If there was a reason, it was most likely to be her loyalty to Melanie Klein. Klein wrote to Jones, berating him for bringing the Freuds to England rather than than sending them on to America. It was a measure of Klein's feelings that she did not consider the effects of a lengthy sea voyage on a fragile, elderly man. As an Anglophile, Freud's wishes were to stay in England. Perhaps Joan's reluctance to visit was a precursor of the intense loyalty Klein was later to demand of her followers.

At first the French and British approach to the Nazi threat was a craven one. Neville Chamberlain and Edouard Daladier met Hitler in Munich on 29th September 1938. They conceded the 'German' part of Czechoslovakia in return for no further Nazi aggressions. Many people, including Joan, had no faith in this attempt at appeasement. Joan called this the 'Munich Complex, the son's incapacity to fight for mother and country'. Gradually, information began to trickle out of Germany about the sadistic aggression directed against their own citizens, particularly the Jews. On a thin pretext on 9th November 1938 an orgy of violence and destruction was unleashed towards the Jews. Shops, flats and synagogues were set on fire. 50,000 Jews were sent to concentration camps. This was Kristallnacht. The Nazis felt free to commit any act of cruelty, however barbaric. However, Hitler had been preparing for war for four years. His next step was to invade Poland. He assumed from his encounters in Munich that France and Britain would not offer any meaningful resistance. He was wrong. On 3rd September, 1939, ultimatums were delivered from Britain and France. Hitler found himself committed to a war across Europe that would ultimately spread across the world.

Meanwhile, back in Maresfield Gardens, in the peaceful house with its secluded garden, Freud was slowly dying. He closed his psychoanalytic practice, but still continued to wind his watch and his clock. He had made a pact with Max Schur that when the pain became too much Schur would help him die. He told Schur that the moment had come but referred Schur to Anna. Anna wanted to postpone the decision, but Schur insisted that it would be too cruel. Schur fulfilled Freud's wishes, and he died peacefully on 23rd September 1939. At Freud's funeral service Ernest Jones gave the funeral oration. The 'liar from Wales' as Freud once called him had proven his loyalty to Freud and his family. It is impossible to think that Joan was not there too.

Almost immediately after Freud's death the doctor's journal *The Lancet* commissioned Joan to write an obituary of him. She must have written it very quickly, or they had commissioned it in advance, as it appeared on 30th September 1939. It is a brilliant pen portrait which gains in liveliness by her account of her first session as a patient with Freud. It is not a piece of hagiography as she suggests that after the operation on his jaw in 1924 Freud's work was not of the same standard. There is a flicker of her anti-Semitism when she says that Freud hardly looked Jewish, but more like a university professor. Joan's anti-Semitism did not prevent her from revering two Jews, Freud and Klein. Joan describes a curious trait in Freud: his naivety. When talking of a young scientist who was interested in psychoanalysis Freud said mournfully 'But I can't regard it as normal you know, that he has married a woman old enough to be his mother!' This should have been no surprise to the discoverer of the Oedipus complex. Interestingly, in his biography of Freud, Ernest Jones gives an example of Freud's naivety which concerned Joan. While she was in analysis with Freud he spoke very angrily during her session about a patient who had complained bitterly about monstrous ill-treatment by an English analyst from Ipswich.

> Mrs Riviere's cool mind at once perceived that this was a cock-and-bull story, but she contented herself with saying that there was no English analyst of the name mentioned, that there had never been an analyst in Ipswich.

Freud was not convinced. However, shortly afterwards a letter arrived from Abraham saying he was referring Freud an English patient who was a 'wild paranoiac' with a fondness for inventing stories about doctors.

In Joan's last public statement about Freud, written in 1952, she amplifies Freud's naivety into a key quality of his genius:

> In using the word naiveté of him, in spite of its usual rather disparaging connotation, I have done so because it alone, I feel, conveys the strength of this immediate acceptance of whatever he met with as valid.

Through this means he gradually built up a picture of the unconscious: 'this world which is unknown to us and yet is so powerful in determining our lives'.

Joan gives the example in her own analysis of Freud making an interpretation to her which she rejected: 'He then said it is *un-conscious*. I was overwhelmed then by the realisation that I knew nothing about it – I knew nothing about it'. Joan wrote to Freud the day he died, so he did not get to read the letter. Anna Freud was touched by it, and forgetting previous hostilities she wrote to Joan acknowledging how much she had loved her father.

Freud's death had spared him the prospect of living through another world war. Initially, Hitler seemed invincible. The German army swept through Denmark and Norway. The British and French forces were driven out and the two countries surrendered. On 9th May, 1940, German troops invaded Holland, which surrendered on 15th May. Hitler seemed to have dithered about whether to invade England, although the British army was cornered at Dunkirk. Hitler's hesitation allowed the allied soldiers to be evacuated, with a savage battering from the German army. Despite the 'Dunkirk spirit' this was a defeat, and 40,000 British servicemen were captured. Meanwhile, the French were forced to surrender on 17th June 1940. Although Hitler had made a plan to invade England, 'Operation Sea Lion', he hoped that England would surrender. German aircraft sank 580,000 tons of shipping. German submarines harried convoys transporting supplies from America. Bombing campaigns against British ports were carried out during 1940–1942, hoping to starve the British into submission. However, the RAF was now retaliating. The most famous was the Battle of Britain on 15th September, 1940, when three waves of bombers and fighter planes came over London. Despite an intense bombing campaign, 'the Blitz', many German planes were lost. In the famous attack on Coventry, 554 people were killed, but 600 German planes were downed. German morale was weakened, while British morale hardened into 'the spirit of the Blitz'. Despite this British resilience the experience of living through these attacks was terrifying. There were many deaths, including children. Clearing out bombed houses was a horrific job. Although bombing and U-boat attacks continued throughout the war, Hitler's megalomania drove him to mount an attack on Russia, although British planes were now carrying the fight into Germany. As the tide of war tuned against Germany there was no let-up of the suffering of civilians and soldiers. The allies took Italy from the Germans. The Red Army took over Germany and moved towards Berlin. After observing the ruin of Soviet lands they were determined to exact revenge. Thousands of German women were mass-raped. German attempts to sue for peace were all rejected. Finally, Hitler and his entourage were cornered in a bunker in Berlin. Hitler shot himself in the head. Eva Braun, now his wife, took cyanide.

Klein's work had revealed horrifically sadistic fantasies in children. Nothing had prepared anyone for their actualisation by adults.

Chapter 16

War

In June 1940, Joan wrote to Klein:

> When the first official mention of invasion began, the possibility of our work all coming to an end seemed so near. I felt we should all have to keep it in our hearts ... as the only way to save it for the future ... so I had the idea of your telling me (and then a group of us) everything you think about these causes ... To me the apathy and denial of the allies, especially England is not clear ... How is it connected with what I shall call 'the Munich complex,' the son's incapacity to fight for mother and country? One great question is why it is so important to be brave?

(Klein or someone else tidily filed this letter together with a paper of Klein's about what death means to the individual.) Joan did not lack for bravery, but the urgency of her wish to know Klein's thoughts was probably linked to Klein's absence from London, and the temporary cessation of their frequent meetings. When war was declared, Joan was out of London herself staying with friends in Hampshire. Her letter to her analysand, Donald Winnicott, is an example of her realism and clearsightedness:

> I am glad that the people of this country are ready to stand up and resist madness and that we can hope to save what this lovely England stands for and that the train loads of children [being evacuated] may yet one day carry it on.

Joan's letters to Winnicott had previously been very formal, but it was an example of the stirring times that she signs it 'your friend'.

In another letter to Winnicott on 21st August, 1940, Joan seems almost exhilarated by the battles in the air, 'Last week there were plenty of night raids and sirens 5 times a day – dog fights overhead ... I was on top of the Downs during most of the activity and saw and heard very little'. This letter is written from Chichester where Joan and Evelyn had bought a house. It is clear from the letter that she planned to restart Winnicott's analysis in the autumn.

Joan's willingness to confide in Winnicott was perhaps a reflection of her feelings. She had nothing to work on without patients to see. She sometimes wrote up to eight letters per day. Some of these were to Klein, who was revising what would become her 1940 paper 'Mourning and its relation to manic depressive states'. This was her second attempt to come to terms with the death, possibly an involuntary suicide, of her son Hans in 1934. Most of Joan's suggestions seem to have been of a stylistic nature:

> I think it is immensely improved by the additions and re-writing ... I feel this paper should really go far to make your new theory about depression become better known and understood.

According to Phyllis Grosskurth, Klein's biographer, the paper was so well written it was assumed that Joan had written it. This is perhaps a reflection of the empathy between Joan and Klein at this point in time.

When war broke out in September 1939, Klein was having her summer holiday in Walberswick – the place where Joan had been in a sanatorium for depression. At first, Klein thought she would stay on there, however, she decided to go and stay with Susan Isaacs. Joan's former patient must have seemed to Klein one of her network of supporters. As we will see, Isaacs was to strike the decisive blow to rescue Klein from her attackers. Unlike Joan, Klein never seemed to be without a patient to work with. She was treating a boy called 'Dick' who we would now describe as autistic. Her work with him was very successful, enabling him to speak and show some emotions. However, Dick's parents, both psychoanalysts, wanted to take him away from the bombs of the Battle of Britain in 1940. They persuaded Klein to follow them to Pitlochry in Scotland.

At first, Klein was enchanted by the scenery. She also started to work with another child patient, 'Richard', whose analysis she wrote up in painstaking detail, as if to ensure the survival of her work. Back in the Institute in London the composition of the analytic group was totally changed. Many of the Kleinian group were absent on war work or taking shelter elsewhere. As well as Anna Freud there were other analytic refugees from Vienna and Berlin. They were not interned but had to stay in London, and formed a cosy group of their own. Freud's death in September 1939 created an anxiety about the survival of psychoanalysis itself. The psychoanalytic societies in Austria and Germany were wiped out by the flight or death of their analysts. The question was, whose psychoanalysis would survive?

When Klein came for a training committee on 24th April, 1940, she found herself under an attack which threatened to destroy her professional position. Anna Freud declared that only she and her colleagues practised Freudian psychoanalysis. What Klein practised was a substitution for it. Klein was shocked to find that Edward Glover, her enthusiastic supporter, was questioning whether Klein's theory should be taught to candidates. Both these attacks threatened Klein's position as a psychoanalyst. If she were not a member of the British Society she could not practice as a psychoanalyst, as the International Psychoanalytic Association insisted that members had to be part of a constituent society. Unfortunately for Klein, the British Society was in a state of flux. Ernest Jones, who had held the society in an iron grip since he founded it in 1919 was gradually retiring to Wales. The lack of his firm pro-Klein leadership probably released hostility to Klein. Edward Glover was desperate to take over from Jones but nothing had been decided. There was an unhappiness among younger members about senior colleagues who held on to positions of power indefinitely. A group composed of Barbara Low, Melitta Schmideberg, and Adrian and Karin Stephen proposed a series of extra-ordinary business and scientific meetings to thrash out these organisational and theoretical matters. These provided Klein with an opportunity to make her case. She was in a deeply painful position. Her greatest enemies were her former supporters, Edward Glover and her own daughter Melitta Schmideberg. Klein turned to Joan to organise her defence. On Christmas Eve, 1941, Joan wrote to Klein:

> I think I can do what you suggest, that is if people consent to be organised … can you get in touch with Dr Payne … Do not let her know that I am organising our views. You might not forget that I do not wish to become a scapegoat again .

This may refer to Freud's anger when she defended Klein's method of child analysis, or perhaps her exchange lecture to the Viennese in 1936. This letter shows two sides of Joan's character. She wanted to defend her friend, and wrote to her on Christmas Eve. On the other hand she was not a 'joiner'. This was to become an issue with Klein.

In reality there were not many Kleinians to organise. John Rickman was an army psychiatrist. Winnicott was setting up a hostel for disturbed children with Clare Britton, who he would later marry. This marriage was far happier than his first – perhaps a tribute to Joan's analysis. Susan Isaacs was in Cambridge, but she travelled up to London for meetings – not an easy thing to do during the war. The controversial discussions were really two sets of meetings. A series of business meetings to discuss how the society was organised, and a series of scientific meetings. One of these meetings was to discuss the topic of unconscious phantasy. This concept of Klein's was considered by the Freudians to be particularly suspect. The speaker was to be Susan Isaacs. Sturdy and clear-thinking, she was ready to take on Klein's enemies. Sylvia Payne arranged for a stenographer to take down the proceedings verbatim.

In the first business meeting, Joan and Susan Isaacs tried to steer the discussion into innocuous areas. They proposed making senior officers (such as Jones and Glover) answerable to the members. They also suggested that no one should hold office for more than two years. However, Walter

Schmideberg made it clear that the anti-Klein faction were not going to be denied their prey. He proposed two items for discussion: 'a) it be reaffirmed that the aim of the society is to further Freudian analysis and b) the meeting to discuss the method of dealing with the deviations from the fundamental principles of Freudian analysis'. Schmideberg used procedural means to attack Klein. Melitta was at least more honest. Her rage spilled out every time she spoke.

In an effort to contain and anticipate Melitta's attacks on her mother, Joan tried to draw her colleagues' attention to the difficult dynamics of the society. 'I submit that it is questionable whether an autocratic organisation is conducive to our aims'. She spoke of the need to empower younger members, as if that would appease Melitta. After this anodyne beginning, Joan grasped the nettle of the attacks on Klein. Certain members were driven by envy and jealousy:

> When members do give each other mutual support, such as sharing and pooling observations ... they are frowned upon and even regarded as unscientific ... In fact any sort of confidence in one's work seems to be regarded with suspicion and dislike.

This was a brave intervention by Joan. Although her analytic technique was purist, her comments on organisational dynamics show how modern her thinking was. Joan's words suggest that she was aware that Melitta's hatred and Glover's machinations to exclude Klein were a response by the British Society to someone like Klein who was unusually creative. Some people in the British Society valued Klein. Others were silently supportive of the envious attacks.

Melitta should have been her mother's crown princess. She was the eldest of Klein's children, pretty and clever, and as Klein recognised from the beginning, devoted to her mother. Like all Klein's children she had to put up with constant upheavals owing to Arthur Klein's work. Later the upheavals were due to Melanie Klein's work. When Melitta was in her teens she was left with Arthur Klein's parents to do her matriculation exams. Arthur and Melanie moved to Berlin so that Klein could have the benefits of the cutting edge Berlin Society. Erich remembered Melitta putting a star on top of the Christmas tree. This family idyll was shattered when Arthur and Melanie separated, this time for good. Melanie, Erich and Melitta moved to cheaper accommodation. Hans went with Arthur to Sweden. Melanie's part of the family were left without a steadying male presence. Klein began a passionate affair, which did not last, but must have further unsettled the children. However, Melanie carried on with her work in the Berlin Clinic and Melitta stuck at her medical studies. As we saw, Abraham died unexpectedly and in the absence of his protection the male members of the Berlin Clinic turned against Klein. On a smaller scale it was the same constellation that would develop in England. Klein fled to England like a comet, trailing controversy in her wake. Melitta stayed in Berlin to do her analytic training in a climate deeply hostile to her mother. In some way this must have mirrored a hostility already active in herself and waiting to flare up.

Once Melitta arrived in England in 1930 she went to live with her mother. Melitta chose to stay with her mother for two years while Walter Schmideberg waited for a visa. Joan may have felt some pangs of jealousy at the arrangement. The letter at the beginning of the chapter makes it clear that she expected to come 'first' with Klein, a state of mind left over from her childhood, when her mother had two subsequent children. Now, Klein and Melitta were able to discuss Klein's ideas, and Melitta's early papers show the influence of her mother's work. What changed Melitta? In 1934 when Hans died, Melitta declared it was suicide and blamed her mother. This was a handy weapon, but the change in Melitta had already begun. When Melitta first came to England she went into analysis with Ella Sharpe, who had supported Klein in her battle with Anna Freud. Sharpe encouraged Melitta to become more independent from her mother. Then, probably before Hans's death, Melitta went into analysis with Edward Glover. After Klein's divorce she may have wanted a father figure, as she had effectively lost Arthur Klein after the divorce. An unanalytic closeness developed between Melitta and Glover. Some people said that Melitta was a substitute for Glover's Down's syndrome daughter. I think that was a *folie à deux*, both shared a sense of raging envy of Klein. Glover had always felt inferior to his elder brother, James, and they were both patients of Abraham. Abraham made it clear that Klein was his star patient. Melitta's envy of her mother had been covered by her idealisation, when this broke down a flood of venom was released.

In 1933, Melitta won a clinical prize for a paper about her work with a three-year-old girl called Vivian. Vivian was envious of her mother, who cannot be allowed to do anything right. Surely an unconscious portrait of herself, but at the same time a development of the concept of envy, which would be continued by Joan and Klein. As the 1930s wore on, Melitta produced a series of papers which were increasingly critical of conventional analytic technique, as well as her mother. Melitta's *coup de grâce* came in 1937 when she read a paper to the British Society called 'After the Analysis' in which she accused unnamed analysts of unscrupulously promoting idealisation of themselves and psychoanalysis. In case the object of her attacks was not clear enough, Melitta included a specific jab at Klein's new concept of the depressive position: 'Other analysts think that no analysis is satisfactory or deep-going enough if the patient has omitted to pass through a phase of depression' (Schmideberg, 1938).

Those like Joan who thought that Melitta's hatred had got out of hand had underestimated her. Fortunately the meetings were recorded word for word by a stenographer or they would have been hard to believe. During the business meeting of 11th March, 1942, both Melitta and Glover spoke against the Kleinians. Melitta excelled herself:

> The Kleinians shelter behind ambiguity and vagueness ... they lack the most elementary scientific discipline. In a manner somewhat reminiscent of Dr Goebbels [the Nazi propaganda minister] they try to impress us by repeating time after time the same slogans.
>
> (King and Steiner, 1991)

Now the comparison to Goebbels may seem ridiculous. But then Hitler was still bombing London. Kristallnacht had taken place in 1938. In 1942 Jews were being gassed in Poland in preparation for large-scale extinction.

Fortunately, Melitta undermined herself by telling the meeting that she had been diagnosed as a paranoic by a senior member of the British Society, who had tried to persuade her husband to take her out of the country 'because I had dared to protest against certain intrigues and organised attacks'. Melitta then gave a list of non-Kleinians whom she thought had been attacked or ill-treated by the Kleinians:

> When Drs Bowlby and Middlemore brought original contributions, they were unfairly attacked ... Mr Strachey has been patronised, disparaging remarks were systematically spread about by Dr Brierly and Miss Sharpe.
>
> (King and Steiner, 1991)

Reading Melitta's diatribe, one is left with the impression that she may indeed have suffered from symptoms of paranoia, particularly as some of the analysts she mentioned protested indignantly that they had not been ill-treated.

What could Klein have felt sitting through all this. Shame? Pity? Humiliation? At this time there was no one as close to her as Joan. Joan came to all the extra-ordinary business and scientific meetings. Her sympathetic presence must have been a support to Klein, and she also coordinated their strategy. However, help came from another source. Sylvia Payne was a highly respected member of the society. She had previously worked as a GP. Her husband remained a GP and referred her patients, thereby freeing her from the mafia-like system of allocating patients. Payne missed the first two business meetings, but read the transcript with mounting horror. She came to the third business meeting in April 1942. After chiding members for reproducing the uncensored atmosphere of an analytic session she read the riot act to Melitta.

> At the last meeting accusations of what in law could be called malpractice were made against Mrs Klein ... the charges were grave and in my opinion such charges cannot be made without the liability of libel actions being incurred.

This successfully curbed Melitta. She partly dropped out of the meetings. However, Glover remained, and even chaired some of the meetings in a snide and partisan way, which was his undoing.

Sylvia Payne's intervention, and the end of the extra-ordinary business meetings marked a change in the atmosphere. There were genuine discussions about theoretical differences. Three papers were given by followers of Klein which were intended to clarify Klein's ideas, but also examine their roots in Freud's work. Susan Isaacs began with a stupendous paper on unconscious fantasy. She drew extensively on Joan's 1936 exchange lecture, which was given in Vienna. She even mischievously quoted papers by Glover and Melitta. There were two other lectures, one by Paula Heimann and Susan Isaacs, and one by Paula Heimann on her own. Joan was silent for most of these meetings, although she made a brief remark in favour of the existence of the death instinct. Perhaps she felt that Klein no longer needed her support, and she no longer came first with her.

The controversial discussions ended with a vindication of Klein's work, although it was to prove a victory with a bitter aftertaste. Anna Freud resigned from the Training Committee. In 1945, Melitta left her husband and went to New York. She did not return until Klein died. Edward Glover had alienated even those who did not support Klein, and Sylvia Payne was elected president of the society. One of her earliest actions was to create two separate training schemes so that Anna Freud and her supporters could stay within the society. Glover was disgusted by this peaceable solution and resigned from the British Society, although, crafty as ever, he kept his membership of the Swiss Society and continued his work with delinquents.

One of the accusations against Klein was that she and her colleagues had grabbed all the candidates and turned them into Kleinians. Klein was able to show that this was factually not the case. However, Klein and Joan between them analysed or supervised all the most dazzling talent from the pre- and post-war years. Susan Isaacs, John Bowlby and Donald Winnicott were analysed by Joan. Hanna Segal, Wilfred Bion and Herbert Rosenfeld were analysed by Klein. Hanna Segal and Herbert Rosenfeld were also supervised by Joan. The relationship with Segal became an important one to Joan, as we shall see. Athol Hughes spoke to Herbert Rosenfeld about his experiences of Joan as a supervisor. He said 'she was fantastically good, a class apart. She was an extremely original person'. Later, after Rosenfeld had qualified, Joan sought his help with a very difficult patient on the grounds that she did not have the training or experience. By this time Rosenfeld was analysing psychotic patients using some of Klein's later ideas. He found Joan unselfconsciously humble. This was a contrast to her reputation with the training committee. When they received a positive report on a candidate they decided it was a first; then Klein remembered there had been one before. Joan was happy to work with someone of equal or superior intellect to herself, but had no tolerance for anyone less well-endowed.

Knowing this, Klein was happy to refer one of her new patients to Joan. Hanna Poznanska Segal was Polish. She had gone to medical school specifically to become a psychoanalyst. Her family fled from the war and Segal ended up finishing her medical course in Edinburgh. She fell in love with Klein's ideas while reading *The Psychoanalysis of Children* and came to London determined to be analysed by Klein, which she achieved, with a struggle. Segal took Melitta's place as Klein's crown princess, although she had developed a sterling reputation in her own right. Segal and Joan found immediate common ground through literature. Both admired Joseph Conrad, and they introduced each other to their favourite writers. Finding a younger woman she could respect was a pleasure for Joan. Her relationship with Diana was a distant one at this time. I managed to meet Dr Segal shortly before she died. Her first impressions of Joan were vivid, 'She was very tall', said Dr Segal, holding her hand way over her head, 'and superego incarnate!' Joan's affection for Segal did not prevent her delivering crushing put-downs. When Segal told Joan she was a member of the Labour Party, Joan responded 'Socialism – that religion of younger siblings'. She must have been sadly disappointed by the Labour government after the war.

Earlier that year Evelyn had died of cancer. His death was a terrible blow to Joan. Despite the difficulties early in their marriage they had developed a close and companionable relationship. They shared the pleasure of their house in Chichester. As the war took hold Evelyn's work dried up, but they were happy to spend time together. They shared a fondness for domestic formality, which Joan derived from her mother, although she would have been reluctant to admit this. Hanna Segal sustained a double loss at this time: her mother died, and her father returned to live in Paris. Thinking Segal would be on her own, Joan invited her to come at Christmas. In fact, Segal had her future husband Michael Segal staying with her. Joan suggested he came too. The visit was a success, and the Segals and Joan became good friends. However, when the Segals went on to have three sons there was a cooling in the relationship. Segal suggested to me that this was because Joan did not like children. She was certainly not a good parent, but her 1936 paper on 'Psychical Conflict in Infancy' shows a tremendous empathy with small children.

In her published account of the Christmas of 1945, Segal tactfully makes no mention of Diana. One would have thought that she would have been with Joan after Evelyn's death. Diana had been close to her father, but she told Athol Hughes that she regarded her Aunt Molly as more of a mother. Perhaps she was with Molly and her husband over Christmas, or away on war work. Joan worried about Diana. According to Segal, Joan made strenuous attempts to persuade Segal to take on Diana as an analytic patient, 'She is very ill'. This may have been true, but Segal refused. Segal also said to me that she thought that Joan longed for Klein to take her into analysis. Segal was one of the most talented analysts of her generation, so her view is worth considering.

Chapter 17

After the war

In the aftermath of the war it was impossible to ignore the needs of children who had lost one or both parents. Europe was awash with orphaned children. Even in England, which had avoided invasion, tens of thousands of servicemen had died for their country, not to speak of the men and women who had died in the Blitz. A committee chaired by Myra Curtis in 1946 began investigating the care of orphaned children in England. With characteristic bluntness Susan Isaacs wrote to the committee to remind them that physical care on its own was not enough: 'The experience of love is just as necessary for the child's mental and moral growth, as good food and medical care are necessary for his bodily health and development'.

In 1945, *New Era Fellowship* magazine decided to devote a whole issue to articles relevant to the bringing up of children during or after the war. Isaacs was asked to write about father-less children. She probably arranged for Joan to write about 'The bereaved wife' as a therapeutic activity. In February 1945, Evelyn had died. The sense of fragility that his colleagues had noticed meant that his relatively early death at 68 was not so surprising. Evelyn died at home of 'metastases of carcinoma in the liver' and carcinoma of the stomach. It sounds a distressing and painful death. For Joan it brought back memories of her father's death in 1909. Then, she was unable to stay in the room. This seems to have also been the case with Evelyn. The death certificate states that 'Mrs W Thomas, sister-in-law was in attendance'. This was Joan's sister Molly.

With characteristic conscientiousness, Evelyn had made his will in 1940. As an expert in the field he had drawn it up himself. Rather surprisingly it is handwritten, and the handwriting looks like Joan's. Was Evelyn ill then too? Evelyn was cremated at Golders Green Cemetery. Ironically this is where Freud was buried. Although Joan could not be with Evelyn when he died, it did not mean she was unfeeling. She was able to use her experience for the *New Era Fellowship* article: 'the catastrophe which the loss of a husband means to a woman, as we know, causes a wound that can only be healed by time'. Joan pays tribute to what Evelyn had given her: 'the husband's love for his wife and need of her, support of her, and belief in her are among the most important assurances that she is of value herself'. Here we get a glimpse of a quality in Joan that hid behind her haughtiness – her humility. Rather surprisingly, Joan suggests that a woman's love for her children keeps alive her belief in herself. This raises the question again of where Diana was at Christmas in 1945, when the recently widowed Joan invited Hanna Segal to come and meet both their needs for company.

The person that Joan was probably closest to at this time was Susan Isaacs. They had both weathered the Controversial Discussions, and Joan appreciated her warmth and sharp intelligence. However, in 1948, Susan lay dying in her bedroom of breast cancer. Her friends gathered in her living room, along with her husband Nathan, and the woman he would shortly marry. Unwilling to tire Susan, small groups of friends took it in turn to visit her in her bedroom. When it was Joan's turn, Susan expressed sadness that the book Joan was editing, containing papers by Susan, Joan, Klein and Paula Heimann, had not yet been published. We do not know what Joan said to her at the time, but she answered her in the introduction to the book when it was published in 1952 as *Developments in Psychoanalysis*:

> the general difficulties of book publication during and after the war … personal difficulties hampering contributors, not the least being the great demand for analytic training by applicants after the war. It would not be surprising if people turned to psychoanalysis after a war characterised by inhuman cruelty and murderousness.
>
> (Riviere, 1952)

Joan naturally does not mention her own personal exigencies. As well as Evelyn's death in 1945, Anna Verrall, Joan's mother, died in 1947. She seems to have been depressed before she died. A small pocket diary of hers has recently come to light. Each page is empty, except for the word 'nothing'. In reality, Molly saw her regularly and Joan saw her less. It was the end of the parental generation for Joan. Her father and mother had died, as had Arthur and Margaret Verrall. Joan and Molly saw each other from time to time. Cuthbert had vanished into the wilds of Canada. Joan's role as editor of *Developments in Psychoanalysis* kept her constructively busy, and in touch with sympathetic colleagues, particularly Klein and Paula Heimann.

Joan got to know Paula Heimann while she was still translations editor for the *International Journal*. Heimann had come to live in England from Berlin at the invitation of Ernest Jones. He was quick to see the risks the Jewish analysts faced with the rise of Hitler. Paula and her husband were already involved with left-wing activities. Her husband made a rapid exit to Switzerland. However, the Swiss refused to take Paula and their son, so they were forced to take up Jones's offer. Not surprisingly the marriage broke down not long after Paula arrived. Klein was still suffering acutely from Hans's death. Longing to speak German with a native speaker, she turned to

Paula. However, Klein soon realised that Paula was herself in need of help, and offered to psychoanalyse her. This was kept a secret, probably because the Kleinians had been accused of psychoanalysing people to convert them to the cause. After the Controversial Discussions the Institute was divided into three groups: the Kleinians, the Freudians and the Independents. This process probably intensified the need to show what was special about each group.

Joan wanted *Developments in Psychoanalysis* to have a range of papers which focused mainly on very young children. The contributors were Joan, Klein, Paula and Susan Isaacs (posthumously). Joan wrote a masterly introduction which examines the similarities between the work of Freud and Klein. She points out Freud's own inconsistencies, and suggests that Klein's work follows from Freud's later theories, particularly the death instinct. Joan points out that there is a class of people for whom Klein's ideas would already be familiar:

> I refer of course particularly to those gifted, intuitive mothers and women who nurse children, who have always taken for granted that a baby does feel and 'think' and 'know' and react and respond emotionally i.e. psychically to whatever happens to him and is done to him.
>
> (Riviere, 1952)

In this generous paragraph, Joan pays tribute to the sort of mother she was unable to be herself, and perhaps an acknowledgement of the emotional support Klein had given to her.

Joan's own contribution to the book is the paper given as an exchange lecture in Vienna in 1936. Although she says she does not work with small children, she describes the development of hating and loving feelings with extraordinary vividness. It feels almost as if she is drawing on her own early experiences. She describes a small child putting stones in her mother's lap, symbolically wanting to replace the babies it has attacked. At the end of the paper Joan lists the work which influenced her. Not surprisingly there are ten papers by Klein. But there are also five papers by Melitta Schmideberg, a reminder of how seriously her work was taken before her paranoid outbursts in the Controversial Discussions.

Tucked away towards the end of *Developments in Psychoanalysis* was the most innovative and controversial paper of all. It was the modestly titled 'Some schizoid mechanisms' by Melanie Klein. This paper proposes a stage of development *earlier* than the depressive position. Because it was not written until 1946 and the other papers in the book do not share its framework. The paper describes how the earliest types of anxiety are kept at bay. The original form of this is the splitting (in phantasy) of the breasts into 'good and bad'. There is also a splitting of the feelings towards the object into love and hate. Various feelings can be split off and denied. An important part of this process is a mental mechanism which Klein calls 'Projective Identification'. This is a phantasy that good or bad aspects of the self (originally the excrements) can be split off and located elsewhere. For example, projection into the mother to control her can be linked to adult feelings of claustrophobia. As Joan says: 'the fixation points of later psychotic disorders are formed in this very early period'.

Joan points out that these concepts, which had originated in Klein's use of the play technique, influence the technique used with adult patients who have psychotic disorders or other severe disturbances. Phyllis Grosskurth, Klein's biographer, suggests that this paper marks a break between Klein and Joan, and that Joan was unwilling to follow Klein into this territory. It is true that Joan did not work with psychotic patients, although we saw that when she found herself with a very disturbed patient she asked Rosenfeld (a psychiatrist) for help. However, it is clear that she thinks that Klein's ideas would be helpful to all analysts. She says: 'every analyst reading it will be reminded of much in his practice and find it exceedingly stimulating'.

Although Joan and Klein did not part company theoretically, this later work of Klein's did produce a rift for other reasons. Many people, particularly those analysts who were psychiatrists, were very interested in the possibility of using Klein's ideas to work with psychotic patients. Herbert Rosenfeld wrote his membership paper on work with a psychotic patient with depersonalisation. Klein was surrounded by very able younger analysts, eager to hear about her work or to be psychoanalysed by her. Hanna Segal came to be regarded as Klein's crown princess. The sheer numbers of people surrounding Klein meant that Joan could no longer feel that she came first with her. She did have that feeling with Evelyn, but he was no longer there. Joan turned to some of her older friends, Ernest Jones and James and Alix Strachey, although all of them lived outside London. Yet in a letter to Ernest Jones it is clear that Joan was still open to new ideas. In the letter Joan was responding to the third volume of Ernest Jones's biography of Freud. Talking about telepathy Joan comments: 'I don't "believe in telepathy", but there is a vast amount of evidence for it ... The apparent telepathy between (*some*) patients and their analysts is amazing'. Joan could have taken it further and suggested that Klein's concept of projective identification could be a mechanism for 'telepathy'.

Klein's talented patient, Wilfred Bion, did develop a theory of the feelings stirred up in the analyst, and how they could inform the work with the patient. However, contrary to Grosskurth's view, Klein could tolerate some differences of opinion. Up until the early 1950s, Joan was still part of the Klein group. In 1952 she was a guest at Klein's seventieth birthday party. In a photograph of the event the guests are sitting round a long table. Klein is standing up. Three guests are standing at the back, separate from the group. These are Rosenfeld, Joan and Winnicott. Joan is standing in an uncharacteristically awkward way. She seems separated from the others. It is remarkably similar to her long-ago photograph at Wycombe Abbey, where she also seemed ill at ease with the group.

Joan could enjoy parties. For her seventy-fifth birthday she declined the offer of a present from her colleagues at the Institute, as she felt there were many new members who would not know her. Instead, she asked for a party. In an unbuttoned moment she described a party when she was a child. Her mother asked her to entertain the guests. She said she would paint a picture and all the guests could watch. Probably not what Anna Verrall had in mind! Perhaps this story represents Joan's wish to have her creativity recognised. However, her normal aloofness cut her off from the growing Kleinian group.

I return to the question which I raised at the beginning of the book. Why did none of the Klein group write an obituary for Joan? As I neared the end of the book I decided to have a final trawl through Joan's archive and also that of Ernest Jones. I found a letter which seemed to answer my question.

The letter was written on 17th December, 1957, from Dr A. Hyatt Williams, one of the younger analysts who was part of the Klein group. It was addressed to Ernest Jones. Hyatt Williams had planned to go to Toronto to take up a leadership role in the Psychoanalytic Society there. He felt for this reason, as well as personal ones, that he would like further analysis. His wife made an appointment for him to see Melanie Klein:

> Meanwhile I met Mrs Riviere at one of the Society's meetings. Mrs Riviere, who I always knew as one of Melanie Klein's admirers, advised me to go to Dr Bion, but on no account to go to Mrs Klein herself. When I went to see Mrs Klein herself, of course I was offered a vacancy.
>
> ...
>
> Mrs Riviere suggests that there would be something too proselytising about the analysis which I would be likely to be given by Mrs Klein at this time in her life. [I] feel inclined to accept the vacancy anyway.

Whatever Ernest Jones said, Arthur Hyatt Williams was Klein's patient until she died in 1960. It would be inevitable that he would speak of this incident in his analysis. Several people have told me that there is a letter from Joan in Klein's archive (which I have not been able to find) that says 'What have I done?' Depending on the date of the letter, it may be about Joan's conversation with Hyatt Williams. Joan would have been aware that Klein would be hypersensitive to any criticism of her work as a psychoanalyst.

It is not clear whether Joan's comments to Hyatt Williams were a momentary jealousy of Klein's popularity, or an envious attack on her. Envy was a topic which fascinated both women. Joan's paper on jealousy as a mechanism of defence against envy of the primal scene was written as far back as 1932. In 1957, Klein began a very long paper on envy. Among other works she refers approvingly to Joan's 1932 paper:

> Joan Riviere ... traced envy in women to the infantile desire to rob the mother of her breasts and to spoil them. According to her findings, jealousy is rooted in this primal envy. Her paper contains interesting material illustrating these views.
>
> (Klein, 1957)

Once again, Joan and Klein are sharing a viewpoint, and Klein seems to have written to Joan to discuss this. Joan responded:

> In your letter you mention your envy paper as again showing that you connect object-relations with instincts: here what I am going to say is not criticism or doubt, I am hoping that you will make it clearer in the book how 'innate envy' can arise. ... It implies an object-relation before birth ... If that is what you mean, it is *new*... and you need to give your evidence for it.
>
> (Spillius, 2015)

The tone of Joan's letter is admiring, but cool. The old warmth is no longer there, although this is not the end of the story.

Chapter 18

The internal world

In 1952 Joan had two papers published in the *International Journal of Psychoanalysis*. This was a special issue in honour of Klein's seventieth birthday. They have similar titles. The first is called 'The unconscious phantasy of an inner world reflected in examples from literature'. The second is called 'The inner world in Ibsen's *Master Builder*'. In the first paper love prevails, even through separation or death. The second paper describes a manic phantasy which comes to a tragic end.

Slowly, and with her characteristically minute care, rather like tiny stitches, Joan builds up a picture of an inner world inside of ourselves. She starts off with a striking image of looking inside an anatomy textbook, and discovering with horror that we have these strange things inside of ourselves. However, in this first paper the inner world is essentially a benign place, where our loved ones can continue to exist despite loss or separation. She quotes a poem which she believes is by Donne. The poet is separated from the woman he loves:

> By absence this good means I gain
> That I can catch her
> Where no-one can watch her
> In some close corner of my brain.
> (Riviere, 1952)

Joan describes how we internalise significant figures in our lives. Originally, these are our parents. At a fundamental level these figures are experienced as either 'good' or 'bad'. The drive to internalise derives from the long period of dependence of the human animal. The repetitive themes in Donne's poems are the rapturous union of lovers, or expectation of loss and its attendant despair. Here, Joan turns to Melanie Klein's suggestion that ultimately the fear of loss is the fear of death.

Joan describes how, from the beginning of life we incorporate other people who are significant – starting with our parents. In our culture we cling to the fiction of our individuality and independence, 'Everyone realises at times, and normally with strong feeling, how much his life and his experience ... is or has been enriched by other men and women'. These feelings of awareness of the importance of the other person are particularly intense at moments of being in love or losing someone.

Here it is impossible not to think that the paper is motivated, at least in part, by the beginnings of Joan's rift with Melanie Klein. She consoles herself with the thought that she still has her memories of Klein, 'when we think such a thought as "I shall always have him or her with me wherever I go"' (Riviere, 1952). These memories of the other person are the representation of the internal world. Although Joan would live another ten years, and Klein would live another eight, the thought of a loss by death was obviously on Joan's mind. She quotes a poem by Samuel Rogers which suggests that we never lose those whom we truly love:

> At moments which he calls his own,
> Then, never less alone than when alone,
> Those whom he loved so long and sees no more,
> Loved and still loves – not dead, but gone before,
> He gathers round him.

As if to make the point more emphatically, Joan tells the reader: 'I tried to show in these two cases the special compensatory connection between external loss and internal acquisition'.

This chapter could have simply portrayed a situation which is *only* benign or comforting. However, as James Strachey observed in his obituary, she *has* to speak the truth, no matter how unpleasant it might be. She acknowledges the never-ending conflict between love and hate and how hate can turn a previously loved person into someone terrifying and evil. Using the work of Joseph Conrad, a novelist Joan greatly admired, she describes how love and hate for the same person can co-exist in the mind. The paper ends with a poem by Apollinaire which is a literal expression of how we are all made of other people. Not only is it a clear illustration of the subject of Joan's paper, but it is a link to Hanna Segal, who had introduced her to Apollinaire. Segal, like Klein, was someone Joan was estranged from. It is as if she is reaching out to people who are important to her.

Having described an internal world of loved or ambivalently loved people it seems strange at first that Joan should turn to Ibsen's *Master Builder*. This is a world of death and terrible damage, and a manic denial of the harm done. It is interesting that when this play was first performed, the critics dismissed it, but it was popular with audiences. Joan shows that the plot of the play only makes sense when we see it as a depiction of the *inner world* of the central character Halvard Solness – 'The Master Builder'. By a mixture of skill and cunning, Solness is at the peak of his success. But he is uneasy and guilty. He is afraid his wishes have a way of coming to pass. By cunning manoeuvres he has enslaved an old but talented architect and his son. The woman who the son loves is in love with Solness. However, Solness's life has also been tragic. His house burned down, and his wife was so disturbed that her milk dried up and their twin babies died. Solness used the insurance from the fire to increase his business. He is now building a new grand house for himself.

The internal world is initially formed of the two parents. Solness derives his power from a magic version of the father's penis. His actual father is represented by the ground-down architect and his son. The other father figure is God. Solness believes he has magic powers building homes for families. In the past he had climbed up the spire of a church to fix a wreath. This event was witnessed by a young girl – Hilda. Now seven years later she comes to claim Solness as her own 'Master Builder'. In contrast to the burned-out mother figure of Mrs Solness, Hilda is radiantly alive. She wants Solness to repeat his earlier feat and place a wreath on the high tower of the new house he is building for himself. She wants to see him 'great and free once more'. However, Mrs Solness is aware that Solness is afraid of heights and tries to stop him. Hilda urges him on and he falls to his death.

Hilda is a strange figure. Unlike Solness and his wife she is able to grieve for their dead children. She is also sympathetic to Mrs Solness. However, in both Hilda and Solness the wish to make reparation to the damaged internal and external figures is ruined by greed, and Hilda is ultimately Solness's nemesis.

The world of *The Master Builder* is very different to the world of Joan's previous paper. In the earlier paper there is a wish to hold on and re-create loved people, particularly parents. The paper ends on a valedictory note. Why then did Joan write a companion paper about a man whose life is dominated by mania and triumph over the internal parents?

I think that consciously, or unconsciously, Joan is trying out two alternative endings for the last stage of her life. One where she is at peace with people in her life, and the other where her life is ruined by the catastrophe of the rift between her and Klein. Klein herself felt lonely in the 1950s. She decided to deal with it by writing a paper about it. Although the paper covers schizophrenia and mental illness in general, in parts she seems to be writing about herself:

> However gratifying it is in later life to express thoughts and feelings to a congenial person, there remains an unsatisfied longing for an understanding without words – ultimately for the earliest relationship with the mother.
>
> (Klein, 1963)

Both Klein and Joan had problematic relationships with their mothers, and I think they provided this wordless communion for each other. This was Klein's last paper. She died in 1960.

When Joan was planning for her own death, she remembered Klein. She also turned more to her old psychoanalytic friends, Ernest Jones and James Strachey. Her letters to James have a real sense of intimacy, which I think was due to their shared link with Arthur and Margaret Verrall, Joan's surrogate parents. During his retirement Ernest Jones and his wife Kitty worked on a substantial biography of Freud. He sent the proofs of the third volume to Joan, as it covered the period when she knew him personally. Her reply, written on 10th October 1957, says as much about her as it does about Freud. She starts off with praise: 'I have nothing but admiration and gratitude for such an amazing piece of work'. She tells Jones how distressing she had found Freud's illness, and adds that she is a fan of voluntary euthanasia. This sounds a bit heartless, but I think it must have had echoes for her of her father's long drawn-out illness and death. Perhaps as an antidote she quickly follows this with an appreciation of a photograph of Freud with his grandchildren in happier days.

Even at this late stage, Joan was still defending Melanie Klein, and chides Jones for taking a 'politic' view of the differences between Klein and Anna Freud:

> Why you have to say that Melanie Klein's work began by exploiting H Hug-Hellmuth's technique or that she worked at a clinic with Ferenczi I can't imagine.

Joan agrees with Ernest's judgement that Freud was superstitious, but she retains her old loyalty for the Society for Psychical Research. Jones does not believe in telepathy, but she does not think that this is compatible with a 'scientific outlook'. As an example she says: 'The apparent telepathy which occurs between (*some*) patients and their analysts is amazing, but is not recorded and studied'. This last point is surely just as relevant today.

In August 1945 James seems to have written to Joan asking her to do some translations. Her reply, from her house in Chichester, throws an interesting light on her preferences:

> I don't really want to give up practice for translation [as James had done]. I would only do much of it if practice gave *me* up, which it may do in the sense I may not be able to go on living in London.

She tells James that her health only allows her to work five hours a day. As she is seeing psychoanalytic patients that would be at least twenty-five hours a week, but she was probably anxious following Evelyn's recent death, 'If you know of a "flat" ... please remember me'. By January 1947 Joan is more cheerful. She has moved to a flat. She tells James that she is editing a book of papers from the Controversial Discussions (*Developments in Psychoanalysis*):

> We are all too busy ... Diana and I were so glad to see you the other evening and that you looked so well again ... I had a very good Christmas – a newish patient brought me an enormous chicken ... which was most luscious. I felt rather guilty about the transference, but put it down chiefly to his showing off! Anyway I had no indigestion.

Perhaps this was one of Joan's 'potboiler' patients.

Ten years later, in 1959, Joan was still involved in Institute matters, arranging the Ernest Jones Lecture (Jones had died in 1958). However, Joan had received bad news:

> Shapland said my eye was a haemhorrage [sic] and was very gloomy – nothing to be done. My sight which was so good is v. badly deteriorated, both near and far – an awful change.

> 13th Jan 1962
>
> Dear James and Alix,
>
> I was hoping you would come and see me in my flat *so* close to Paddington – then in July 1960 I was suddenly taken ill with virulent pneumonia and everything stopped. I was ill for many months and am now an aged and feeble creature, can't walk or see much. I can still read good print.

In this letter, Joan's usual firm and flowing script has become wavering. On 20th May 1962 she died. The death certificate says 'cor pulmonaris', which would have meant suffocation. She was not alone, her housekeeper was there.

Her will left most of her money and possessions to Diana. Half the residue of her estate was to go to the Melanie Klein Trust, to set up a Joan Riviere Fund. The other half went to the South Downs Preservation Society. Although she seemed exquisite, she loved to walk on the downs, even in wartime. She was not afraid.

Epilogue

Looking idly through old copies of the *International Review of Psychoanalysis*, I discovered what is, in effect, the appreciative Kleinian obituary for Joan which was missing which she died. It was a review of the collection of Joan's papers, edited by Athol Hughes, written in 1992 by Dr Ronald Britton, perhaps the most creative psychoanalyst of a more recent generation.

The thirty years which had passed since Joan's death allowed her to emerge more clearly from the shadows of her dazzling peers and the following generation, Herbert Rosenfeld, Hanna Segal, Donald Winnicott and John Bowlby. As well as Joan's talents as a supervisor and psychoanalyst, Dr Britton pays tribute to her talent as a writer: 'It is probably the case that she was second only to Freud as a writer of genuine quality amongst psychoanalysts'. (It is perhaps this talent that contributed to making her Freud's favourite translator.)

As a working analyst with major contributions of his own, Dr Britton fillets out Joan's key ideas, some of which were many years ahead of their time. Perhaps the best known is in 'A contribution to the analysis of the negative therapeutic reaction', written in 1936. Joan introduced the concept of a 'defensive organisation'. Dr Britton describes this as a complex phantasy system which is clung to as a defence from an imagined psychic catastrophe. This concept has spawned a book by the distinguished contemporary analyst John Steiner and countless other papers. In 'Womanliness as a Masquerade', written in 1924, Joan 'introduces us to her profound, subtle and inspiring view of her own sex'. Britton points out that Joan did not hesitate to contradict Freud's ideas of female sexuality.

Joan's skills as an expositor made her a natural choice as a public speaker. In 1936 the Institute of Psychoanalysis put on a series of public lectures on 'The Emotional Life of Civilised Men and Women'. Klein lectured on 'Love, guilt and reparation', Joan spoke on 'Hate, greed and agression':

> Riviere's paper is a beautifully written account of emotional development with recognisably original ideas merged into a general descriptive account … Is this the first emergence of the notion of a confusion

> between good and bad as the source of psychosis? Is this the first use of the terms me and not-me in the baby's struggle for distinction?
>
> (Britton, 1992)

James Strachey's obituary presents a picture of Joan as uninterested in the world outside her own consulting room. This is contradicted in a paragraph which Dr Britton quotes at length from 'Hate, greed and aggression':

> Another point, which economists realise much better perhaps than other people do, is the degree of dependence of the human organism on its surroundings. In a stable political and economic system there is a great deal of apparent liberty and opportunity to fulfil our own needs, and we do not as a rule feel our dependence on the organisation in which we live – unless, for instance, there is an earthquake or a strike! Then we may realise with reluctance and often with deep resentment that we are dependent on the forces of nature or on other people to a terrifying extent. Dependence is felt to be dangerous because it involves the possibility of privation.

Britton feels this captures the essence of modern psychoanalysis as met with in clinical practice. I think Joan's statement goes far beyond psychoanalytic practice. There is, for example, a hatred of vulnerable, dependent people, such as refugees and those on benefits. There is little support for mothers who want to stay at home with their babies. She even points out our reluctance to accept our dependence on the environment. The current American president, Donald Trump, is an excellent example of climate-change denial.

Dr Britton takes us back to the fine grain of Joan's theory. He suggests that she anticipates Bion's theory of containment. This is (initially) the mother's capacity to receive and process the baby's projections of difficult feelings. As well as helping us understand psychosis, this theory has had a huge influence on modern psychoanalytic practice. Joan puts her version of this very clearly:

> It is probable that our need in babyhood to project our dangerous, painful states of anger out of us into someone else and identify someone else with them, and ourselves only with our good states, is one of the main stimuli towards recognising other people at all.

She concludes that we need other people for two reasons: for love and for hate. Although Joan was not a political person, her views illuminate relationships between countries and people.

At the end of Britton's review of Riviere's collected papers, he identifies one key facet of her personality and attitude:

> her unflinching statement of unwelcome truth, so boldly stated as to transform pessimism into heroic acceptance recalls Sigmund Freud. Riviere herself wrote of Freud: 'One could say that his simple direct personal response to whatever he perceived as valid in itself was the unique characteristic of genius'.

Britton suggests that this was what Riviere most admired and sought to emulate.

Bibliography

Primary Sources

Institute of Psychoanalysis Archive

Diaries:

Anna Verrall, 1883–1906, P02/C/01.
Joan Riviere, 1905–19, P02/C/03.
Correspondence from Joan Riviere to:
James Strachey, G10/BG/F02/04; CSF/F03/03; CSF/F03/10; CSF/F03/24; CSF/F01/48; CSF/F01/49; 19/04/1959 (part missing).
Susan Isaacs, CIB/F03/05; CIB/F03/06.
Ernest Jones, CKB/F07/34; CRB/F07/01; P04/C/E06 (x7).
Mrs P. S. Florence, P02/C/02/05.
Letter from Arthur Hyatt Williams to Ernest Jones: CWA/F20/02.

Photographs:

Molly Verrall, P02/D.
Joan and Father, P02/D/01.
Joan c.1895, P02/D/03.
Joan and Diana, P02/D/08.
Joan in the 1920s (book cover), P02/D/07.
Joan in the 1930s, P02/D/11.
Evelyn Riviere, P02/D/16.

Wellcome Library Klein Archive

Correspondence to Klein from Riviere, PP/KLE/A.58; PP/KLE/C.96; PP/KLE/A.6.

Victoria and Albert Theatre Archive

Correspondence: to Ida Nettleship from Ellen Terry, THM/14/20; TMM/14/20.

Tate Britain Archive

Diary: Elspeth Phelps, n.d.

Secondary Literature

Bakman, N. (2013). Thirty years on: K. R. Eissler's interviews with Joan Riviere (1953). *Psychoanalysis and History*, 15(1), 91–104.
Beard, M. (2002). *The Parthenon*. London: Profile Books.
Beeton, I. (1861). *Mrs Beeton's Book of Household Management*. Edited by N. Humbe, 2000. Oxford: Oxford Worlds Classics.
Beller, S. (1995). *Vienna and the Jews*. Cambridge: Cambridge University Press.
Bion, W. R. (1962). The psycho-analytic study of thinking. *International Review of Psychoanalysis*, 43, 306–310.
Boll, T. E. M. (1962). May Sinclair and the Medico-Psychological Clinic of London. *Proceedings of the American Philosophical Society*, 106, 310–326.
Bowerman, E. (1965). *Stands There a School*. Sussex: Dolphin Press.
Britton, R. (1992). Review of *The Inner World and Joan Riviere: Collected Papers 1920–1958*. In: A. Hughes (ed.), *International Review of Psychoanalysis*, 19, 505–507.
Brome, V. (1986). *Ernest Jones, Freud's Alter Ego*. London: Caliban Books.
Brook, A. (1995). The eye and I: psychological aspects of disorders of the eye. *Journal of the Balint Society*, 23, 13–16.
Caine, B. (2005). *Bombay to Bloomsbury*. Oxford: Oxford University Press.
Crawford, E. (2002). *Enterprising Women*. London: Francis Boutle.
Danto, E. (2005). *Freud's Free Clinics*. New York: Columbia University Press.
Davey, L. (1977). *The Inns of Lewes*. Lewes: Pomegranate Press.
Davis, M. E. (2006). *Classic Chic: Music, Fashion, and Modernism*. Berkeley and Los Angeles: University of California Press.
Etherington-Smith, M. and Pilcher, J. (1986). *The IT Girls*. London: Hamish Hamilton.
Flanders, J. (2003). *The Victorian House*. London: Harper Perennial.
Florence, B. M. (1978). *Lella Secor: A Diary in Letters 1915–1922*. New York: Burt Franklin.
Frank, C. (2009). *Melanie Klein in Berlin*. Sussex: Routledge.
Freud, S. (1912–1913). A note on the unconscious in psychoanalysis. *Proceedings of the Society for Psychical Research*, 26(66), 312–318.
Freud, S. (1927). *The Ego and the Id*. Translated by J. Riviere. London: Hogarth Press and Institute of Psychoanalysis.
Freud, S. (1930). *Civilisation and its Discontents*. Translated by J. Riviere. London: Hogarth Press.
Friedman, S. S. (2002). *Analyzing Freud*. New York: New Directions Books.
Gay, P. (1988). *Freud: A Life for Our Time*. New York: Norton.
Glendinning, V. (2006). *Leonard Woolf*. London: Simon and Schuster.
Graham, P. (2009). *Susan Isaacs*. London: Karnac.
Grosskurth, P. (1986). *Melanie Klein*. London: Hodder and Stoughton.
Harrison, J. (1925). *Reminiscences of a Student's Life*. London: Hogarth Press.
Heimann, P. (1963). Contributions to Memorial Meeting for Joan Riviere held by the British Psycho-Analytical Society, London, 3 October 1962. *International Journal of Psychoanalysis*, 44, 228–235.

Herzog, D. (2017). *Cold War Freud*. Cambridge: Cambridge University Press.

Holroyd, M. (1996). *Augustus John*. London: Pimlico.

Hughes, A. (1991). *The Inner World and Joan Riviere: Collected Papers 1920–1958*. London and New York: Karnac.

Hughes, A. (1992). Letters from Sigmund Freud to Joan Riviere (1921–1939). *International Review of Psychoanalysis*, 19(3), 265–285.

Hughes, A. (1997). Personal experiences – professional interests: Joan Riviere and femininity. *International Journal of Psychoanalysis*, 78, 899–911.

Hughes, K. (1993). *The Victorian Governess*. London: Hambledon Press.

Hughes, M. (1991). *A London Family 1870–1900*. London: Atlantic Books.

Jones, E. (1957). *The Life and Work of Sigmund Freud, Vol.3*. London: Hogarth Press.

Kardiner, A. (1977). *My Analysis with Freud*. New York: Norton.

King, P. and Steiner, R. (1991). *The Freud Klein Controversies, 1941–45*. London: Routledge.

King, P. and Steiner, R. (eds.) (1992). *The Freud–Klein Controversies 1941–1945*. London, New York: Tavistock/Routledge.

Klein, M. (1928). Early stages of the Oedipus conflict. *International Journal of Psychoanalysis*, 9, 167–180.

Klein, M. (1935). A contribution to the psychogenesis of manic-depressive states. *International Journal of Psychoanalysis*, 16, 145–174.

Klein, M. (1940). Mourning and its relation to manic-depressive states. *International Journal of Psychoanalysis*, 21, 125–153.

Klein, M. (1946). Notes on some schizoid mechanisms. *International Journal of Psychoanalysis*, 27, 99–110.

Klein, M. (1957). *Envy and Gratitude*. London: Hogarth Press.

Klein, M. (1963). On the sense of loneliness. In: R. Money-Kyrle (ed.) (1975), *Melanie Klein, Envy and Gratitude and Other Works, 1946–1963* (pp. 300–313). London: Hogarth Press.

Klein, M. and Riviere, J. (1937). *Love, Guilt and Reparation*. London: Hogarth Press.

Kris, A. O. (1994). Freud's treatment of a narcissistic patient. *International Journal of Psychoanalysis*, 75(4), 649–664.

Lee, H. (1996). *Virginia Woolf*. London: Chatto and Windus.

Maas, J. (1969). *Victorian Painting*. New York: Abbeville Press.

Maddox, B. (2006). *Freud's Wizard: The Enigma of Ernest Jones*. London: Murray.

Maroni, L. (2004). The observant mother. *Journal of Infant Observation*, 6(3), 60–70.

Meisel, P. and Kendrick, W. (eds.) (1986). *Bloomsbury Freud: The Letters of James and Alix Strachey, 1924–25*. London: Chatto and Windus.

Mitchell, J. (1986). *The Selected Melanie Klein*. London: Hogarth Press.

Morris, J. (1993). *Travels with Virginia Woolf*. London: Pimlico.

Moyle, F. (2012). *Mrs Oscar Wilde*. London: John Murray.

Oppenheim, J. (1985). *The Other World*. Cambridge: Cambridge University Press.

Ornston, D. G. (1992). *Translating Freud*. New Haven and London: Yale University Press.

Overy, R. (2010). *The Third Reich*. London: Quercus.

Paskauskas, R. A. (ed.) (1993). *The Complete Correspondence of Sigmund Freud and Ernest Jones*. Cambridge and London: Harvard University Press.

Peacock, S. (1988). *Jane Ellen Harrison: The Mask and the Self*. Massachusetts: Yale University Press.

Peck, W. (1952). *A Little Learning*. London: Faber.
Raitt, S. (2000). *May Sinclair*. Oxford: Clarendon Press.
Raverat, G. (1952). *Period Piece*. London: Faber.
Reid, M. (2007). The loss of a baby and the birth of the next infant. *Journal of Child Psychotherapy*, 33(2), 181–201.
Riviere, J. (1920). Three notes. *International Journal of Psychoanalysis*, 1, 200–202.
Riviere, J. (1920–1921). The Theory of Dreams. *Women's Supplement* [of *The Guardian*].
Riviere, J. (1921). Review of C. W. Valentine *Dreams and the Unconscious*. *British Journal of Medical Psychology*, 2, 244–246.
Riviere, J. (1923). Review of Sigmund Freud *Group Psychology and the Analysis of the Ego*. *International Journal of Psychoanalysis*, 4, 183–199.
Riviere, J. (1924). The Castration Complex in a child. *International Journal of Psychoanalysis*, 5, 467–468.
Riviere, J. (1929). Womanliness as a masquerade. *International Journal of Psychoanalysis*, 10, 303–313.
Riviere, J. (1930). Magical regeneration by dancing. *International Journal of Psychoanalysis*, 11, 340.
Riviere, J. (1932). Jealousy as a mechanism of defence. *International Journal of Psychoanalysis*, 13, 414–424.
Riviere, J. (1934). New introductory lectures on psychoanalysis: By Sigmund Freud. *International Journal of Psychoanalysis*, 15, 329–339.
Riviere, J. (1936a). A contribution to the analysis of the negative therapeutic reaction. *International Journal of Psychoanalysis*, 17, 304–320.
Riviere, J. (1936b). On the genesis of psychical conflict in earliest infancy. *International Journal of Psychoanalysis*, 17, 395–422.
Riviere, J. (1937). Review of Freud's autobiography. *British Journal of Medical Psychology*, 16, 72–77.
Riviere, J. (1939). An intimate impression. *The Lancet,* 30 September 1939.
Riviere, J. (ed.) (1952). *Developments in Psychoanalysis*. London: Hogarth Press.
Robinson, A. (2002). *The Life and Work of Jane Ellen Harrison*. Oxford and New York: Oxford University Press.
Robinson, J. (2010). *Bluestockings*. London: Penguin.
Rodman, F. R. (2003). *Winnicott, Life and Work*. London: Da Capo.
Schmideberg, M. (1934). The play-analysis of a three year old girl. *International Journal of Psychoanalysis*, 15, 245–264.
Schmideberg, M. (1936). A note on suicide. *International Journal of Psychoanalysis*, 17, 1–5.
Schmideberg, M. (1938). After the analysis… *Psychoanalysis Quarterly*, 7, 122–142.
Segal, H. (1991). Foreword. In: A. Hughes (ed.) *The Inner World and Joan Riviere: Collected Papers*. London and New York: Karnac.
Sherborne, M. (2012). *H. G. Wells, Another Kind of Life*. London: Peter Owen.
Sherwin-White, S. (2017). *Melanie Klein Revisited*. London: Karnak.
Showalter, E. (1987). *The Female Malady*. London: Virago.
Smith, H. (2010). *The British Women's Suffrage Campaign*. Harlow: Longman.
Spillius, E. (2015). *Journeys in Psychoanalysis*. London: Routledge.
Steinbach, S. (2004). *Women in Great Britain, 1760–1914*. London: Weidenfeld and Nicholson.

Strachey, J. (1963). Obituary. *International Journal of Psychoanalysis*, 44, 228–235.
Sutherland J. (ed.) (1958). *Psychoanalysis and Contemporary Thought*. London: Hogarth Press.
Tims, E. and Segal, N. (eds.) (1988). *Freud in Exile*. New Haven and London: Yale University Press.
Uglow, J. (1993). *Mrs Gaskell*. London: Faber.
Van Dijken, S. (1998). *John Bowlby: His Early Life*. London and New York: Free Association Books.
Vicinus, M. (1985). *Independent Women*. Chicago: University of Chicago Press.
Wetz, E. (2007). *Weimar Germany*. Princeton: Princeton University Press.
Young-Bruehl, E. (1988). *Anna Freud*. London: Macmillan.

Index

For Product Safety Concerns and Information please contact our EU
representative GPSR@taylorandfrancis.com
Taylor & Francis Verlag GmbH, Kaufingerstraße 24, 80331 München, Germany

www.ingramcontent.com/pod-product-compliance
Ingram Content Group UK Ltd.
Pitfield, Milton Keynes, MK11 3LW, UK
UKHW021307260926
475702UK00048B/807
* 9 7 8 0 4 1 5 5 0 7 6 8 4 *